1776

1776

The British Story of the American Revolution

Sponsored by The Times,
The Sunday Times and Barclays Bank

National Maritime Museum, Greenwich, London 14 April to 2 October 1976

First published 1976
Catalogue by Kenneth Pearson and Patricia Connor
Copyright © Times Newspapers Limited 1976
All rights reserved
ISBN 0 7230 0147 2

Produced and published for the 1776 Exhibition by
Times Books, the publishing imprint of
Times Newspapers Limited, Gray's Inn Road, London WC1X 8EZ

Grateful thanks are extended to the owners and photographers who kindly provided photographic material for the 1776 Exhibition and for reproduction in this catalogue

Designed by Anthony Cohen
Cartography by David Penney
Printed by Balding and Mansell Limited, Wisbech, Cambridgeshire

Contents

Foreword

The 1776 Exhibition at the National Maritime Museum is the major celebration in the United Kingdom of the Bicentenary of the United States of America. It has not been an easy exhibition to present. Scholarship could not be sacrificed to dramatic effect, yet the complex series of often unco-ordinated events which led to the American War of Independence had to be made coherent. The serious student and the wondering child must be gripped for an hour by the story of how Britain lost a Colony yet, in fact, was handing over to the United States its ultimate destiny to assume one day the leadership of the English-speaking world.

How the Exhibition came about is told elsewhere in this catalogue, and there are references on nearly every page to those who by their loans and by their labours have made it comprehensive and comprehensible. No single individual has done more for the Exhibition than Her Majesty The Queen, who has been kept closely informed about the celebrations planned on both sides of the Atlantic. Her Majesty will be creating history by visiting, at her own wish, so many of them. We are grateful to Her Majesty for agreeing to open this Exhibition, in the company of the Duke of Edinburgh; by so doing the Queen will have an opportunity to see in a new context the many wonderful things she has graciously provided from the Royal Collections.

Our thanks to the Royal Family go further. The Prince of Wales readily agreed to take part in a unique recording of the words spoken when his ancestor, King George III, received the first U.S. Minister, John Adams, to the Court of St James. In the Exhibition His Royal Highness speaks the King's words and the Hon. Elliot Richardson, until recently U.S. Ambassador to Britain, those of his most famous predecessor.

Mr James Callaghan, M.P., Secretary of State for Foreign and Commonwealth Affairs, has been co-patron of the Exhibition with Mr Richardson, and we record our thanks to them both for their readiness to help and to place their staffs and services at our disposal. Following the appointment of the Hon. Mrs Anne Armstrong as the new United States Ambassador, she immediately consented to be a patron. We warmly welcome her to London.

The decision to hold the Exhibition at Greenwich was a deliberate one. The English exploration and colonisation of America began at Greenwich when the monarchs had their palace there, and was finally confirmed by Royal Charter 'as of the Manor of East Greenwich' – a legal term that was used in the grants to the first of the Colonies in the 17th century. Greenwich served as the home of inspiration, the source of patronage and the port of embarkation for a century of mercantile expansion that saw the origins of the New World.

We are indeed fortunate that a rebuilt main wing of the National Maritime Museum has been made available by an imaginative gesture of the Trustees, whose Chairman,

Admiral Sir Charles Madden, has given us every encouragement. Mr Basil Greenhill, Director of the Museum, has day by day for two years assisted wholeheartedly in the planning and organisation of the Exhibition.

The Chairman of the organising working parties has been Mr Philip Taverner, who occupied a similar central directing role with outstanding success and flair with the Tutankhamun and Chinese Exhibitions. Millions of British people owe a great deal to him for his remarkable talents. The conception of this Exhibition has been in the inspired hands of its Director, Kenneth Pearson, whose researches will prove to be of enduring importance; he and the designer, Robin Wade, have, not for the first time, co-operated to great good effect.

The financial burden of organising exhibitions on this scale are now heavy and hazardous in an inflationary world. On this occasion Times Newspapers turned to Barclays Bank Limited to co-sponsor the Exhibition. The Bank's Chairman, Mr Anthony Tuke, responded immediately. His father, the late Mr A. W. Tuke, a former Chairman, has told in the official history that Barclays was founded prior to 1694, and Gosling's (a part of Barclays since 1896) history dates back to 1649–50. For a century and a half Gosling's, and subsequently Barclays, have provided a banking service for *The Times*. It is therefore a very appropriate sponsor partnership, and we are grateful for the physical as well as the financial contribution of Barclays.

Finally, we welcome all those citizens of America who are coming to Greenwich this year. Though inevitably they will be tracing the British story of great events two centuries ago, this Exhibition is for many of us a tribute to that nation of nations, the United States, and to its people whom we honour for their deathless attachment to freedom. We have wanted to be generous in our treatment of their cause in 1776, partly in recognition of our debt to them for the blood they shed when the two countries were on the same side in two world wars this century.

C. D. HAMILTON

Acknowledgements

The Exhibition is presented in collaboration with the National Maritime Museum, a number of whose representatives served on the various committees. In addition many members of the staff of the Museum have contributed advice and help to the Exhibition. We also acknowledge the active support we have received from the National Army Museum and in particular from Mr William Reid, the Director.

A special word of thanks is due to the Department of the Environment, notably Mr Charles Collins and Mr Roland Greatrex, who have worked closely with the design team on the difficult task of making recently modernised galleries suitable for a temporary exhibition.

The response to requests for loans to the Exhibition has been overwhelming. The names of those persons and institutions who have participated are included at appropriate points in this catalogue. The sponsors would like to pay particular tribute to the generous support we have received from the United States. This is particularly important in view of the many exhibitions and events being staged in the United States in 1976 to mark the bicentenary.

Mr Ian Pearson, Director of W. Wingate and Johnston Limited, has acted as consultant on packing and transportation. His company or their agents have been responsible for packing the exhibits and transporting them to Greenwich.

Professor Esmond Wright has acted as academic adviser to the Exhibition and on the catalogue. Kenneth Pearson of *The Sunday Times* has directed the Exhibition with the help of a research team led by Patricia Connor, with Ann Gould, Joanna Dejardin, Duffy White, and Sara Day in Philadelphia.

Times Newspapers invited Robin Wade Design Associates to design the Exhibition. The designer in charge was Mrs Pat Read. Michael Knight worked with Robin Wade Design Associates on the Prologue and Epilogue. MacKay and Partners are the advertising agents to the Exhibition. Miss Fay Jenkins was the Account Manager responsible.

Most of the publications associated with the Exhibition and almost all the items sold in the Sales Area have been devised by Times Newspapers Publishing Division. The Marketing Manager of that Department, Mr Bruce Howell, has participated at Working Party and Publications meetings, as has Mrs Candida Hunt of Times Books, who produced this catalogue.

The British electronic sales registers used at the various sales points have been kindly loaned by Gross. We also wish to thank Jaeger, who once again have most generously provided the clothes worn by the sales girls.

The 1776 Exhibition is sponsored by Barclays Bank, *The Times* and *The Sunday Times* and was organised on their behalf by Carlton Cleeve Limited.

Main Contractor
Clements & Street Limited, Birmingham

Sub-contractors
Theatrical contractor – Victor Mara Limited, London
Electrical contractor – Savoy Electrical Limited, London
Special lighting effects – Theatre Projects Services Limited, London
Photographic enlargement and mounting – Brook-Tella Limited, London
Special maps – Harold King   Special models – Thorp Modelmakers Limited, London
Tentage in and outside exhibition – John Edgington & Company Limited, London
Special dressed figures – Ray Scott   Declaration of Independence costumes – Derek West

P. A. TAVERNER

Introduction

The search for 1776 has taken us 13,000 miles by car in the United States, Canada, France and Great Britain, snapping up clues in countless museums, libraries and historical societies on the trail of those 18th-century items which were to represent the colours on our palette. For it was my intention that we should paint a portrait of the 18th century; one which might capture a moment when great political and social forces were at work, and which even now have their reverberations.

The decision taken more than two years ago to embark on this project was based on the belief that there *was* another side of the story to be told; the subsequent journey of discovery reconfirmed our original thoughts as a documentary note led to a painting, as an army list pinpointed the fortunes of an officer, as a cargo manifest broke the trail to a gun, as a letter confirmed the ownership of a ring . . . the web of cross-references gave life to our cast-list of players who fought a war with so much regret.

There was, we found, among the original Thirteen States a greater desire to lend precious and significant items to use in London than there existed to exchange such objects between themselves. The idea that the British should want to take a look at this celebration was a gesture which provoked both amusement and envy. Many an American director confessed his wish to have assembled the exhibits we have collected and to have told such a story as we have attempted to do.

It was impossible to travel so far in the United States without wanting to learn much more about those twin poles of the Revolution, Virginia and Massachusetts; for it was these two States above all others which provided the dominant drive and organisation to the movement for independence. It is most fitting that this exhibition should be held at Greenwich, for it was from the Royal palace once situated on this bend of the Thames that the founding charters of Virginia and what was then Massachusetts Bay were issued.

The connection between Greenwich and the American colonies is even closer than this would suggest. The Queen's House, now the focal point of the National Maritime Museum complex, was in fact a gift from James I to his wife, Queen Anne of Denmark; and in 1616 Inigo Jones was commissioned to build her residence near Greenwich Palace on the river. Almost at the same time, 3000 miles away, the first permanent English settlement in America was taking root in Virginia – at Jamestown on the James river. And it was the Pilgrim Fathers, sailing from Plymouth in the *Mayflower* in 1620, with a land grant in North Virginia (the Colony stretched north then to the New York area), who were driven from their intended landfall by adverse weather, landed at Cape Cod, and sat tight where they were, to create Massachusetts.

The climate, the land, religion and the social organisation of these two Colonies moulded their character: the one, witness to the spread of plantation life with profitable tobacco crops and plenteous slave labour; the other, sitting for a third of the year in the grip of a mean winter, peopled by tough farmers and merchants forced to be skilled at sea by terrain that was none too charitable. It is no accident that 150 years later these two Colonies still dominated American life and offered complementary services to the Revolution.

This year in London sees in fact two exhibitions dedicated to the study of America and Britain in the 18th century. Besides '1776', the Victoria and Albert Museum, under Dr Roy Strong, will mount an exhibition called 'American Art: 1750–1800; Towards Independence'. Produced in conjunction with Yale University Art Gallery, this particular display is due to bring together the very best examples of the fine and applied arts of an emerging nation. 'American Art', which opens in July, and '1776' will produce between them an almost total view of Anglo-American politics and art of the day.

It remains to me to express my gratitude to two people who have made my efforts possible. The first is my wife, Patricia Connor, historian, researcher, writer and untitled deputy, who suffers the disadvantage, unlike my office colleagues, of being available for conferences at all hours of the day and night. The second is my Chairman, Sir Denis Hamilton, who one day said 'yes', and made it all work.

KENNETH PEARSON

From the National Maritime Museum

As Director of the National Maritime Museum I am delighted that our plans to mark the Bicentenary of the American Revolution have culminated in the holding at the Museum of the largest special exhibition *The Times* and *The Sunday Times* have yet sponsored. We have collaborated to fulfil one of the most important functions both of a great national museum and of great national newspapers – to make information readily and attractively available and in so doing to provide an educational service for the public. We are delighted on this occasion to have Barclays Bank as joint sponsors of the exhibition.

For the last eight years we have been reorganising and expanding the National Maritime Museum and, in collaboration with the Department of the Environment, reconstructing all the public displays and the research facilities in one of the largest programmes of comprehensive modernisation recently undertaken by a national museum. The last stage of this reconstruction was the building of a new gallery system with additional floors inside the existing shell of the West Wing. The opening of this exhibition, held in these new galleries, marks the completion of this great rebuilding programme. In 1977, when the exhibition is over, the new galleries will be opened permanently, with displays illustrating, among other subjects, the archaeology of the ship, the history of yachting, Captain Cook and the exploration of the Pacific, and the long naval campaigns that led to Nelson's triumph at Trafalgar.

BASIL GREENHILL

The Timetable of Revolution

1492   Christopher Columbus, voyaging from Spain to discover a western route to India, lands in the New World.

1497   John Cabot sails from Bristol, under the patronage of Henry VII, to discover and settle new lands across the Atlantic. He explores the Newfoundland coast.

1607   After several unsuccessful attempts to establish British settlements in North America, particularly in Virginia, Jamestown is founded on the James river, Virginia, as the first permanent English colony.

1620   The Pilgrim Fathers sail from Plymouth in the *Mayflower* and establish an English colony in what becomes Massachusetts.

1632–1732   During this century the colonies of Maryland, Connecticut, Rhode Island, Carolina, New York, New Hampshire, Pennsylvania, New Jersey, Delaware and Georgia are one by one granted Royal charters and become established as British colonies.

1756   War breaks out against the French over territorial boundaries in North America.

1758   British capture Louisburg, Canada.

1759   The year of British victories at Minden, Germany; Quiberon Bay off Brest; and at Quebec, Canada.

1760   Accession of George III, aged twenty-two.

1763   Britain's victories in the Seven Years War earn her good terms at the Peace of Paris, including the accession of Canada, Nova Scotia, Cape Breton, St Vincent, Tobago, Dominica, Grenada, Senegal, Minorca and Florida.

1765 March   The Stamp Act, devised to tax the American colonies, ostensibly to help pay for the French war and provide defence for the Colonists.

1766 March   Stamp Act repealed, but followed by the Declaratory Act asserting Parliament's right to tax the Colonies.

1767 June   Chancellor Townshend introduces duties on glass, paper, dyestuffs and tea.

September   Colonists respond by drawing up non-importation agreements.

1770 January   Lord North becomes Prime Minister.

March   The Boston Massacre; Redcoats, provoked by a mob, fire and kill five civilians.

April   The Townshend duties abolished; tea tax is retained to maintain the right to tax.

1772 June   British revenue cutter *Gaspée* burnt by Rhode Island mob.

1773 May   Tea Act passed, restricting free tea-trade in the Colonies to protect the East India Company.

December   The Boston Tea Party, at which Rebels destroy 342 cases of East India Company tea.

1774 March   The Boston Port Bill passed. It closes the harbour to shipping as punishment for the Tea Party.

April   The Quebec Act, granting toleration to Roman Catholics in Canada, thus securing Canadian loyalty. Edmund Burke attacks the Government's American taxation policy in the House of Commons.

May   Accession of Louis XVI to throne of France.

September   First Continental Congress convenes in Philadelphia (see 'Steps to Independence' on page 71).

1775 April   First shots of the war exchanged at Lexington and Concord.

May   Rebels under Ethan Allen and Benedict Arnold capture Fort Ticonderoga.

June   George Washington appointed Commander-in-Chief of the Continental army. Battle of Bunker Hill.

December   Germain becomes Secretary of State for the Colonies.

1776 March   British evacuate Boston.

May   American mission in Paris secures secret loan of one million *livres*.

July   Declaration of Independence passed by Continental Congress.

September   British occupy New York.

December   British occupy Rhode Island. Washington retreats across New Jersey into Pennsylvania, then crosses Delaware river and defeats the Hessians at Trenton.

1777 January   Washington defeats British at Princeton.

April   Lafayette, with other French volunteers, arrives in America.

September   British defeat Rebels under Washington at Brandywine and occupy Philadelphia.

October   Burgoyne surrenders his army to Gates at Saratoga.

1778 February   France signs treaty of commerce and friendship with the Rebels.

April   Chatham collapses while addressing the House of Lords on American policy and dies five weeks later.

June   Conciliation offers from peace commission under the 5th Earl of Carlisle rejected by Congress. British, under Clinton, evacuate Philadelphia.

July   Comte d'Estaing's fleet arrives in American waters.

September   French capture Dominica.

November   British sieze St Lucia from the French.

December   British occupy Savannah, Georgia.

1779 June   Spain declares war on Britain. The siege of Gibraltar begins.

July   French capture Grenada.

August   The 'false armada' (the French fleet) occupies the Channel, threatening invasion.

September   *Bonhomme Richard*, under John Paul Jones, captures H.M.S. *Serapis* off Flamborough Head from Captain Richard Pearson. Convoy under escort of *Serapis* escapes.

October   A combined French-American siege of Savannah ends in Rebel retreat.

1780 May   British capture Charleston, South Carolina.

June   Riots in London, instigated by anti-Catholic Lord George Gordon. Army camps established in Hyde Park and on Blackheath.

July   Rochambeau and his troops arrive at Newport, Rhode Island.

August   Gates trounced by Cornwallis at Camden.

October   John André hanged as a British spy following Benedict Arnold's defection. Patrick Ferguson killed in major Loyalist defeat by Rebels at King's Mountain.

November   Holland enters the war following a British declaration.

1781 January   Tarleton defeated by Daniel Morgan at Cowpens.

March   Cornwallis wins a pyrrhic victory over Nathanael Greene at Guilford Court House.

May   Washington and Rochambeau meet at Wethersfield and draw up strategy which leads to Yorktown.

June   French forces move from New England to a rendezvous with the Rebel army.

August   De Grasse arrives with reinforcements in the Chesapeake while the allied Franco-American troops move south to Virginia.

September   Indecisive Battle of the Capes prevents naval relief of Yorktown.

October   Cornwallis surrenders his army after the siege of Yorktown.

1782 February   Spain takes Minorca from the British.

March   Lord North resigns; succeeded by a Whig coalition under Rockingham.

April   Rodney saves the West Indies by defeating de Grasse at the Battle of the Saints.

July   On Rockingham's death, Shelburne forms Ministry. British evacuate Savannah.

October   Admiral Lord Howe relieves Gibraltar.

November   Preliminary Articles of Peace agreed in Paris.

December   British evacuate Charleston.

1783 February   British and Americans proclaim the cessation of hostilities.

September   Treaty of Paris signed.

November   Final evacuation of New York begins.

1785 June   John Adams presents credentials to George III as first American Minister to the Court of St James.

Prologue

1

General Sir Banastre Tarleton, 1754–1833
Sir Joshua Reynolds

London, 1782. Oil on canvas
236·2 cm × 145·3 cm
The Trustees of the National Gallery, London

Tarleton in this portrait is traditionally given the rank and title he attained later in life. Here, in fact, he is seen as the young cavalry officer, a lieutenant-colonel at twenty-six, whose victories in the southern American colonies in 1780 and 1781 earned him the reputation of a fearless fighter. The Rebels called him 'Bloody Tarleton'.

Reynolds' portrait was painted in 1782 and the artist records the first sitting as taking place on 28 January. It was exhibited at the Royal Academy that same year when Gainsborough's equestrian portrait of Tarleton, now untraced, first appeared. Reynolds shows him in the uniform of the British Legion, a unit of American Loyalist cavalry. The flag is emblazoned with the letter 'L', presumably for 'Legion'. Tarleton's pose disguises the fact that he had lost two fingers of his right hand at the Battle of Guilford Court House in March 1781. (For further details of his career see item 513.)

The red-haired cavalryman, impetuous and daring, typifies those field officers who won moments of great victory for King and Country in the American Revolution.

2

General James Wolfe, 1727–59
The Chaulette Brothers

Quebec, 1779. Painted wood
152·4 cm high, including pedestal; 91·4 cm wide, including extended arm
Literary and Historical Society of Quebec

This statue of General Wolfe was carved from a life portrait by Hervey Smyth, Wolfe's aide-de-camp. Smyth's picture was a study for a full portrait and was done just before the battle for the Heights of Abraham and the capture of Quebec in 1759.

In the 1770s a burgess of Quebec, George Hipps, grew disturbed that there was no monument in the town to the man who had in effect taken Canada from the French. Hipps bought a house on the corner of a street with a niche over the front door. He then commissioned two French wood sculptors named Chaulette to carve an exact likeness of the General. When completed, it stood in its niche until the end of the 19th century. (Ref: Casgrain, P. B., 'The Monument to Wolfe on the Plains of Abraham and the Old Statue at Wolfe's Corner', *Transactions of the Royal Society of Canada*, vol. 10, 1904.)

Wolfe symbolises here the strength of British forces in the Seven Years War (1756–63). The French defeat ensured that France would take her revenge at the first opportunity. The American Revolution was that moment.

THE PROLOGUE

The Prologue to the Exhibition celebrates in photographic form the personalities on both sides of the Atlantic whose contact in their various professions cements understanding at a number of levels. Pop music, diplomacy, the sciences, drama, scholarship, sport, etc., mark those fields in which a similarity of endeavour and a common language expressing those achievements are seen to be part of the bonds which attract Britain and America to each other. The Prologue spans the last thirty-five years or so to a moment when the United States chose to return to Europe as our Allies.

There was a time in 1776 when . . . but that is another story. Here it is.

Colour Plates

I

88

62

43

139

124

408

The BLOODY MASSACRE perpetrated in King — — Street BOSTON on March 5. 1770 by a party of the 29th REG.t

Unhappy BOSTON! see thy Sons deplore,
Thy hallow'd Walks besmear'd with guiltless Gore:
While faithless P—n and his savage Bands,
With murd'rous Rancour stretch their bloody Hands;
Like fierce Barbarians grinning o'er their Prey,
Approve the Carnage and enjoy the Day.

If scalding drops from Rage from Anguish Wrung
If speechless Sorrows lab'ring for a Tongue
Or if a weeping World can ought appease
The plaintive Ghosts of Victims such as these;
The Patriot's copious Tears for each are shed,
A glorious Tribute which embalms the Dead.

But know, Fate summons to that awful Goal,
Where JUSTICE strips the Murd'rer of his Soul:
Should venal C—ts the scandal of the Land,
Snatch the relentless Villain from her Hand,
Keen Execrations on this Plate inscrib'd,
Shall reach a JUDGE who never can be brib'd.

The unhappy Sufferers were Mess.rs SAM.l GRAY, SAM.l MAVERICK, JAM.s CALDWELL, CRISPUS ATTUCKS & PAT.k CARR
Killed. Six wounded; two of them (CHRIST.r MONK & JOHN CLARK) Mortally

Engrav'd Printed & Sold by PAUL REVERE BOSTON

22

375

Thayeadanegea
Joseph Brant
the Mohawk Chief.

328, 332

332

The First, Second, and Last Scene of Mortality. Prudence Punderson.

466

357

565, 498

A Question of Duty

ALL BEGINNINGS ARE ARBITRARY. There was no magic change in North America in 1763 following the signing of the Treaty of Paris, which ended the Seven Years War between Britain (with Prussia) and France (with Austria). Britain had won Canada from the French 'on the Plains of Germany' in Pitt's phrase, largely by giving such financial aid to Frederick the Great of Prussia that the French were tied down in Europe. Canada had been won also by Pitt's strategy and by the skill and courage of his commanders, notably the young Wolfe and his even younger colleague William Howe, who had scaled the steep cliffs of the Heights of Abraham in 1759 and captured Quebec.

With French threats removed, the American colonists now had a totally new sense of security. They could safely look north and west to the New Country, and felt not only relief but pride. The conquest, however, was primarily the work of British regulars on British pay; the Colonists had every reason to be grateful to Pitt the Elder and his commanders.

The British Empire in North America in 1763 was extensive. It stretched from the stormy seas off Labrador, from Anticosti Island and from Hudson Bay down to the steamy swamps of Florida, and inland to the heights of the Appalachians. The newly-conquered country of Canada was thinly peopled with missionaries and fur trappers scattered across the St Lawrence and on to the Great Lakes, with posts in the Old North West and with outposts on the Mississippi at Kaskaskia and Vincennes. As part of the Treaty terms, the French settlement of New Orleans went to Spain.

Until 1763 the scattered and diverse bits of empire, casually and haphazardly acquired, were not parts of a system. The Board of Trade and Plantations directed it with a light rein, and laws were as often evaded as honoured. Its guardian was the navy. From it, however, the middle class grew and prospered by trade and commerce on both sides of the ocean, in London and Bristol, Liverpool and Glasgow, Boston and Philadelphia. The Navigation Acts (1651, 1663, 1696) ensured a British monopoly of trade but gave bounties to colonial products, guaranteed markets for the staple crops of tobacco and sugar, and fostered an active colonial ship-building industry. By 1776 one in four of the 7000 ships engaged in the Atlantic trade were American or West Indian built. It is true that New England did not benefit from this mercantilist system nearly as much as the plantation colonies, but by discreet evasion of the law and a rich smuggling industry with the British West Indies, Boston, as well as the Chesapeake Bay colonies, was booming.

The conquest of Canada, and the extent of the North American empire, posed a military problem: the security of half a continent, most of it unmapped. The British Government had nine under-strength battalions spread in a great arc from Pensacola up to Halifax. It posted them in small detachments of regulars, drawn mainly from the 60th (Royal American) Regiment. It had first and last to guarantee that there would be no resumption of the French threat, and, in particular, that those Indian tribes who were allies of the French would stay quiescent. For their part, the Indians were afraid of the British who came to settle, whereas the French were first and last traders and trappers. Coinciding with the treaty of Paris, the Ottawas rose in rebellion and in their chief, Pontiac, produced an outstanding leader. Thus while both in London and in North America there was a wave of rejoicing at the signing of the Peace, it was not in fact until a year later that the trouble with the Ottawas was ended. It seemed not only wisdom but liberalism for the British Government to draw a firm line at the peaks of the mountains, the Proclamation Line, and say 'thus far and no farther'. The Indians were to be protected in their hunting lands and given some reasonable security. If, however, it seemed to be counsel of wisdom and kindness in London, the curbing of the westward movement of the white settlers seemed, to enterprising men like George Washington and wily Ben Franklin, the Pennsylvania agent in London, to be an attempt at restriction. Many of them ignored the rules and even George Washington instructed his agent in the Youghiogheny country, William Crawford, to buy up all the land he could. Crawford did well for his patron.

All of this – defence, security, liberal Indian policy and the control of a restless white frontier movement – required an increase in the number of troops and in the money with which to finance it. Accordingly in 1763, George Grenville, the Chancellor of the Exchequer, decided to invite suggestions for methods whereby a larger army could be financed. He waited for a year and none of the colonial agents were able to offer suggestions, so in 1764 he brought forward his proposal for a Stamp Act through which the revenue from stamps imposed on legal documents and newspapers, cards and dice, would be devoted to this purpose. This was an entirely familiar practice in Britain and seemed in no way unusual; moreover, the revenue from the stamps would produce only one-quarter of what was going to be needed to pay for the defence of the newly-won territories.

The Stamp Act made good sense and seemed legitimate. In Britain there was also a sense of pride. The new spirit in London was imperial, aware of the commerce that bound the recently acquired territories together but aware also of a need for order and – given the size of the debt and land tax at four shillings and six pence in the pound – for economy. Very few people in Britain, and indeed very few in North America, envisaged the wave of protest that would follow the Stamp Act. Benjamin Franklin even recommended a friend for the job of Stamp Distributor. The opposition, unexpected and all but spontaneous, caught Britain unawares.

ESMOND WRIGHT

6

11

3
The Right Honourable George Grenville, 1712–70
Attributed to George Romney

1762–3. Oil on canvas
78·7 cm × 60·9 cm
The Earl of Halifax, Garrowby, Yorkshire

George Grenville was the Father of the Stamp Act, 1765, one of the means by which Parliament tried to raise money from American sources to defray the expense of keeping British troops on the frontiers of the thirteen colonies. Grenville, educated at Eton and Oxford, was a master of finance and Parliamentary procedure. He held many government posts until he was appointed First Lord of the Treasury and Chancellor of the Exchequer (and therefore Prime Minister) in April 1763.

On 7 February 1765, fifty-five resolutions, imposing nearly the same stamp duties on America as there existed in England, were unanimously agreed in the House of Commons. Grenville, brother-in-law of William Pitt, the first Earl of Chatham, was dismissed from office in July 1765, when George III grew tired of his Minister's tedious manners and temper.

The Stamp Act was designed to collect £60,000 a year to pay part of the £350,000 estimated as the cost of maintaining troops across the Atlantic. The duties would be payable on a great deal of printed matter, including newspapers and legal documents.

4
Charles Watson Wentworth,
2nd Marquess of Rockingham, 1730–82
Sir Joshua Reynolds

1774. Oil on canvas
124·4 cm × 99 cm
The Earl of Rosebery, South Queensferry, West Lothian

Rockingham, a Whig and a friend of Pitt, became First Lord of the Treasury in July 1765. A young, inexperienced politician, he was at once under great pressure to repeal the Stamp Act. Countless violations of the Act in the Colonies and the lobbying of British merchants, who had suffered a twenty-five per cent drop in trade through American boycotts, brought quick results: the Act was repealed in March 1766.

But behind the ever-present desire to tax the colonies, there lay the need of Parliament to assert its sovereignty. Support for the Repeal of the Stamp Act was assured by the concurrent passage of the Declaratory Act making Parliament's position clear.

This, in turn, was followed by the Mutiny Act which indirectly required Provincial Assemblies to provide quarters for British troops in the Colonies. Rockingham's Ministry was short-lived: it fell in July 1766.

5
Charles Townshend, 1725–67
Sir Joshua Reynolds

1766. Oil on canvas
238·7 cm × 147·3 cm
The Marquess Townshend of Raynham, Norfolk

Seen in this portrait in the robes of the Chancellor of the Exchequer, Charles Townshend took up this Cabinet post in Pitt's last Ministry in August 1766. In May 1767, the wit who could keep a club table 'in a roar till two o'clock in the morning', brought in proposals to deal with the rising temper of the Americans and the financial needs of his budget. Among other proposals, Commissioners of Customs were to be established in America to superintend the laws of trade, and a port duty was to be imposed on glass, red and white lead, painters' colours, paper . . . and tea.

News of the impending duties provoked Americans to riot. Further anti-importation associations were formed, and customs officers began to suffer brutal consequences. Townshend never lived to see the results of his actions. On 4 September 1767 he died of 'a neglected fever'.

6
The 3rd Duke of Grafton, 1735–1811
Pompeo Batoni

1762. Oil on canvas
73·6 cm × 60·9 cm
The Duke of Grafton, Thetford, Norfolk

Augustus Henry Fitzroy, Duke of Grafton, was appointed First Lord of the Treasury in July 1766. In this case, the post did not entitle him to lead the administration. William Pitt had formed the Government, but as he was ill he had retired to the House of Lords as the Earl of Chatham, a long-expected rise to the ranks of the peerage. Grafton would execute the daily business.

The Duke had great ability, and with Chatham's later retreat to the country, he effectively took over the Ministry. At thirty-one he was the youngest Prime Minister to that date. In office, his American sympathies led him to believe that all the Townshend duties should be repealed, but 'to his great surprise and mortification' his Cabinet voted, against his ad-

vice, not to rescind all taxes. Grafton lost by a vote of one, and the tax on tea was retained. It was in the spring of 1770, after Grafton's resignation, that Lord North's new Ministry repealed all the Townshend duties except that one.

The problem of Parliamentary sovereignty still exercised the Government's mind. The right to tax Americans had once again to be asserted.

7
William Pitt, Earl of Chatham, 1708–78
Richard Brompton

1772. Oil on canvas
116·2 cm × 85·6 cm
The National Portrait Gallery, London

A shaper of victory against France in the Seven Years War, Pitt's direct method of administration (ministers leaving the King at St James's Palace would find Pitt slipping instructions into their hands on the way out), a necessary dynamic in war, was not always the most winning expedient in peace. Nevertheless, he had been a mountain of a politician, and his presence threw its shadow across generations of government.

On the question of taxing the American colonies, Pitt had no doubts. The Stamp Act should be repealed, he said in 1766, 'absolutely, totally and immediately'. He was, however, no supporter of American independence. His defeated Bill of February 1775 was meant to declare the supremacy of England over the Colonies in all matters except taxation. When in December 1777, he recommended the withdrawal of troops from the Colonies, he was still 'an avowed enemy to American independency'.

Pitt, in his last years, was afflicted with mental and physical disorders. In April 1778, when the Duke of Richmond moved in the House of Lords for the withdrawal of troops, Pitt had shifted his ground. Wrapped in flannel and supported on crutches, he protested against 'the dismemberment of this ancient and most noble monarchy'. When he rose to speak a second time, he collapsed with a fit. He died on 11 May at his country house at Hayes, Middlesex.

8
John Wilkes M.P., 1727–97
Robert Edge Pine

1768. Signed and dated above chair: 'R. E. Pine, pix, 1768'. Oil on canvas
127 cm × 101 cm
The Speaker of the House of Commons, London

Wilkes, son of a City malt distiller, free-thinker and rake, and in no way disconcerted by his perpetual squint, entered Parliament in 1761 as a loyal supporter of Pitt. Having already made some mark as a controversial pamphleteer, Wilkes launched early attacks against George III and the Tory Government, which reached their historical climax with edition number 45 of his newspaper *The North Briton*. (Its title epitomised much English hatred of the Scottish Lord Bute, the King's early favourite, and therefore of all Scots.) In it Wilkes had attacked the King's Speech at the Opening of Parliament, and insinuated that the King had countenanced a deliberate lie.

Law officers, who believed the article a seditious libel, had Wilkes committed to the Tower of London. Through the long struggle that followed, Wilkes was dismissed from Parliament, imprisoned and forced to suffer exile in France. At issue, in reality, was the question of Parliamentary privilege and the freedom of speech that privilege might permit. King, Government, Opposition and the country at large were passionately exercised by the conflict. Finally recovering his position, Wilkes became a City of London Alderman (the City backed his views) and later Lord Mayor.

Wilkes, Pitt and the 'No. 45' were all embraced by the American colonists as symbols of the liberty of speech and the individual.

9
The 2nd Earl of Dartmouth, 1731–1801
Thomas Gainsborough

1769. Oil on canvas
124·4 cm × 99 cm
The Earl of Dartmouth, Kings Langley, Hertfordshire

William Legge, second Earl of Dartmouth, took his seat in the House of Lords in May 1754. He was appointed President of the Board of Trade and Foreign Plantations in July 1765. In August 1772 he took up the post of Secretary of State for the Colonies. He was a sensitive man and although he came down on the side of coercion of the Colonies, his decisions were not easily arrived at. Benjamin Franklin called Dartmouth 'a truly good man', who 'wishes sincerely a good understanding with the Colonies, but does not seem to have strength equal to his wishes'. He was succeeded as Secretary of State for the Colonies in November 1775, by Lord George Germain.

10
Carved plaque of the Royal Coat of Arms
Boston, 18th century. Carved and painted wood
78·7 cm × 92·6 cm
Massachusetts Historical Society, Boston

These carved Royal Arms hung over the doorway of the Province House in Boston, home of the Royal Governors of the Colony of Massachusetts Bay from 1716 until the Rebels forced the British to evacuate the city. Under this symbol of Royal government, Britons and Americans passed daily on political and commercial business.

11
'No Stamp Act' teapot
English, *c.* 1765. Creamware, lead-glazed earthenware
12 cm high
Colonial Williamsburg Foundation,
Williamsburg, Virginia

Domestic items of all kinds were used to carry propaganda during the Revolution.

12
A sheet of twenty Stamp Act seal impressions from Boston
24 cm × 30 cm
Massachusetts Historical Society, Boston

13
Stamp Duty stamps
Two loose-leaf sheets from proof volumes of stamp impressions, 18 April 1765
20 cm × 25 cm
Trustees of the British Library, London

1. Page 34 of larger 1d. (one penny) stamps for newspapers and pamphlets
2. Page 45 of smaller 4d. (fourpenny) stamps for almanacs

Following the Stamp Act, the Stamp Commissioners authorised designs for the various values of stamps to be used. These two sheets are typical of those submitted for approval in May 1765.

14
The Stamp Duty Register
The Register of the Dies and Stamps used in the service of the Stamp Duty Revenue for America and West Indies Isles etc. Book A.
48·2 cm × 30·4 cm
Trustees of the British Library, London

A symbol of the early trouble between Britain and the American colonies, this register contains examples of the dies, impressed on to paper, issued for the printing of legal and commercial documents listed under the Stamp Act. There is one other register held in the collections of the Inland Revenue.

15
The seal of Andrew Oliver, Lieutenant-Governor of Massachusetts Bay

Amethyst; incised arms and motto
2·5 cm × 2·2 cm
Mr Andrew Oliver, Boston, Massachusetts

This elliptical seal is carved with the Oliver family arms, crest and the motto 'Pax Quaeritur Bello' – 'peace is obtained by war'. Attached is a silver label bearing on one side: 'The original Seal of Andrew Oliver, Lieut. Governor of Massachusetts, 1771. Ob. 1774.'

Andrew Oliver (1706–74), a graduate, moved early into governing circles in colonial Boston. He was overseer of the poor, collector of taxes, member of the school inspection committee and of the Provincial Council, and secretary of the colony. Later, when the Stamp Act was passed, he accepted the office of Distributor of Stamps. On 14 August 1765, he was hanged in effigy on Boston Common between the figures of Lord Bute and George Grenville. The next day Oliver signed a pledge refusing the job.

By December 1765, under the pressure of economic distress, the temper of the Boston mob grew worse. On 16 December, Oliver received a letter demanding his full resignation as Stamp Distributor. 'Your non-Compliance, Sir,' the note said, 'will incur the Displeasure of the Trueborn Sons of Liberty.' The next day, before 2000 spectators, he swore not to enforce the Stamp Act.

In October 1770, he was appointed Lieutenant-Governor of Massachusetts. He died in Boston in March 1774. A howling mob followed his coffin to the grave.

16
Silver spoon celebrating 'the Repeal of the American Stamp Act'

English, 1766. Silver
20 cm long; bowl 4·1 cm wide
Virginia Historical Society, Richmond

Inscribed on the back of this spoon are the words: 'L.C. 1766 the Repeal of the American Stamp Act'. The spoon first belonged to Landon Carter (1710–78) of Sabine Hall, Richmond County, Virginia. Carter

19

9

was a leading Virginian critic of the Stamp Act which he denounced as a 'sinister conspiracy'. It is recorded that Carter ordered these spoons from London, the order to be executed in silver only if the Act was repealed; otherwise they were to be made of horn.

17
'Pitt' mug
Richard Chaffers

Liverpool, c. 1760. Transfer-printed porcelain
11·9 cm high
Merseyside County Museums, Liverpool

Another form of communication. Only by these means could the majority of people know what their leaders in London looked like. This mug was printed in Liverpool by Sadler and Green. The likeness of Pitt was taken from a Thomas Billinge engraving of the Hoare canvas of 1756.

18
'The Last Shift'
1765. Engraving, apparently a book plate
10·4 cm × 13·3 cm
Ref: BM 4118
Trustees of the British Museum, London

The engraving shows a British officer of the Government holding up a party of Americans. Lord Bute tells George III that the new taxes will provide welcome funds. Bute, formerly the King's tutor and still at this time reckoned to exert great influence at Court, was supposed to have prompted a series of measures, of which the Stamp Act was one.

19
'The Able Doctor, or America Swallowing the Bitter Draught'
1774. Engraving from the *London Magazine*
9·2 cm × 15 cm
Ref: BM 5226
Trustees of the British Museum, London

This print illustrates a report on the debate of the Boston Port Bill passed on 31 March 1774, as a punishment for the Boston Tea Party (see 'Storm in a Teacup', page 40).

In this print America is held down by Lord Mansfield, Lord Chief Justice, while Lord North pours tea down her throat and America spews it back. From North's pocket there protrudes a copy of the Boston Port Bill, which was to close the harbour to all shipping. Lord Sandwich, First Lord of the

17

Admiralty, holds America's legs. Behind Mansfield stands a shocked Britannia and Lord Bute with a sword engraved 'Military Law'. To the left the figures of France and Spain watch the proceedings.

20
South Battery certificate
Thomas Johnston

Boston, before 1765. Line engraving, signed under picture: 'T. Johnston, Sculpt.'
19·6 cm × 27·3 cm
American Antiquarian Society, Worcester, Massachusetts

Men who served at the Boston fortresses as 'montrosses', or artillerymen, were given these certificates as a form of identity card. The North and South Batteries were Boston's main seaward defences at this period. The engraving of the fort testifies to Johnston's skill.

21
'A View of Part of the Town of Boston in New England and British Ships of War Landing their Troops! 1768'
Paul Revere (see item 38)

Boston, 1770. Line engraving, signed lower right: 'Engraved, Printed and Sold by Paul Revere'
33 cm × 48·2 cm
The Boston Athenaeum, Massachusetts

Increasing violence in New England provoked the British Government into reinforcing its troops in the Colonies. Here Paul Revere, silversmith, engraver and despatch rider, catches the moment when the Redcoats land at Boston Long Wharf. The forces included the 14th and 29th Regiments of Foot, a detachment of the 59th, and a train of artillery with two cannon. Revere owed much here to the influence of Christian Remick, master mariner and an amateur artist of some talent (see item 25).

22
'The Bloody Massacre perpetrated in King Street'
Paul Revere

Boston, 1770. Line engraving, signed lower right: 'Engrav'd Printed & Sold by Paul Revere Boston'
31·6 cm × 28·5 cm
The Boston Athenaeum, Massachusetts

On 5 March 1770, a wild mob began to taunt a British sentry on duty outside the Customs House in Boston. The soldier was abused and ice and snow were thrown at him. Six privates and a corporal appeared from a guardhouse and were joined by the officer of the day, Captain Thomas Preston. The shouting crowd pressed closer and closer. Suddenly shots rang out and five Americans fell dead or mortally wounded.

The print, plagiarised from that of another engraver, and first on the market twenty-three days after the event, was a piece of propaganda which achieved its aim. The picture is inaccurate. The Redcoats did not line up and fire in this manner. The trial of the soldiers, defended by American lawyers who later became Rebel leaders, found only two of the soldiers guilty of manslaughter. The six others were acquitted.

Henry Pelham, from whom Revere had stolen the idea, wrote to the engraver on 29 March 1770 describing what Revere had done as 'one of the most dishonorable Actions you could well be guilty of'.

STORM IN A TEACUP
Long-established laws ensured that the American colonies traded only through Britain. The mother country imported raw materials – timber for ships, iron, skins, tobacco, rice, fish, flour and dyes. In return the Colonies were provided with all the manufactured goods they needed: woollens, metalware, linens, cottons, silks, paper, tea, hardware, hats and shoes. By the early 1770s this imbalance in trade left the Colonies with an annual deficit of £1·6 million.

Discontent across the Atlantic reached a peak in 1773, when the British Government tried to rescue the East India Company from a financial crisis. (The growth of American smuggling, principally through Dutch ports, had contributed to the glut of tea overflowing from the Company's warehouses.) The consequent Tea Act of May 1773 allowed the East India Company to undercut the price of all tea sold in America, and named specific consignees in the main cities to handle the trade. For the colonists this new set of limitations was the last straw. On 16 December 1773, a crowd of Bostonians threw 342 chests of East India Company tea into the harbour.

The destruction of about 105,000 pounds of tea, valued by various authorities at between £11,000 and £18,000, was considered by the British Government a flagrant criminal act: it responded with the Boston Port Bill in March 1774, which closed the port to all shipping. The American boycott of British goods intensified and after 1774 trade ground to a halt. The value of British imports dropped from £2,590,000 to £201,000. In December 1775, with 600 ships idle in the Thames, the Government imposed a total ban on colonial trade.

23
Green Dragon Tavern
John Johnston

Boston, 1773. Pen and ink with watercolour wash, signed bottom centre: 'John Johnson'
21·5 cm × 31 cm
American Antiquarian Society, Worcester, Massachusetts

Taverns and church meeting halls were the traditional gathering places in the American colonies. The Green Dragon Tavern, in the North End of Boston, was the meeting place for the local Sons of Liberty, a self-appointed association of colonists dedicated to fighting the Stamp Act and subsequent legislation. It was here, according to this contemporary sketch, that the Boston Tea Party was planned in December 1773. These were men who had been moulded by the hard life of the colony of Massachusetts Bay, a province of 250,000 inhabitants focused on Boston.

Few watercolour views of 18th-century Boston survive. This small sketch has probably been saved by the importance of the Green Dragon as a revolutionary headquarters.

24
Castle William
Artist unknown

Boston, 1773. Ink and watercolour
10 cm × 20 cm
Ref: LC-USZ62-45381
Library of Congress, Washington, D.C.

Castle William, on Castle Island, defended the outer reaches of Boston Harbour. During the Stamp Act troubles it provided refuge for Government officials from the mobs who wrecked their houses. After the Boston Massacre, British troops were withdrawn from the town to Castle William.

25
'A Perspective View of the Blockade of Boston Harbour'
Christian Remick

Boston, c. 1768. Watercolour, signed in the shield upper right: 'Christian Remich'
41 cm × 162·8 cm
Massachusetts Historical Society, Boston

Soon after the British landed troops in Boston in October 1768, Remick produced six similar watercolours of the event, several dedicated to patrons, including Rebel leader John Hancock (see item 99).

26
'A New Method of Macarony Making, as practised at Boston'
London, 12 October 1774. Mezzotint, 'printed for Carrington Bowles, No. 69 in St Paul's Church Yard'
35·5 cm × 25·4 cm
Ref: BM 5232
National Maritime Museum, Greenwich, London

Two Bostonians tar and feather an unfortunate customs officer. The rope around his neck suggests he has been half-hanged. The cockade on the hat on the right marks the man out as one of the Sons of Liberty. The '45' on the other hat refers to the 'No. 45' issue of John Wilkes's *The North Briton* (see item 8). The satire is based on the treatment handed out to John Malcom or Malcomb, Commissioner for Customs in Boston, who in January 1774 was tarred and feathered, led to the gallows and forced to drink great quantities of tea.

The 'Macarony' in the title gives it an ironic twist. It was the name applied to 18th-century English dandies whose clothes exaggerated the height of fashion.

27
'The Bostonians in Distress'
London. Mezzotint, 'printed for R. Sayer, & J. Bennett, Map and Printsellers, No. 53 Fleet Street, as the Act directs, 19 Nov 1774'
35 cm × 25 cm
Boston Public Library, Massachusetts

When the British closed the port of Boston, many Americans were distressed by unemployment and the expense of bringing supplies overland from Salem, the nearest operating port. The satire shows British troops and cannon surrounding the Liberty Tree on Boston Common. In the background four British warships blockade the port. Gifts of food were sent to Boston from all parts of the continent. A knowledge of America is shown by the Bostonians' punishment. This method was employed in the colonies for slaves convicted of capital offences. They were imprisoned in this manner and starved to death.

28
The Boston Tea Party
This drawing by Johann Ramberg (1763–1840) was an illustration for a German yearbook of 1784 covering the American Revolution. It is the earliest known sketch devoted to the Tea Party itself; the original is in the Metropolitan Museum of Art, New York.

The Road to Bunker Hill

TWO LANTERNS SHONE in the tower of Boston's North Church on the clear, moonlit night of 18 April 1775. Units of the British army were on the move to destroy rebel powder stores and supplies. Signals across the New England countryside were warning American militia companies of General Gage's 'secret' intent. The people of Massachusetts were roused.

Across the waters of Boston harbour Paul Revere, express rider for the Rebels, rowed from the town to the opposite Cambridge shore. One lamp was to shine if the British marched across the Boston Neck towards Lexington and Concord. Two indicated that they would be taking the shorter route by boat to Charlestown, then marching the twenty-one mile route from there. Revere was ahead of them.

The British plan to seize the stores was the outward sign of the tensions which existed by 1775 between the British administration and the American population. Those Parliamentary acts provoked by the Boston Tea Party, which had brought economic distress to Massachusetts, had done nothing to reconcile American opinion to the British point of view, though there were hundreds of New England colonists who still looked to George III as their king.

Executive power in the Colony was beginning to move away from the Royal assemblies and to be assumed by self-appointed American bodies. The first Continental Congress had met in Philadelphia in September 1774, and the Massachusetts Provincial Congress had set itself up in Concord as a revolutionary government. Thomas Gage, commander-in-chief of the British forces and Governor of Massachusetts, had informed London that it would take 20,000 men to reconquer New England. London might not be sending reinforcements on anything like that scale (Gage had about 3500 men in Boston), but some sort of action was demanded at once. Local spies had told him of the stores.

Paul Revere was not alone that night riding the news to the farming communities. Dr Joseph Warren, soon to be president of the Provincial Congress and living in Boston, had asked a neighbour, William Dawes, to take the land route to Lexington and Concord. With Revere in the lead at Lexington, Rebel leaders John Hancock and Sam Adams, staying at a local house, were warned that the British were coming and they might be arrested. Dawes, Revere, and a new recruit, Samuel Prescott, now made for Concord. Not long on the new road, the riders were surprised by patrolling British officers. Dawes and Prescott escaped and headed for Concord. Revere was taken into custody.

Back in Boston, Lieutenant-Colonel Francis Smith of the 10th Foot had been given the task of leading the Redcoats on the raid. He had eight light infantry companies – the fastest men – and eight grenadier companies – the toughest men in a regiment. By 2 a.m. his force was ashore on the Cambridge side of Boston harbour, wading through marsh, fording a stream to avoid noise on a bridge, each man with one day's rations and thirty-six rounds.

By the time Colonel Smith and his 700 men had reached Menotomy it was clear that the entire countryside was party to the operation. Smith had sent on the 52-year-old Major Pitcairn with a detachment to secure the bridge which they would use to cross the Concord river. Now he sent back a message to Gage that reinforcements would be needed. Gage gave the order at 4 a.m. that Lord Percy, colonel of the 5th Foot and a brigadier-general under Gage, was to take his First Brigade to help the Redcoats on the road. One of the orders involved in this move was misdelivered; there was a four-hour delay.

Meanwhile, as the British force approached Lexington, John Parker, captain of the local militia, had drawn up some seventy Rebels across a part of Lexington Green. Major Pitcairn called on his soldiers not to fire 'but to surround and disarm them'. But soldiers had broken ranks, officers were shouting. Parker ordered his men to disperse. There was a general melée . . . and suddenly a shot. No one knows who fired that first shot. There is no evidence. But the British fired a volley after that, and then another. And then there were dead Rebels lying on the Green.

When Colonel Smith caught up with the action, he was horrified. He rode on to the Green, shouting for a drummer. As soon as the rattle of a drum rose above the clamour, the Redcoats obeyed its orders, formed ranks, and marched away to Concord. But then, as they came near to their target, Smith's column of soldiers became aware of a phenomenon that was to haunt the British army for the next six years of the conflict. Marching along the ridges parallel with their own route were scores and scores of Rebel militia, growing in number by the minute, as from the surrounding country volunteers joined in to march with the expanding column.

At Concord, detachments moved off to search for supplies, breaking open barn doors, burning gun carriages, pouring ammunition and flour into the town pond; the rest marched on to the North Bridge towards their final destination. At the bridge, soon after the Redcoats had been deployed to search, Captain Walter Laurie of the 43rd Foot watched anxiously as a long snake of some 400 Rebel militia advanced upon the bridge from the other side of the river. Some British units were recalled in time for the second confrontation of the Revolution. This time the nervous Redcoats suffered no inhibitions about firing first. They shot at the Rebels, and began their retreat.

There was, a minute before that retreat, a silence across the bridge at Concord, when men in uniform had no wish to attack, and men in homespun jackets and familiar deep-crowned hats said, 'We were the more careful to prevent beginning a rupture with the King's troops . . .'. But in the distance the fires in Concord looked as if the British were burning the town, and to the Redcoats the American militia posed a threat to a safe return to Boston. So there was killing.

The British, despite what may have been said, had accomplished their mission: to get to the stores, destroy them, and return to Boston. On their way back through Concord, Rebels fired from the surrounding fields, crouching low behind stone walls, not a phalanx of another colour to be outwitted, out-shot and overrun. Back through Lexington, where with two cannon set up for action, Lord Percy's relief force waited. Fourteen hundred men were deployed to swallow up the exhausted grenadiers who staggered in, low on ammunition. For the next 15 miles back, the British troops, now with flankers in the outer fields, fought their way home, as the Rebel militia fired and ran on and fired again.

Near to Boston Lord Percy was faced with a large American force awaiting him at Cambridge. Instead of taking the expected route, Percy feinted in that direction and then swung north towards the Charlestown peninsula and the safety of Royal Naval guns. As night fell, his weary troops were ferried across the water to Boston. British casualty figures vary according to different authorities, but they can be put at seventy-three killed, 174 wounded and perhaps twenty-six missing. The Rebels lost forty-nine killed, about forty wounded and five missing. But the figures were not strategically important. The British were back in Boston; the Americans now surrounded the town. The siege of Boston had begun.

The fight at Lexington and Concord changed British attitudes. The Rebels were no longer to be despised as fighters. 'Whoever looks upon them as an irregular mob,' Lord Percy wrote to London, 'will be much mistaken.' On their side, the Rebels used a grossly exaggerated report of the action with false stories of atrocities (that is not to say there were none) to challenge opinion in London by getting there first.

The rest of April, and then May, went by in Boston. At Cambridge, the Rebel army grew in size. The senior British ranks in Boston had been reinforced by three major-generals: Burgoyne, Clinton and Howe. There were plans to attack the Rebels, first of all by occupying two points of high land from which Boston could be dominated: Dorchester Heights to the south on the mainland; and Breed's Hill and Bunker Hill on the Charlestown peninsula. Two days before the British were due to move onto Dorchester Heights, the Rebels in one night threw up a redoubt almost invulnerable to cannon on Breed's Hill (confused by 18th-century map-makers with Bunker Hill and known as that to historians from then on) and by their threatening presence there, took the offensive.

On an exceedingly hot day, 17 June 1775 (the day Washington in Philadelphia was appointed to lead the Rebel army), General Howe led the attack on the enemy position. Though there were obvious ways to deal with the situation involving flanking movements, Howe chose to tackle the position and the Rebel forces head on. Howe landed at 1 p.m. with 1500 troops and twelve guns and established his positions at the foot of the hill. Later in the afternoon he was reinforced.

In the first two attacks, the heavily loaded Redcoats were shot down by concentrated musket fire which rang out in synchronised waves. Flanking movements along the banks of the Mystic River ran into stoutly defended stone and fence walls from which the Rebels produced a devastating fire. Finally a concentrated attack by the Redcoats, now without their packs but with musket and bayonet, during which Major Pitcairn was mortally wounded, carried the King's men to victory at the redoubt – at a terrible cost.

The total American strength has been considered as in excess of 3000 men, of whom 140 were killed and 301 were wounded. The British total reached about 2500 during the day. Of this number reported casualties reached 226 killed and 828 wounded, forty per cent of all those involved. There is no better definition of a Pyrrhic victory. Stunned by the figures, the British withdrew into inactivity for the winter; and when the Rebels occupied Dorchester Heights and armed it with the guns the Rebel colonel, Henry Knox, had dragged from Ticonderoga, Howe ordered the evacuation of Boston on 17 March 1776. A new phase of the American Revolution was about to begin.

KENNETH PEARSON

30

35

29
Four views of the Battles of Lexington and Concord, 19 April 1775
1. The Battle of Lexington
2. A View of the Town of Concord
3. The Engagement at the North Bridge in Concord
4. A View of the South Part of Lexington
New Haven, Connecticut, 1775. Hand-coloured line engravings, signed lower right: 'A. Doolittle Sculpt.'
Each 34·2 cm × 45 cm
Connecticut Historical Society, Hartford

When General Gage, Commander of the British Forces in America and Governor of Massachusetts Bay, sent out troops to destroy hidden provincial military supplies, he had set light to the Revolution. The march to Lexington and then on to Concord, twenty-one miles north-west of Boston, produced a reaction from American militia unforeseen by Gage. The news of the fighting spread quickly through the colonies. From the south marched the Connecticut Guard under the command of Benedict Arnold. The Guard stayed three or four weeks at Cambridge, just outside Boston, before returning home.

With that militia unit was Amos Doolittle, a New Haven engraver, who, with another artist-soldier, Ralph Earl, visited the Lexington and Concord sites within days of the battles. Earl sketched the topography of the skirmishes. In that autumn of 1775 Amos Doolittle transferred the four scenes to engravings and the series was announced for sale on 13 December 1775. There are few complete sets in existence. All authorities agree that this is the finest.

As with Revere and the print of the 'Boston Massacre', Doolittle used considerable artistic licence in depicting the battles, although he was very close to them. Neither at Lexington nor at Concord were the Redcoats positioned in such orderly array. Rebel sentiment responded to the sight of the tough, tyrannical British troops advancing on the poor disorganised colonials. Men whose rural lives relied heavily on the gun could shoot as straight as, perhaps straighter than, the young trained soldier.

The prints show (1) The encounter on Lexington Green, with Major Pitcairn on horseback directing the British fire. (2) The Redcoats marching through Concord with Colonel Smith and Major Pitcairn in the foreground. In the left background a British detachment destroys provincial stores of gunpowder, etc. (3) British troops and American militia confronting each other across the bridge at Concord. (4) The British under attack from behind farm walls as Lord Percy's rescue units meet retreating Redcoats on their way back to Boston.

30
The Royal Oak Tavern Sign
Medford, 1769. Painted maple and pine
132 cm × 95·2 cm
Royall House Association, Medford, Massachusetts

The Royal Oak Tavern stood in the village of Medford, five miles north-west of Boston. Paul Revere, on his ride to warn the countryside that Gage's men were coming, rode beneath this sign on the way to Lexington. Tradition has it that the hole in the sign was caused by a musket shot fired by one of the Medford militia on his return from Lexington.

Jonathan Porter owned the inn from 1774 to 1786. The sign was made in 1769, and Porter had his name painted over that of the previous owner.

31
Lieutenant-Colonel George Maddison and family
Artist unknown

1763. Oil on canvas
45·7 cm × 35·5 cm
Brigadier T. F. J. Collins, Saffron Walden, Essex

Maddison was lieutenant-colonel of the 4th, or King's Own, Regiment of Foot from 1763 to 1775. The 4th Foot sailed to America from St Helen's, Lancashire, and arrived in Boston in the middle of June 1774. Maddison commanded his regiment in Boston. The light company of the 4th Foot was at Concord Bridge. Another unit of the regiment joined Lord Percy's rescue column out of Boston. Maddison returned to England some time between 1775 and 1776.

32
Hugh, Earl Percy, 1742–1817
Pompeo Batoni

Before 1776. Oil on canvas
71·6 cm × 60·9 cm
The Duke of Northumberland, Alnwick

Lord Percy, later to become the second Duke of Northumberland, was colonel of the 5th Foot and a brigadier-general under Gage in Boston. He had a first-class military mind, was most popular with his men, and was to fight in many of the most important engagements in the early part of the revolutionary war.

Percy, a Member of Parliament until 1776, and at one time aide-de-camp to George III, commanded the brigade which rescued the British troops returning from Concord. Percy's men marched thirty miles in ten hours during that day and were under incessant fire for fifteen of them. On the Boston side of Lexington he set up his cannon with the Redcoats establishing a line between them. Colonel Smith's retreating grenadiers and light infantry were covered by Percy. He later wrote home, as he did regularly, that he had 'had the happiness of saving them from inevitable destruction'.

33
Lord Percy's Return Route from Lexington
1775. Manuscript sketch map of the roads in the Boston area between Cambridge, Menotomy, Charlestown and Medford
39 cm × 59 cm
The Duke of Northumberland, Alnwick

A rare map showing Percy's road back to Charlestown from Lexington. He avoided the Rebel militia camped at Cambridge. It is a practical military map marked with such significant phrases as 'hilly broken ground but no trees' . . . 'fine plain country' . . . 'steep easy descent'. Crude as it was, it would have had great tactical value.

34
Lord Percy's Diary
1774. Manuscript
The Duke of Northumberland (at the Northumberland Fusiliers Museum), Alnwick

Lord Percy left for America on 7 May 1774 from Ireland, where many of the British regiments were stationed, 'On Board the Symetry, Cove of Cork'. His regiment, the 5th, filled the *Symmetry*, the *Father's Goodwill*, the *Alicia* and the *Henry*. The 38th Foot was on board the *Empress of Russia*, the *Humber* and the *Lively* 'being all bound for Boston, however as the Wind was at West we only went into the Lower Road & came to anchor again . . .' He arrived on 4 July.

35
Lord Percy's wallet and colonial currency
1774–6
The Duke of Northumberland (at the Northumberland Fusiliers Museum), Alnwick

It is likely that Lord Percy was carrying this wallet in his engagement between Boston and Lexington. The American money contained in it is slightly later. It comes from Massachusetts, Rhode Island and Philadelphia. The Massachusetts note was engraved by Paul Revere.

36
A Draught of the Towns of Boston and Charles Town
John Montresor

Boston, 1775. Coloured manuscript
43·8 cm × 42·5 cm
The Duke of Northumberland, Alnwick

The full title of this manuscript map reads: 'A Draught of the Towns of Boston and Charles Town and the Circumjacent Country shewing the Works thrown up by His Majesty's Troops, and also those by the Rebels during the Campaign 1775'.

Montresor's map, dedicated to Lord Percy, details the military situation in 1775 with great clarity. The British are camped in Boston and guard the narrow neck which connects the peninsula with the mainland. All around the Rebels dig themselves in. To the north, across the water, lies Charlestown overlooked by Breed's Hill and Bunker Hill (shown but not identified). To the south-west of Boston are Dorchester Heights, soon to be occupied by the Rebels.

John Montresor (1736–99), an army engineer, first fought in America in the Seven Years War. He was promoted to captain in 1775 and made chief engineer in America. He was much concerned with map-making (of the highest quality) and with constructing or improving fortifications around New York, Philadelphia, Boston and the West Indies.

37
Paul Revere
This portrait of Paul Revere by J. S. Copley was painted in 1768–70, and is one of few paintings showing a colonial American at work. Revere holds in his hand a teapot identical to that exhibited here (see item 38), before the engraving is applied.

The original painting, of which this is a photograph, hangs in the Museum of Fine Arts, Boston, Massachusetts.

38
Teapot
Paul Revere

Boston, 1773. Silver
16·6 cm high; 23·3 cm wide overall
Worcester Art Museum, Massachusetts

This teapot is inscribed 'LO' for Lois Orne, with the coat of arms and the crest of the Ornes, a Massachusetts family. This fine example of Revere's work may well be the piece he is seen engraving in the Copley portrait. It was fashioned in the new rococo style, with its pear-shaped body and the cast pineapple finial on the lid.

The political and professional lives of Paul Revere (1735–1818) were in many ways interconnected. He was a Freemason and also a member of the Sons of Liberty organisation. No doubt members moved freely between the two. His skill as a silversmith and an engraver are testified to by the quality of his work. Though he rode as a messenger for the Massachusetts Committee of Correspondence, Revere was not so adept as a politico-soldier. His military career ended in disaster in an ill-fated attack on the British in 1779.

39
Pair of sauceboats
Paul Revere

Boston, 1760–70. Silver, marked 'Revere'
13 cm high; 20·3 cm long
Pauline Revere Thayer Collection, Museum of Fine Arts, Boston, Massachusetts

40
Tankard
Paul Revere

Boston. Silver
22·5 cm high; 13·9 cm in diameter
Museum of Fine Arts, Boston, Massachusetts

41
Lieutenant John Dutton of the 38th Foot
Artist unknown

c. 1770. Oil on canvas
45·7 cm × 35·5 cm
Mr Robin Duff, Old Meldrum, Aberdeenshire

John Dutton was killed at Bunker Hill. As the battle faded in the evening, afflicted by gout, Lieutenant Dutton sat down to change his stockings. Two American soldiers approached him, to surrender as he thought. They shot him and his servant.

42
Lieutenant David Graeme of the 52nd Foot
McLaughlan

1772. Oil on canvas
82·6 cm × 69·9 cm
Mrs L. G. Bladon, Salisbury, Wiltshire

Lieutenant Graeme (1750–75) joined the Army and was gazetted as an ensign in the 52nd Regiment of Foot in June 1773. He was promoted to lieutenant early in 1775. He took part in the attack on Bunker Hill, where the 52nd moved along the banks of the Mystic River in a flanking attack to turn the American left wing. In the early stages it was the hottest part of the battle. Graeme, severely wounded, was moved to Charlestown below the hill and died there on 3 July.

43
Light infantry helmet of the 5th Foot
c. 1774. Leather, metal and hair plume
17·1 cm high
Wallis and Wallis Military Heritage Museum, Lewes, Sussex

The helmet belonged to William Herd, who enlisted in the 5th Foot at eighteen years of age, in 1774. He was with Lord Percy at Lexington and later fought in the battles of Bunker Hill, Brooklyn, the Bronx, Brandywine and Germantown. The 5th also covered Clinton's withdrawal from Philadelphia. In one of these engagements Herd was shot in the left hand. He returned with his regiment to Ireland in 1781.

Leather in this type of headdress was treated to toughen it. The metal badge, depicting St George slaying the dragon, must be one of the earliest insignia employed by a regular regiment which is still in use today. The regiment became the Royal Northumberland Fusiliers.

44
British grenadier cap of the 35th Foot
Before 1768. Embroidered cloth
26·6 cm high
Rhode Island Historical Society, Providence

This grenadier's mitre cap is traditionally held to have been captured at Bunker Hill. In 1768 British army regulations brought in the grenadier's bearskin cap but, as with most changes, some time would have elapsed before the entire Army was re-equipped.

45
Sword of Corporal Thomas Holden of the 52nd Foot
Steel blade, white bone hilt decorated with gilded brass. Leather scabbard with belt loop
81·2 cm overall length
Trustees of the Oxfordshire and Buckinghamshire Light Infantry (43rd and 52nd) Museum, Winchester, Hampshire

The sword was carried by Corporal Holden as the 52nd attacked along the banks of the Mystic River at Bunker Hill. The white bone hilt suggests this sword was navy issue, perhaps picked up by Holden on the battlefield.

46
Bunker Hill gold medal
Made and presented 1785
Obverse: '43' in centre of a device, inscribed round the edge: 'A TESTIMONY OF REGARD TO A WORTHY SOLDIER'.
Reverse: inscribed 'Given by the Officers of His Maj[ys] 43rd Reg[t] in the year 1785 to T. Loftus, to perpetuate the memory of his disting[ed] conduct at the Battle of Bunker's Hill 17th June 1775'.
Trustees of the Oxfordshire and Buckinghamshire Light Infantry (43rd and 52nd) Museum, Winchester, Hampshire

Medals given to British forces in the revolutionary war were extremely rare. This one was awarded for bravery and won on the left wing of Howe's troops as the 43rd attacked straight up Bunker Hill towards the American redoubt.

47
Bunker Hill medal awarded to Royal Marine Subaltern Peter Ewing
Engraved on the obverse: 'A Testimony of Public Regard' in a garter, 'GR' crowned in centre.
Engraved on the reverse: 'By order of the King, with 300 Pounds for the Wound Capt. Ewing Recv[d] the 17th of June, 1775' in a wreath.
Mr Edward Charol, Stamford, Connecticut

Peter Ewing (1756–94) was commissioned as a subaltern and posted to the *Cerberus* on which he crossed to Boston with Generals Howe, Clinton and Burgoyne. In May 1775, he was discharged from his ship to join the 1st Marine Battalion. He was severely wounded at Bunker Hill. Ewing moved to Halifax when Howe withdrew from Boston, and on learning that his unit was to return to England, he volunteered for further service in the war and joined H.M.S. *Flora*. He served with her until she was scuttled, along with the *Cerberus*, at Rhode Island in August 1778, when threatened by a major French fleet (see item 502).

48
American officer's pistol powder horn
1775. Cow or ox horn
Mr Crosby Milliman, Georgeville, Quebec

41

46

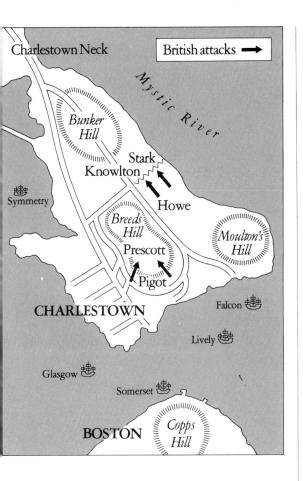

This horn belonged to Joseph Caswell, a Rebel, and was carved in Roxbury Camp in 1775. The Rebel lines at Roxbury were to be found just over a mile from the British defences at the Boston Neck.

Powder horns were used by both sides as long as powder and ball were carried separately, that is to say, before the use of cartridges became more widespread. The horn was sawn off at each end. The tapered end was bored to make a spout; the wide end was plugged with wood. Most of them were engraved by their owners, by someone more experienced in the regiment, or by professionals. They were often engraved with slogans or decorated with informative maps.

49
American fowler musket
46½ inches (118 cm) barrel length
Mr Crosby Milliman, Georgeville, Quebec

This musket was carried by William Whetcomb at Lexington and Concord. It is typical of the guns borne by the Rebels at Bunker Hill and other early battles. At the beginning of the war, with a great shortage of military guns, American militia were urged to bring along any shoulder arms they owned. As a result, many were armed with hunting pieces such as the Hudson Valley and New England fowlers.

50
View of Charles Town and Bunker Hill
Samuel Biggs, Lieutenant in the 5th company of the 2nd Battalion, Royal Marines

Boston, *c.* 1776. Grey wash watercolour
44·3 cm × 60·9 cm
The Duke of Northumberland, Alnwick

A pencil-and-ink drawing of this view was executed by one 'S. Biggs, Marines' in November 1775. It was taken from the site of the Copps Hill Battery in Boston, just across the water from Charlestown. This watercolour version is likely to be of a slightly later date and is dedicated to 'Earl Percy'. Five months after the Battle of Bunker Hill, the ruined houses of Charlestown can be seen. Breed's Hill, in the centre, where the Rebel redoubt stood, is now covered with tents. Between Breed's Hill and the sails of the ship stands Bunker Hill in the distance, now covered with British army barracks. At the far left, a flag flies over Rebel entrenchments.

51
A Correct View of The Late Battle at Charlestown
Robert Aitken

Philadelphia, 1775. Line engraving
18·4 cm × 24·7 cm
*Anne S. K. Brown Military Collection,
Providence, Rhode Island*

The Pennsylvania Gazette for 20 September 1775 advertised this print for sale. Robert Aitken (1734–1802) was printer and publisher of *The Pennsylvania Magazine* as well as an engraver, and it was in this magazine that the engraving first appeared in September 1775. The word 'correct' is somewhat misleading.

52
'Noddle-Island · or How · are we decieved'
London, 12 May 1776. Coloured engraving, published by 'M. Darly strand'. Inscribed: 'J. S. sc.'
21·5 cm × 15·8 cm
Ref: BM 5335
Trustees of the British Museum, London

As a result of Bunker Hill, General Gage had been recalled for incompetence and replaced by General William Howe, the new commander-in-chief in America. The move changed very little. After a long siege by the Rebels, Boston was finally evacuated by the British in March 1776. The satirists were not slow to respond: this engraver lampoons the withdrawal.

Noddle's Island was another name for William Island in Boston Harbour. The title contains the pun on 'Howe'. At the top of the coiffeur opposing sides shoot it out. Some authorities believe it is the British who are flying flags with an ass and a fool's cap and bells. Lower down, Redcoats march away, while others row out to the waiting ships.

53
The Battle of Bunker Hill
John Trumbull

London, *c.* 1786, or later. Oil on canvas
50·8 cm × 76 cm
Private collection

Bunker Hill was the only event of the Revolution which Trumbull actually witnessed, albeit at some distance, and painted. At the time he was nineteen, and adjutant to the commander of the 1st Connecticut Regiment. He was later, briefly, second aide-de-camp to Washington before leaving military service to concentrate on painting.

54

57

Trumbull has focused his picture on the death of Dr Joseph Warren, president of the Massachusetts Provincial Congress and newly-elected major-general of American militia. Warren, however, chose to fight in the ranks at Bunker Hill and was killed as the redoubt was stormed.

The artist painted this subject as the first in a series of Revolutionary War pictures in London in 1786. That picture, considered his finest in the series, now belongs to Yale University art gallery. The study here, which is almost identical, could have been painted for that picture, or for a later copy.

54
General Thomas Gage
Jeremiah Meyer

Undated miniature, London
4 cm × 5 cm
National Portrait Gallery, London

Thomas Gage had spent twenty years of his life fighting alongside and dining with Americans. He distinguished himself in the Seven Years War and in 1758 married Margaret Kemble, daughter of a New Jersey politician. His American wife bore him six sons and five daughters. His arrival in Boston, in May 1774, put him into a situation in which his duty conflicted with his inclinations. Events overwhelmed him as the growing circle of Rebel troops outside the town drove Gage deeper and deeper into inactivity. He resigned his command in October 1775 and returned home. As Lord George Germain, Secretary of State for the American Colonies, wrote: 'General Gage, with all his good qualitys, finds himself in a position of too great importance for his talents.'

55
General Gage's bank account
Ledger
42·1 cm × 29·2 cm
Lloyds Bank Limited, Cox and King's branch,
Pall Mall, London

General Gage banked with Cox and Company, now part of Lloyds Bank. His accounts are interesting for the information which they provide on his expenditure. They make clear, too, that though he had retired from Boston, he was still collecting £1500 a year as Governor of Massachusetts. His absence was looked upon as temporary.

56
Proclamation: a death warning for traitors
Boston, 1775. A broadside
31·5 cm × 19·5 cm
Massachusetts Historical Society, Boston

Four months or so after the Battle of Bunker Hill, the tension in Boston was approaching breaking point. Boston was under siege from the Rebels outside, and those who supported them were slipping out of the town to join them. General Howe threatens death for anyone caught doing so.

57
A Committee of Safety journal
North Carolina, 1775. Booklet of twelve pages
18·6 cm × 24 cm
North Carolina State Archives, Raleigh

Committees of Safety were organised in 1775 by the Rebels to function as a form of local government. They had, among other powers, the right to mobilise militia. The committees, therefore, consisted of very radical politicians. But how radical? This journal contains a diary of events of the Surry County, North Carolina, Committee of Safety. Here, between concentric circles, someone has written that daring legend, 'Liberty or Death'. And then, just to be on the safe side, the Rebels remind the world that their quarrel is only with the British Parliament: 'God save the King', they cry.

58
George III's Proclamation for suppressing Rebellion and Sedition
London, the Court of St James's, 23 August 1775
44·3 cm × 59·6 cm
Ref: PRO C83/148/14
Public Record Office, London

George III could not have regarded the American colonies with anything but a paternal eye. All his training had moulded him into a father-figure whose attitudes, both domestically and politically, would prove disastrous when sons, daughters and a nation came of age. For some time before the outbreak of hostilities, the King had talked of his colonial children. But both Pitt and, more explicitly, the American, Thomas Jefferson, were asking George to accept a political principle (the concept of some sort of commonwealth) many decades before such an ideal became a possibility. But, for the moment, the die is cast. The colonies, claims the King, are in rebellion.

The Look of London 1776

IN 1776 THE METROPOLIS of London was one of the wonders of the world. It was the biggest city in Europe, with about 740,000 inhabitants (one of every ten Englishmen), and far outnumbered its two nearest rivals within the Empire, Philadelphia and Bristol. The city's central core extended from Hyde Park in the west to Mile End in the east, encompassing the elegant residences and neighbourhoods of the rich, of which the most recent were Portland, Portman and Manchester squares, as well as the ramshackle lanes and alleys of Shadwell, Wapping and the Radcliffe Highway.

London was a place of pains and pleasures. The death rate was far higher than in the countryside and only constant immigration (each year 8000 more people came to the city than left it) increased the city's numbers. Though better paved and lit than Paris, much of the city stank. Air pollution from domestic coal fires caused smog and black rain. The streets were packed with traffic, and the rattle of wheels, together with the cries of hawkers and ballad-singers created a deafening noise. Food was often tainted or stale; the drinking water also tasted foul and could, moreover, prove fatal. Widespread prostitution – it was possible to buy a guide to London whores called *The New Atlantis* – attested to widespread poverty. Crime, though less prevalent than in other large European cities, was commonplace: in 1776, for instance, the Lord Mayor was held up at gunpoint at Turnham Green.

Yet nearly all classes enjoyed themselves in style. They gambled away their guineas at White's Club or their pennies in the tavern; in 1776 both patricians and plebs attended David Garrick's final theatrical performance; and, if Ranelagh and Vauxhall pleasure gardens were playgrounds of the rich and middling sort, the poor could still go to the gardens at the Dog and Duck and watch the frolics of famous highwaymen and *filles de joie*. Every Londoner seems to have belonged to a club. Gentlemen, including Lord Sandwich, patronised the Sublime Society of Beefsteaks in Covent Garden; the famous Literary Club whose members included Johnson, Reynolds, Burke and Goldsmith, met at the Turk's Head in Gerrard Street; artisans and apprentices belonged to a self-styled 'free and easy' society.

Rich and poor shared the same pleasures and vices; it was simply that they enjoyed them in different places. This was also true of politics. Without exception, Continental visitors to London were struck by the universal preoccupation with politics. The pleasures of polite society, they complained, were ruined by acri-

facing page: item 65
(detail)

monious political debate: mealtimes were changed to fit parliamentary sittings; families and friends quarrelled; and ladies' soirées were less concerned with light conversation than with matters of state. Even those wearing leather aprons or with calloused hands were eager to give the benefit of their political wisdom.

In 1776 this thriving political culture centred upon two institutions, the coffee house and the press, and was absorbed by one issue, America. By the mid-18th century there were over 550 coffee houses in the metropolis; many had their special clientele. The coffee house served as an exhibition hall, a debating club, a business address and a social venue but, above all, it was a political forum. Pro-American radicals like Thomas Hollis, backbench M.P.s like Sir Roger Newdigate and statesmen like Ben Franklin all went to the coffee house to read the latest newspapers or political pamphlets – usually provided gratis by the management – and to discuss the latest news. By 1776 they could draw on a mass of information. The year before, over 40,000 newspapers were sold in England each day; London had seventeen papers; there were over thirty-five provincial journals. Nearly all the ninety-five political pamphlets discussed by *The Monthly Review* in 1776 were on the American question, and print-shops displayed political cartoons in abundance.

British opinion on America, both in London and in the provinces, was sharply divided. Some believed that the Americans ought to be brought to heel by force; others argued that only conciliation could reunite Britain and her colonies. The first view was that of George III, his ministers, and the majority of M.P.s; it dominated Government policy from Westminster throughout the period, but also won considerable support in the provinces which in 1775 had sent 141 loyal addresses condemning the American rebellion. It was based on the belief that the colonial rebellion began because, as George III put it, 'the too great lenity of this country increased their pride and encouraged them to rebel.' All the earlier conciliatory moves had failed to prevent further American defiance. Colonial intransigence showed that they were determined to challenge Parliamentary sovereignty. Armed conflict and the Declaration of Independence, therefore, came as no surprise to the King, Prime Minister Lord North and his colleagues. These events confirmed the need to defeat and punish a band of factious, self-interested rebels.

This view was scorned by the Rockinghamite and Chathamite Whigs, and by the radicals of the city of London. They saw the Americans as loyal subjects who had been forced to defend their rights from the depredations of an incompetent and corrupt government. Only the genuine restoration of American rights could bring them back into the fold. Apparent agreement on this issue concealed the unfortunate disarray amongst the defenders of America. They could muster an average of only sixty votes in the House of Commons, and about twenty-five in the Lords. Chatham was fatally ill, quarrelled constantly with Burke, Richmond and the Rockinghams, and came out adamantly against independence. Nearly all Opposition attempts at conciliation (even that of Burke) were insufficient to win back the Colonists, and until Britain suffered military defeat no one was willing to countenance the full range of American demands.

JOHN BREWER

59
Yachts of the Cumberland Fleet starting at Blackfriars
English School
Late 18th century. Oil on canvas
44·3 cm × 64·7 cm
Royal Thames Yacht Club, London

Unruffled by the troubles in America, London society continued to patronise its sports. In July 1775 Henry Frederick, Duke of Cumberland, George III's younger brother, presented a cup to be competed for by 'Pleasure Sailing Craft' on the Thames, between Westminster and Putney. At the first race, the eighteen or twenty gentlemen who took part agreed among themselves to sport 'aquatic uniform', perhaps the first appearance of yachting gear. In this picture the Cumberland fleet, later to become the Royal Thames Yacht Club, is seen mustering by Blackfriars, London's newest bridge, completed in 1770.

60
Cumberland Cup
1776. Silver, engraved with the winner's name, 'Kingfisher'
30·4 cm high

Royal Thames Yacht Club, London

A new silver cup was presented to the winner of the race each year. The whereabouts of only four are now known. This one, presented for the second race, was won in 1776.

61
Westminster from Old Somerset House
Paul Sandby

Before 1775. Watercolour
12·2 cm × 57·1 cm
Trustees of the British Museum, London

The view of Westminster, looking up-river from Somerset House terrace, was a favourite among 18th-century artists. Spanning the river is Westminster Bridge. Completed in 1748 at a cost of £393,189, it was the first new bridge to be built across the Thames since the 12th-century London Bridge. At its northern end stand Westminster Abbey and Westminster Hall, home of Parliament. And fringeing the river's north shore are some of the great buildings which faced Whitehall and the Strand, including Scotland Yard, Inigo Jones's Banqueting Hall and, just out of sight, the new Adelphi.

59

62
Cheyne Walk, Chelsea
James Miller

1776. Watercolour, signed and dated
41 cm × 63·1 cm
Victoria and Albert Museum, London

Cheyne Walk was the main Thames-side thoroughfare of the village of Chelsea, two miles west of
London. Battersea, across the river, was still countryside. Chelsea was a popular resort, particularly because of its fashionable pleasure gardens at Ranelagh,
and became a favourite area for New York Loyalists
to settle.

63
Bloomsbury Square, looking north
Edward Dayes

1780. Watercolour
53·3 cm × 38·1 cm
Trustees of the British Museum, London

Bloomsbury Square was laid out in front of Lord
Southampton's new mansion in 1661, and was the
first of London's specifically designated open spaces.
With St James's Square, which followed a year or
two later, it set the pattern for the West End's 18th-
century development. By 1776, however, the newer
squares north of Piccadilly, Cavendish and Hanover,
Berkeley and Grosvenor, were favoured by the
fashionable, and Bloomsbury Square was occupied by
bishops and barristers. In 1780 Lord Mansfield's
house, 11 Bloomsbury Square, was attacked by the
mob who resented his prosecution of their favourite,
John Wilkes.

64
Queen's Palace, St James's Park
Artist unknown

1768. Tinted drawing
26·6 cm × 20·3 cm
Trustees of the British Museum, London

In 1762 George III bought Buckingham House for
£28,000. It was a red brick mansion facing the Mall,
built in 1705 by the Duke of Buckingham. The King
spent more than that sum, and two years, refurbishing
it. Renamed the Queen's Palace, the house became the
Royal home. Royal business was carried on round the
corner in St James's Palace where visitors to soirées
or levées often commented on the cramped quarters
and lack of grounds. 'The Kings of England live in

66

E, O, OR THE FA

Pub.ᵈ Oct. 28.1781 as the Act dir

ONABLE VOWELS.

St James's Palace like pensioners, while army and navy pensioners live like kings at Chelsea and Greenwich,' said one European witness. The Queen's Palace was demolished in 1825; George IV built the present Buckingham Palace on its site.

65
Windy Day, St Paul's Churchyard
Robert Dighton

1783. Watercolour
31·9 cm × 24·4 cm
Victoria and Albert Museum, London

St Paul's Churchyard was a centre for London's print shops, the most notable being Carrington Bowles Map and Print Ware-House, at No. 69, whose window is seen in the painting. Their speciality was the very popular hand-coloured mezzotints and portrait caricatures by Robert Dighton. The topical illustrations and satires were, in the 18th century, one of the chief means of circulating news, gossip and opinion. Many concentrated on the American war. They could be studied in shop windows (the crowds frequently caused serious obstruction), in coffee houses and taverns, or as they circulated in private houses. The sudden gusts of wind around St Paul's, caused by the high buildings, were notorious and attributed to the devil, for shops displaying pornography clustered in the churchyard.

66
E.O. or the Fashionable Vowels
Thomas Rowlandson

Published London, 28 October 1781. Engraving
18·4 cm × 25 cm
Ref: BM 5928
Trustees of the British Museum, London

Gambling was one of the chief preoccupations of fashionable society in 18th-century London, the men in their clubs, the ladies in their drawing-rooms. The addiction to gaming in all forms – wagers, dice, cards, roulette, lotteries – meant that exclusive clubs such as White's, Boodle's, Crockford's, Almack's and, later, Brooks's prospered under the patronage of such leaders as 'Gentleman Johnny' Burgoyne, Banastre Tarleton and Charles James Fox. £5000 might be lost on a single stake, £70,000 dropped in a night. Rowlandson himself was a confirmed gambler and these punters seated at the E.O. table (the initials standing for Even and Odd) were probably caricatures of well-known gamblers of his day.

67
The Magic Lantern
Paul Sandby

Date uncertain. Watercolour
37·3 cm × 53·9 cm
Trustees of the British Museum, London

London in 1776 offered a rich choice of entertainment at all levels to its population of 700,000. The pleasure gardens (see item 71), the theatres, the cockfights appealed to all, provided they could afford the entrance. Subscription concerts and balls, the 'spectacles' at the Pantheon in Oxford Street, the British Museum and the Royal Academy were the province of the wealthy. Drawing-room entertainment was another diversion for the rich – musical evenings, gaming or magic-lantern shows, which had been popular now for over a century. Sandby's illustration of all the aids to vision reflects the fact that London was the world centre for the manufacture of optical instruments. The coloured servant-boy was one of the 15,000 negroes living in England at the time.

68
High Life Below Stairs
James Caldwell, from a painting by John Collett

Published London, 1772. Engraving
26·6 cm × 35·4 cm
Trustees of the British Museum, London

Poverty, unemployment and crime were chronic problems in the London of 1776. Unskilled workers poured into the city each year and were lucky if they found jobs paying as much as twelve shillings a week, the price of a pound of tea. The discontent bred in overcrowded, unhealthy conditions meant that mob violence could erupt at the slightest instigation. The few who gained employment in domestic service, with the security of board and lodging, were well off and could indulge, as the engraving shows, in fashion and leisure.

69
Coffee House
Henry W. Bunbury

1780. Sepia ink, pencil and grey wash drawing, signed, dated and inscribed: '*London Gazette*'
33·3 cm × 30·7 cm
The Lewis Walpole Library, Farmington, Connecticut

Coffee and chop houses, clubs, taverns and ale houses were the social centres of 18th-century London (see

'Gossip in a Coffee House' page 64). Bunbury's drawing was engraved and published in 1781 under the title 'The Coffee House Patriots; or news from St Eustatia', to mark the arrival of news of a British victory over the Dutch in the West Indies earlier that year.

70
Club Night
Henry W. Bunbury

1785. Sepia ink, pencil and grey wash drawing Signed, dated and inscribed: 'Matlock'
Oval, 33·2 cm × 39 cm
The Lewis Walpole Library, Farmington, Connecticut

71
Vauxhall Gardens
Thomas Rowlandson

1784. Pen, ink and watercolour
48·2 cm × 74·8 cm
Victoria and Albert Museum, London

Of London's fifteen pleasure gardens, Vauxhall, or Spring Gardens, in Lambeth was the oldest, gayest and most popular. Rowdier than its nearest rival, élite Ranelagh in Chelsea, it drew enormous crowds: the concert audience could number 10,000; the supper room seated 400. Open in summer, when theatres closed, the gardens appealed to all classes. Samuel Curwen, a Massachusetts emigré loyal to George III, visited Vauxhall on 18 July 1775, 'where paying each the customary 1/- we entered a most enchanting spot, consisting of fine graveled walks, shrubberies, covered alcoves and boxes, all lighted by Lamps properly disposed round about the Orchestra or open music gallery; before it were placed under the trees in a regular order, tables covered and spread with glasses, decanters, plates etc for the entertainment of the company.' His dinner of beef, ham, custards, cheese-cakes and cranberry pie, washed down with a bottle of port, cost two shillings.

Rowlandson's illustration of this scene, later engraved, includes caricatures of society figures: Dr Johnson, Boswell and Mrs Thrale are in the left supper-box, the Duchess of Devonshire and her sister, Lady Duncannon, are in the centre, regarded by two leading journalists, Captain Topham, in the foreground with an eyeglass, associate of Wilkes and Sheridan, and Sir Henry Bate-Dudley, 'the Fighting Parson', editor of *The Morning Post*. To the right, the popular actress Perdita Robinson is being seduced by gallant. For their entertainment, François-Hippolyte Barthelémon, who with Johann Christian Bach and Samuel Arnold composed for Vauxhall, conducts the orchestra, and Madame Weischel, Bach's pupil, sings.

72
Rural Beauty or Vauxhall Gardens
London, 1737–8. Music sheet, engraved after Gravelot
31·6 cm × 19 cm
Mr Peter Jackson, London

Much of the music played in the pleasure gardens of London has survived and is still enjoyed today. Many of the well-known composers wrote for Ranelagh, Marylebone or Vauxhall. The gardens were cultural centres rather than the fairgrounds one might imagine. Dr William Boyce wrote the music for 'Rural Beauty', John Lockman the words, and it was published under a vignette view of Vauxhall Gardens themselves.

[Plays, concerts, sporting and charity events were sponsored in 18th-century London by subscription from the wealthy.]

73
Nine admission tickets/invitations
Trustees of the British Museum, London (Banks Collection)

● Walton Bridge Regatta
18 July 1775
Engraved on yellow paper, with red seal
21·5 cm × 27·3 cm

● *The Way to Keep Him*, a play
Friday 4 May 1787, at Richmond House, Whitehall
Rt. Hon. General Burgoyne's ticket
Printed card
7·6 cm × 12 cm

● *The Way to Keep Him*, a play
17 May 1787. Invitation sent to Miss Tryon from The Duke and Duchess of Richmond.
'Ladies are Desired to come in Night Gowns, Robes à la Turque, or other dresses Without hoops, and not to wear Feather or High Caps.'
Printed paper
23·4 cm × 18·4 cm

● *Jane Shore* with *The Guardian*, two plays
Monday 30 April 1781, at Hall Place, at half past six
Printed card
6·9 cm × 9·5 cm

● A sight of the British Museum
1776
Blank pass
Printed card
6·3 cm × 9·5 cm

● A sight of the British Museum
24 December 1777, at one o'clock
Mr Banks's ticket
Printed card
6·3 cm × 9·5 cm

● Annual pass to the British Museum Gardens
1 January 1779
Miss Henley's ticket, signed 'S. Harper, Secretary'
Printed card
6·3 cm × 9·5 cm

● Benefit Night for Mr Rayner
1785, Sadler's Wells
Engraved card
6·3 cm × 9·5 cm

● Benefit night for Mr Wilkinson
1780, Mr Astley's Amphitheatre at Westminster Bridge
Pit and Gall. 1/-
Engraved card
6·3 cm × 9·5 cm

[1776 was one of the most outstanding years in publishing that London had ever seen. In that year three books, each of which radically altered accepted opinion in its own sphere, appeared for the first time.]

74
An inquiry into the nature and causes of the wealth of nations
Adam Smith, LL.D and F.R.S.

Vol. 1, London: Printed for W. Strahan and T. Cadell in the Strand, 1776
Quarto. First edition
University of London Library (Goldsmith's Library of Economic Literature)

Smith worked for ten years before *The Wealth of Nations* first appeared on 9 March 1776. He was paid £500 and the edition was exhausted in six months. It rapidly became a handbook for both statesmen and philosophers at a time when the Industrial Revolution was forging change in both home economics and foreign trade; and the century-old laws regulating trade between Britain and her colonies were being thrown aside by revolutionaries.

75
The history of the decline and fall of the Roman Empire
Edward Gibbon Esq

Volume the first, London: Printed for W. Strahan and T. Cadell in the Strand, 1776
Quarto. First edition
University of London Library (Sterling Library)

Gibbon's *Decline and Fall* was a runaway success, hailed for its literary style and its historical accuracy. Three editions were rapidly sold and the conservative author, a staunch supporter of North's Ministry throughout the American war, earned £490. His belief in the superiority of Britain was regarded cynically by some intellectual sceptics at a time when the principles of the existing parliamentary system were being challenged.

64

76
Fragment of Government, or a Comment on the Commentaries
Jeremy Bentham

London, printed for T. Payne, 1776
University College Library, London

Bentham's work, published anonymously, was a strong criticism of Blackstone's Commentaries, the standard law-text at that time. By attacking it, Bentham was challenging the immutability of law, government and sovereignty as set out by Blackstone, in a period when society was changing so fast that it needed laws to adapt to new demands and situations. His *Fragment* was held to be a model of controversial literature.

77
A box for the card game Loo
18th century. Wood, red paint and lacquer. The box, one of a set of four, contains flat ivory and bone counters. On the top, a circular rotating disc
Box: 8·8 cm × 6 cm, 3·1 cm high
Long counters: 6·9 cm × 1·2 cm
Short counters: 4·1 cm × 2·6 cm
National Society of the Colonial Dames of America, Wethersfield, Connecticut

Loo, based on the four suits of cards, was very popular in the 18th century. 'Loo is mounted to the zenith. The parties last until one and two in the morning,' wrote Horace Walpole in 1759.

Originally French, the game was also played a good

71

deal by gentlemen and officers during transatlantic crossings. Stakes could be very high. In 1761 Walpole wrote, 'The Duke of Cumberland lost £450 at Loo last night.'

78
Playing cards
English, 18th century
One set of 50 cards, printed in red and black
5·5 cm × 3·1 cm
Ten court cards in the standard suits 9·5 cm × 6·3 cm
National Society of the Colonial Dames of America, Wethersfield, Connecticut

18th-century playing cards, so popular with a public addicted to gambling, were no different from those of today, except that numbers were omitted and the court cards were single-headed.

79
Playing Cards
English, *c.* 1780. Engraved by Rowley
8·8 cm × 6·3 cm
Guildhall Library Collection of the Worshipful Company of Makers of Playing Cards, London
(Henry D. Phillips Collection)

This complete set of playing cards is in its original paste-board box. The four suits are coloured red, blue, pink and green, and the devices are unusual: the Hearts are contained in chalices, the Spades are spontoons, the Diamonds faceted stones and the Clubs shamrocks. The single-headed court cards depict 18th-century monarchs: George III and Queen Charlotte are King and Queen of Hearts, the Spanish royal couple are the Diamonds, Persian royalty the Clubs, and Louis XVI and Marie Antoinette of France are Spades. Each knave is a military figure in an oval frame.

80
Grocer's receipt, at the Sugar Loaf and Canister
1776. Engraved, and ink on paper
18·5 cm × 22 cm
Davison, Newman & Company Limited, London

Tea, coffee and chocolate had been popular drinks since the 17th century, when they were introduced by the East India Company, and were staple fare in the coffee houses. Despite seemingly exorbitant prices (coffee, five shillings and six pence a pound; chocolate, five shillings a pound; tea, twelve shillings and six pence a pound), many people were drinking tea in their own homes by 1767. In that year Arthur Young wrote, in his *Farmer's Letters*, 'As much superfluous money is expended on tea and sugar as would maintain four millions more subjects on bread.'

81
Wooden shop sign: 'Ye Crown and Three Sugar Loaves'
Sign of Davison, Newman and Company which hung over their Fenchurch Street premises in 1776
33 cm × 24·1 cm
Davison, Newman & Company Limited, London

The city firm of Davison, Newman was traditionally one of the shippers of the tea thrown into Boston harbour during the Tea Party. They were general grocers, and dealt in coffee, cocoa, snuffs, sago, vermicelli, spices, dried fruits, rice and nuts. They also handled sugar – three cones (the form in which all sugar was sold) appeared on many grocers' signs.

GOSSIP IN A COFFEE HOUSE
Although London's coffee-houses existed ostensibly to provide refreshment, for they served food and liquor as well as tea, chocolate and coffee, they were even more important as an essential cog in the wheel of society. They were meeting places where men of like mind and sympathies could gather to discuss, argue or simply read.

'No noise is made, everybody speaks low, that he may not disturb his neighbour', wrote an 18th-century European visitor. 'People go to them chiefly for reading the papers, an occupation which in England is one of the necessaries of life. The most frequented houses take in ten or twelve copies of the same paper, not to make people wait, together with the best periodical publications.' Political pamphlets, topical satires and propaganda broadsides would have littered the tables and plastered the walls.

Loyalist Samuel Curwen was perhaps more aware of the debates, however. 'America furnishes matter now and then for disputes in Coffee houses,' he wrote from London in 1775. 'The disputants talk loud, and sometimes warmly, but without rudeness or ill manners or ill nature and there it ends. 'Tis unfashionable and even disreputable here to look askew on one another for difference of opinion in political matters; the Doctrine of toleration if not better understood, is, thank God, at least better practised than in America.'

Coffee houses became even more club-like when certain groups favoured them. American loyalists each adopted a different rendezvous as their own small colonial centre in London. Letters headed 'from the Massachusetts Coffee house' or 'the Carolina Coffee house', were shipped across the Atlantic in great numbers during the war. For as a patron became a regular customer, the landlord of a coffee house would offer his establishment as a mailing address, a message centre, a rendezvous – a true home from home.

82
Edmund Burke, 1729–97
James Barry

London, 1774. Oil on canvas
127 cm × 99 cm
National Gallery of Ireland, Dublin

Edmund Burke was private secretary to the Marquess of Rockingham, a leading Opposition Whig, from 1765 to 1782. Burke entered Parliament in 1766 as Member for Wendover, and, as a Dublin-born Irishman, immediately attracted attention as a poetic and commanding speaker. He was animated by two main themes. He first feared that a conspiracy of the Establishment would erode the democratic rights of Parliament itself: the Cabinet might be 'a certain set of intriguing men . . . [determined] to secure to the court the unlimited and uncontrolled use of its own vast influence under the sole direction of its own private favour'. And he shared a passionate belief in the liberty of the American individual: 'An Englishman is the unfittest person on earth to argue another Englishman into slavery.'

Burke's words could move, but could change very little. On 22 March 1775 he made perhaps the greatest speech of his life. For three hours in the House of Commons he spoke on the need for peaceful conciliation with the colonists. He held the House in his grip, and he sat down to the 'highest strains of applause'. His resolution was then defeated by a vote of 270 to 78.

83
Lord North, 1732–92
Nathaniel Dance

London, *c.* 1770. Oil on canvas
130·7 cm × 99 cm
The Earl of Rosebery, South Queensferry, West Lothian

Francis, Lord North, who later succeeded to the family title as the 2nd Earl of Guilford, became First Lord of the Treasury, succeeding Grafton's Ministry, in January 1770. For twelve years, he held his office not as the architect of dynamic policies, but more as the politician who rises to fill a vacuum when stronger, conflicting forces produce a self-defeating opposition.

He supported the tea tax as the right of the Mother Parliament, but he knew he was not the best of leaders to execute the consequent policy of war. 'Upon military matters,' he said, 'I speak ignorantly, and therefore without effect.'

Several times, when fortunes of war went badly, North tried to resign, but each time the King – never sure his Prime Minister meant it – prevailed upon him to stay in office. (Any alternative choice from the Opposition might have produced a man who challenged the King's own political role.)

North was expert at controlling the business of the House of Commons and showed great skill with Treasury matters. He had a wry sense of humour and was much liked. But gradually the burden of controlling the country's finances, together with his counterpointing role as War Minister responsible for heavy expenditure, drove North into a mood of gloom and distraction, and made him even more reluctant to take positive action. He resigned on 20 March 1782, five months after the fall of Yorktown.

84
The Earl of Sandwich, 1718–92
Thomas Gainsborough

London, 1783. Oil on canvas
233 cm × 152 cm
National Maritime Museum, Greenwich, London

In 1771, under Lord North, John Montagu, the 4th Earl of Sandwich, became First Lord of the Admiralty, organiser of naval affairs. He was a man of great charm, who ran a London house renowned for its relaxed social atmosphere and the music that pervaded it. But no man in his lifetime was more under assault for his private and public immorality.

In the 18th-century world of patronage, where allegiance and votes were bought with the offer of lucrative posts, Sandwich, with seventeen assured followers in the House of Commons, wielded a power which he exploited with little regard for his Cabinet colleagues. In a period when the Admiralty guarded its independence with great jealousy, the national need during the American Revolution was for a leader whose political foibles would be placed subservient to greater strategic demands.

Sandwich was not this man. His running of the navy became a matter of personal whim; the Cabinet

might decide wide naval issues, but if its First Lord thought little of their plans, the ships were not made available. 'I could never understand the real state of the fleet,' Germain once wrote to Lord North. The Whig Opposition and its historians combined to denigrate Lord Sandwich, but others thought him energetic, shrewd and dedicated.

In Gainsborough's portrait, Lord Sandwich is seen with the Royal Hospital at Greenwich in the background, the plans of its infirmary in his hands. Sandwich was Governor of the Hospital in 1763 and 1771–82.

85
George, Viscount Sackville, 1716–85
Thomas Gainsborough

London, 1783–5. Oil on canvas
124·4 cm × 99 cm
The Lord Sackville, Sevenoaks, Kent

Viscount Sackville, Secretary of State for the Colonies, was generally known during the Revolution and through later history by his earlier title – Lord George Germain. Germain, who joined Lord North's Cabinet in November 1775, was responsible for policy in the Colonies and thereby for the conduct of the British army during the war. It was his orders to generals in the field and his marshalling of recruits and regiments to American bases which provided the Redcoats with their effectiveness in the field.

But the crucial problem in such an exercise was one of distance and weather. Messages from London to any one of the thirteen colonies could take as much as three months to arrive – and they sometimes never reached their destination. Ships were becalmed or driven off course by 200 miles or more. Whatever Germain might plan, its execution was uncertain.

Germain had already served as a major-general with the army in Europe during the Seven Years War. After the Battle of Minden he was found guilty of disobeying orders and was, it was claimed, 'unfit to serve ... in any military capacity whatever'. George II had been unduly harsh, and Germain's return to politics some years later was welcomed by the public. But this experience must have coloured his later role. His industry and expertise were unchallenged. It was his personal judgements which were in question, as he allowed his own responses to others to cloud his relations with certain British generals. He preferred Burgoyne and Cornwallis for the independence of their operations. With the end of the war he retired from politics in 1782.

86
Charles James Fox, 1749–1806
Sir Joshua Reynolds

London, 1784. Oil on canvas
124·5 cm × 101·6 cm
Lady Teresa Agnew, Dorchester, Dorset

Entering Parliament in 1768, Charles James Fox was
a young man of wit and wealth. The son of Lord
Holland, Fox was an inveterate gambler, a vice which
in no way disguised the broad, cultured education he
had received and which stood him in good stead as an
orator. His political ambitions were curtailed almost
at once when he was dismissed from a Government
post in 1774 for offending the King. George III had
already found that he must give 'the young Cub . . . a
severe rap on the paws'. Fox crossed to the Opposition, joining Burke and Rockingham, where he
dedicated himself to challenging the power of the
King and his friends. It was this attitude which led
him to defend American liberty. Fox would not consent, he said, to 'the bloody consequences of so silly a
contest about so silly an object conducted in the
silliest manner . . .'

87
**First study for the Collapse of the
Earl of Chatham**
J. S. Copley

London, *c*. 1779. Oil on canvas
63·5 cm × 76·8 cm
Trustees of the Tate Gallery, London

In April 1778, William Pitt, the Earl of Chatham, was
opposing the policies of the Duke of Richmond who
wished to see British troops withdrawn from the
colonies. Pitt, opposed to the complete severance of
Britain from her overseas territories, collapsed as he
spoke. He died a month later.

88
**The 3rd Duke of Richmond
out Shooting with his Servant**
Johann Zoffany

c. 1765. Oil on canvas
107·8 cm × 134·6 cm
Trustees of the children of Hugh Leggatt

Charles Lennox, 3rd Duke of Richmond and Lennox
(1735–1806), took his seat in the House of Lords in
March 1756. Although by 1760 he held a Court post,
a quarrel with the King led to his dismissal. There-

83

84

85

89

after he attached himself to the Opposition, as had his nephew Charles James Fox. He served as Ambassador in Paris under the Rockingham Ministry in 1765. It was during a debate in 1766 that Richmond called Chatham 'an insolent minister'. From then on, it is said, Chatham did not reappear in the House of Lords during his own administration. Throughout the Revolution the Duke of Richmond, most radical of the Lords, sought to conciliate the Colonies.

89
Dr Johnson, 1709–84
Sir Joshua Reynolds

London, 1775. Oil on canvas
74·8 cm × 62·1 cm
Courage Limited, London

Samuel Johnson, wit, raconteur, distinguished and prolific author, represented in 18th-century English society the most conservative Tory view of the Colonists, epitomising the attitudes of thousands: 'They are a race of convicts and ought to be content with anything we may allow them short of hanging'. Johnson believed that 'in sovereignty there are no gradations'.

He published two pamphlets on the American problem, 'The Patriot', 1774; and 'Taxation no Tyranny: an answer to the resolutions and address of the American Congress', 1775. Both produced a flood of debate. 'I am willing to love all mankind,' he said, 'except an American.'

90
A View of London Bridge
William Marlow

c. 1762. Oil on canvas
101·6 cm × 126·4 cm
Her Majesty the Queen

Marlow painted four known versions of this picture, one of which was exhibited at the Society of Artists in 1762. It shows the north end of London Bridge (the 12th-century bridge had just been refurbished and the last buildings on it demolished in 1757) viewed from Fresh Wharf or Cox's Quay. The scene must have been a familiar one on London's bustling riverside, which fed the thriving economy of the city in 1776. The barrels and bales, shipped up and down the Thames, wait outside the warehouse for horse-drawn carts to distribute them. The church is St Magnus the Martyr; behind are Fishmongers' Hall, the tower of St Michael's, Cornhill, and St Paul's.

Ideas of Revolution

THE AMERICAN REVOLUTION was not a social but a political one. It was not intended to bring a new class to power, and many of its leading ideals were neither novel nor socially subversive. Its chief concern was with individuals' rights and the political, not social, mechanisms designed to preserve them. But what was distinctive and revolutionary was the way in which familiar ideas were transformed from pious ideals into political action and European theories adapted to special, American conditions. The Declaration of Independence began the process which only ended with the American constitution of 1787. It was a watershed in the conflict between the British Government and the American colonies. On the one hand the bulk of its text looks back, surveying and recapitulating American grievances against George III and his ministers; on the other, it looks forward, laying down in the bold clear prose of Thomas Jefferson's opening paragraphs the principles on which any future American government would be based: the equality of men and the existence of 'unalienable Rights'.

The Declaration, therefore, was revolutionary in two ways. First, it put the formal stamp of approval on colonial resistance to the British. Secondly, it signalled not only American rejection of Britain but American faith in the New World. All of the American leaders, including Jefferson, Franklin and John Adams, knew that independence committed them to the creation of a new set of political institutions, a distinctively *American* type of politics. Independence destroyed British political authority at a stroke; it also permanently removed from America what many contemporaries considered to be the two greatest pillars of political order and stability, monarchy and an hereditary aristocracy. The decks were cleared for American republicanism, a novel experiment whose outcome could not be predicted, even by its most ardent supporters. Independence, therefore, was both a rejection of the past and a leap into the dark; it was a terrible risk.

Most of the leading supporters of Independence (except Paine, who was not an American anyway) were reluctant revolutionaries. Rich and well-established, like John Hancock, they stood to lose much if the revolutionary experiment went wrong. Nevertheless the Americans who began by defending their rights ended by creating a new state. This was an act of astonishing temerity, especially for a group of men who were reluctant to discard their deeply felt allegiance to British culture and British traditions. It needed an enormous sense of the justice of their cause to take such chances and sever such ties. The American Revolution, in other words, was not possible without the revolutionary ideals, the spirit of 1776.

What were these ideals and what were American assumptions about politics? One that they shared with many of the great figures of the European Enlightenment was a belief in man's capacity to cope with political and social problems, and the view that improvement and reform were real possibilities. Man's reason, provided it was not distorted or restrained by those bugbears of the Enlightenment, superstition, censorship or external compulsion, could comprehend and change the world. This idea is most obvious in Paine: common sense, he says, is all you need once you have thrown off tradition; politics are simple, not complex, and within the understanding of all men, however humble.

A second view that European philosophers, most notably Voltaire, shared with the Americans was the belief that America was a very special society, the only one in which Enlightenment ideas of toleration, humanitarianism and progress were not merely aspirations, but were actually put into practice. This reinforced the notion that many Americans had long held, and which stemmed from their puritan view of divine providence: America was God's chosen land and Americans His chosen people. Independence, therefore, was part of America's destiny.

The most important single ideological influence on the American Revolution was republicanism; it shaped Americans' understanding of British Government policies and gave them a set of values on which to base their new society. It was the steam in the political machine. American republicanism was British in origin. Although many of the European philosophers, including Rousseau, Voltaire and, most notably, Montesquieu, grappled with the problems of republican liberty and the ideal state, the men who most influenced the Americans were such 17th-century English radicals as Harrington, Milton and Sidney – the so-called Commonwealthmen. English and American republicans shared a simple creed. All men had natural rights; they must be free to enjoy 'Life, Liberty and the pursuit of Happiness'. It followed that the prime purpose of politics was to create a system that preserved these rights. Government, therefore, had to be based on law, the protector of liberty, and not on the arbitrary whim of an absolute ruler.

Yet what all republicans most feared, with an obsessiveness that verged on paranoia, was a plot or conspiracy to undermine men's rights. Republican Whigs were sure that power corrupts; they believed an attack on liberty to be virtually inevitable. The colonial view of George III's Government, summarised in the long list of grievances in the Declaration of Independence, is therefore a republican account of the plot to destroy American freedom. The republican ideal, in American eyes, was no longer protected by British political institutions, which had become tyrannical and corrupt. In these circumstances Americans *had* to invoke the right, enshrined in republican ideology though usually associated with John Locke, to dissolve the social contract and begin anew. They valued republicanism more than their connection with Britain and, turning their back on Europe, gave republicanism a new home.

JOHN BREWER

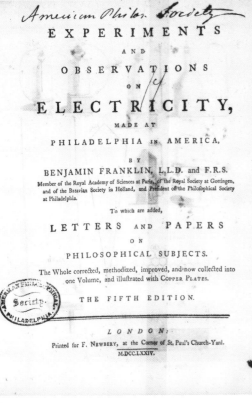

95

102

THE STEPS TO INDEPENDENCE

5 September 1774

The First Continental Congress convenes in Phila-delphia. Fearing punishment like that inflicted on Boston, which has been forced to cease trading, twelve colonies (Georgia does not attend) meet for a six-week session 'to consult on the present state of the Colonies . . . and determine upon wise and proper measures . . . for the recovery of their just rights and liberties, civil and religious, and the restoration of union and harmony between Great Britain and the Colonies . . .'

10 May 1775

Three weeks after Lexington and Concord, the Second Continental Congress meets in Philadelphia, this time with Georgia. This body becomes, in effect, the national government. It establishes the Conti-nental army, with George Washington as com-mander. It authorises the issuing of Continental cur-rency and a United Colonies Post Office, under Benjamin Franklin.

23 August 1775

George III issues his Proclamation for suppressing Rebellion and Sedition (see item 58).

26 October 1775

The King opens Parliament, referring in his speech to 'rebellious war . . . manifestly carried on for the pur-pose of establishing an independent empire'.

22 December 1775

American Prohibitory Act gets Royal Assent, making all American vessels and cargoes liable to confiscation by the Crown.

10 January 1776

Paine's *Common Sense* proposes independence.

23 March 1776

Resolution passes through Congress establishing Americans' rights to fit out privateer ships to seize enemy vessels.

6 April 1776

American ports open to world trade, severing com-pletely economic dependence of the Colonies on Britain.

April and May 1776

Colonies begin to set up local governments as the Royal Governors realise their positions are untenable and withdraw.

North Carolina, Rhode Island and Virginia declare independence.

7 June 1776

Richard Henry Lee, acting on instructions of the Virginia Convention, presents to Congress the Lee

Resolution: 'That these United Colonies are, and of right ought to be, free and independent States, that they are absolved from all allegiance to the British Crown, and that all political connection between them and the State of Great Britain is, and ought to be, totally dissolved.'

10 June 1776

Congress defers a decision on this drastic proposal, but appoints a five-man committee to consider and prepare a Declaration of Independence.

4 July 1776

The Lee Resolution having passed through Congress on 2 July, the first step to implement it is to issue the Declaration. After several days' debate in committee, the document, drafted by Thomas Jefferson and approved by John Adams and Benjamin Franklin, is accepted by Congress. Independence is declared.

91
Benjamin Franklin, 1706–90
Joseph Wright

1782. Oil on canvas
80·6 cm × 64·7 cm
Pennsylvania Academy of the Fine Arts, Philadelphia
(Bequest of Mrs Joseph Harrison, Jr)

By 1770 Benjamin Franklin, agent in London for the colonies of Pennsylvania, Georgia, New Jersey and Massachusetts, had reached an eminence in the worlds of science and literature which marked him out as one of the greatest intellects of the period.

His record speaks for itself. He was a printer and an editor. He had established in Philadelphia the American Philosophical Society, the first circulating library, the first fire company, and an academy which was to become the University of Pennsylvania. He had demonstrated the identity of lightning and electricity with the aid of a kite, among a host of other scientific experiments. His clarity of thought in all fields was reflected in the style of his prose. He was much sought after by the greatest company in France and in England, where he had become a member of the Royal Society of Arts.

As early as 1767 he had foreseen the coming conflict, and advised in a letter to an English friend that the only way to avoid it was a union in which all sides were represented in Parliament. But the pride of the British people, he thought, would make this unacceptable. 'We must all hang together,' he once said, 'or assuredly we will all hang separately.'

He left for Philadelphia in 1775 to fight for the Rebel cause in his own country; but he left a sad man.

94

93

'I have lived so great a part of my life in Britain, and have formed so many friendships in it,' he once wrote, 'that I love it . . .'

92
Bust of Benjamin Franklin
Jean-Jacques Caffieri

Paris, *c.* 1779. Plaster
66 cm high
Royal Society of Arts, London

This plaster cast of the bust of Franklin was taken from a terracotta original. This in turn was, according to the inscription, 'fait à Paris par J. J. Caffieri en 1777'. The subject was so well known in Paris, where by this time he was a representative of Congress, that the bust enjoyed its first exhibition in the Parisian Salon de Correspondance as early, it is thought, as 1783. The Royal Society of Arts acquired this image of its distinguished member in 1791.

93
Stencil printing set given to Benjamin Franklin in Paris
c. 1780. Box, wood and brass with 25 stencils
26 cm × 32 cm × 8 cm
American Philosophical Society, Philadelphia, Pennsylvania

'Printer', in the 18th-century meaning of the word indicated both printer and publisher. Paris honoured Franklin's early profession with this gift.

94
Benjamin Franklin's travelling chess set
Silver thimble case; chessmen and board
Case: 8 cm long. Chessmen: 1 cm high
American Philosophical Society, Philadelphia, Pennsylvania

Chess was one of Franklin's favourite games. He carried this set with him to play while travelling.

95
Five volumes from the library of Benjamin Franklin
American Philosophical Society, Philadelphia, Pennsylvania

Any five books taken from Franklin's library would show the breadth of his vision and the range of his interests. This selection illustrates the point:
Franklin's own *Experiments and Observations on Electricity*, 1774; *Les Droits de la Grande Bretagne,*

Etablis contre les prétentions des Américains, 1776; *An Essay on the History of Civil Society*, 1767, by Adam Ferguson; *Histoire de l'Académie*, the volume of 1778; *The Art of making Common Salt . . . for Use in the British Dominions*, 1748, by William Brownrigg

95a
Sign of the Three Squirrels
from Benjamin Franklin's London bank
Mid-17th century. Paper on pewter
73·6 cm × 60·9 cm
Barclays Bank Limited, London

In the 1650s this sign hung outside the premises of a London goldsmith and banker. The address, 19 Fleet Street, was later taken over by Messrs Gosling, Bennet and Gosling, bankers to Benjamin Franklin during his stay in London. Gosling's adopted the Sign of the Three Squirrels.

'THOSE DAMN'D REBELS'
The Rebel leaders were motivated by philosophical theories in the air throughout the 18th century. These had their foundation in the work of John Locke. His *Two Treatises on Government*, published in 1690, arose out of the Glorious Revolution of 1688 and became the handbook to Whig philosophy thereafter. Government derives its authority from the people's consent, and they may overthrow any government which threatens their fundamental rights, he argued. Men are naturally equal, all have rights of life, liberty and property which the state exists to protect.

Locke's words made him, in many eyes, the father of the American Revolution. But other philosophers were shaping similar arguments. In 1762 Rousseau extended the ideas of a social contract, seeking to guard against power being exercised by one individual or group over another. Montesquieu, in 1751, advocated the distribution of political power between independent sovereignties, neutralising the strength of government to extend civil liberties.

Between 1764 and 1783 nearly 1400 pamphlets, which constituted the principal medium for political debate outside Parliament relating to the American colonies, were published in Britain. In all these, the fundamental questions posed by Locke and later philosophers were discussed from every point of view. In America a host of others appeared. American leaders, such as Sam Adams, John Adams, Patrick Henry and John Hancock, had this corpus of work on which to base their persuasive arguments. But the one work which was, perhaps, the culmination of the debate was Tom Paine's *Common Sense*.

96
Patrick Henry, 1736–99
Virginia lawyer, one of the most extreme revolutionary leaders bred in the sybaritic atmosphere of slave-owning Virginia. A brilliant orator whose speeches became the basis for agitation from Charleston to Boston. 'Caesar had his Brutus, Charles I his Cromwell, and George III – may profit by their example . . . if this be treason, make the most of it,' he said in 1765. Ten years later he led the call for armed resistance: 'Give me liberty, or give me death.'

The original of this miniature by Lawrence Sully is part of the Dupuy Collection at the Museum of Art, Carnegie Institute, Pittsburgh, Pennsylvania.

97
John Adams, 1735–1826
Massachusetts lawyer. Cautious, logical, honest and less radical than his second cousin, Sam Adams, but he rejected British attempts to recruit him as a Government officer, recognising their desire to divide him from his rebellious compatriots. He was reconciled slowly to the need for a complete break with Britain, but once convinced, was called 'the Atlas of American Independence'. 'Infringements and violations' of the Colonists' rights as British citizens in the 1760s 'demonstrate a system formed to enslave America'.

The original painting by J. S. Copley belongs to Harvard University, Cambridge, Massachusetts.

98
Sam Adams, 1722–1803
Boston tax collector, incapable of managing his own business successfully. Skilled at organising political strength, 'a professional patriot' with little original revolutionary thought. He enjoyed a decade of power from the Stamp Act to the Declaration, when the rallying of rebels was vital, then fell into obscurity. He was described by Jefferson as 'truly the Man of the Revolution'.

'True Americans have no need for constitutional arguments for they are on better ground. All men have a natural right to change a bad constitution for a better one when they have it in their power.'

The original painting by J. S. Copley is in the Museum of Fine Arts, Boston, Massachusetts.

99
John Hancock, 1737–93
Millionaire Boston merchant, closely allied with Sam Adams who recognised Hancock's usefulness. Pomp-

ous, vain, called 'The American King', but popular. Became President of the Continental Congress, and as such was first to sign the Declaration of Independence. Hancock and Sam Adams were the only two Rebels not offered pardons by Gage as a last-minute conciliation attempt before Bunker Hill. Their treason was too extreme. But he was never fully trusted by his compatriots. 'Such a leaky vessel is this worthy gentleman,' commented John Adams.

The original painting by J. S. Copley is in the Museum of Fine Arts, Boston, Massachusetts.

100
Tom Paine, 1737–1809
Born in Thetford, Norfolk, Paine went to America in 1774 with an introduction from Franklin, after his dismissal as an excise man for leading an agitation for a pay increase. He entered radical politics and edited the *Pennsylvania Magazine* for eighteen months. Initially Paine hoped for a peaceful solution to the situation, but after 1775, with fighting in New England, the meeting of the second Continental Congress, Washington's appointment as commander-in-chief and the American invasion of Canada, his views altered.

Paine set these out in *Common Sense*, which was published anonymously in Philadelphia on 10 January 1776. The 47-page pamphlet cost two shillings. It urged the immediate declaration of independence to unite the Colonies and secure French and Spanish support. A continent, he said, could not remain tied to an island. An immediate success (120,000 copies sold in the first three months; half a million in all according to contemporary sources), Paine's pamphlet paved the way towards 4 July and galvanised many Rebels into active support for the cause.

Paine, when his authorship became known, was much credited and was appointed secretary to Congress's Committee on Foreign Affairs.

The original of this painting by Matthew Pratt is at Lafayette College, Easton, Pennsylvania.

101
Common Sense, Addressed To The Inhabitants of America, . . .
Thomas Paine

Philadelphia, 1776. R. Bell
The Boston Athenaeum, Massachusetts

George Washington's own copy, inscribed on the title page in his own hand.

102
Thomas Jefferson, 1743–1826
Jefferson was thirty-three when he wrote the Declaration of Independence, the youngest of the Virginia delegates to Congress and a wealthy man in terms of land and slaves. Income from his assets supported him when he had to abandon his law practice, on the closure of the courts in 1774.

A tall, red-haired man, Jefferson was a prolific writer, inventor and philosopher, but proved himself a bad administrator and a failure as a leader during the war. It took him a little over a fortnight to draft the Declaration before, with amendments from John Adams and Franklin, it was ready for debate.

Much to Jefferson's chagrin, Congress deleted some of his rhetoric and eliminated some of the more extravagant charges. Nevertheless his eloquent phrases, particularly at the beginning and end, survived.

The original painting by Mather Brown is reproduced by courtesy of Mr Charles Francis Adams and the Thomas Jefferson Memorial Foundation.

103
First printing of the Declaration of Independence
A broadside entitled 'In Congress, July 4th, 1776. A Declaration by the Representatives of the United States of America, in General Congress Assembled.' Philadelphia, 4–5 July 1776. Printed by John Dunlap 46·9 cm × 34·2 cm
Ref: PRO ADM 1/487
Public Record Office, London

On 4 July 1776, Congress ordered the printing of its Declaration for distribution to the army and state assemblies. The text was signed by the President, John Hancock, attested by the Secretary, Charles Thomson, and despatched to John Dunlap, a Philadelphia printer, who delivered the printed broadsides to Congress on the morning of 5 July. Independence was declared in each state as the broadsides arrived – not until mid-August in the case of remote Georgia.

THE SIGNERS
On 19 July Congress ordered an engrossed copy of the Declaration of Independence. This was signed by all delegates present on 2 August, and six absent then were added later. The names of the signers were kept secret, in case things went badly for the Rebels; but in January 1777, after Washington's victories at Princeton and Trenton, an authenticated copy with the names of the signers was issued.

Fifty-five delegates signed the document under the name of their President, John Hancock, in groups representing the thirteen states. Most delegations had three or four members, except for New Jersey with five, Virginia with seven, and Pennsylvania with nine. These men were the leaders of American society. Many were wealthy merchants, farmers, planters; nearly half were lawyers. Many also had close links with Britain. Eight were born here, several had honorary degrees from British universities, and many of the lawyers studied in London, five of them at the Middle Temple.

104
Windsor sack back armchair
Francis Trumble

18th century. Black painted wood
96·5 cm high
Independence National Historical Park,
Philadelphia, Pennsylvania

Francis Trumble (1716–98), a Philadelphia craftsman, supplied the State House with seventy-eight of these chairs between 1774 and 1776. This particular chair stood in the chamber when Congress met and signed the Declaration.

105
Rectangular inkstand with double-lidded, hinged cover and solid cast ball feet
Probably Birmingham, England, *c.* 1805. Pewter
20 cm × 12·7 cm; 5 cm high
Independence National Historical Park,
Philadelphia, Pennsylvania

Although this is a slightly later version, inkstands similar to this would have been in use on the tables in the Congress chamber in 1776.

106
Tricorn hat belonging to William Williams of Connecticut
Black felt
8·8 cm to height of crown
National Society of the Colonial Dames of America,
Wethersfield, Connecticut

Three-cornered hats like this were typical of the revolutionary period, and many of the Signers would have worn them in Philadelphia. Tradition says that William Williams, who signed for Connecticut, was wearing this hat on 4 July.

99

100

In CONGRESS, July 4, 1776.

A DECLARATION
By the REPRESENTATIVES of the
UNITED STATES OF AMERICA,
In GENERAL CONGRESS ASSEMBLED.

103 (detail)

104

107
Commentaries on the Laws of England
Sir William Blackstone

1774. Volumes 1 and 2, 6th edition
*The Honourable Society of the
Middle Temple Library, London*

The first volume of Blackstone's *Commentaries* appeared in 1765, the year of the Stamp Act. It was highly regarded and quickly became the standard text in legal affairs; it was used in courts in the Colonies, just as in Britain, and was certainly on the table in Philadelphia when the Congress delegates met to draft their Declaration of Independence.

In an age when philosophers were debating the role of men *vis-à-vis* society, Blackstone declared that all law, including statute law, owed its validity to its conformity with natural law. (Natural law was equated by 18th-century lawyers with the common or customary laws of England.) This conformity was assumed in the case of the British Parliament: 'There is and must be in every state a supreme, irresistible, absolute and uncontrolled authority, in which the . . . rights of sovereignty reside. This supreme power is by the constitution of Great Britain vested in the King, Lords and Commons.' Against such a rigid acceptance of authority, Bentham published his *Fragment of Government* in 1776 (see item 76). The Americans could not support such an authority, even if it were to be reformed, because to them it had become foreign and unrepresentative.

108
The Congress voting Independence
This photo-mural is an enlarged detail of an engraving believed to be among the earliest and most accurate representations of the signing of the Declaration of Independence in July 1776. The painting from which the engraving was taken was begun by Robert Edge Pine, an Englishman who arrived in America in 1784 to paint scenes from the Revolution. Pine died in Philadelphia in 1788 before completing this work, which was added to a little later by the American artist, Edward Savage.

The original painting hangs in Independence Hall, Philadelphia.

The Court of George III

GEORGE III HAS HAD THE ILL FORTUNE to be remembered in history for two events he could not control: his own illness, ending in total mental alienation, and the loss of the American colonies. Until recent years he has received a bad press from historians, who tend to worship power and are intolerant of failure. Certainly George III was an indifferent politician; yet he had many qualities which in more fortunate circumstances might have been remembered to his honour.

To Americans he is their last king, denounced by Jefferson in the Declaration of Independence as 'unfit to be the ruler of a free people'. The greater part of that document consists of a catalogue of the alleged misdeeds of George III, which were held to justify the Americans in their rebellion. But the Declaration of Independence is an exercise in propaganda, not a sober statement of historical fact. Many of the charges made against George III could equally well have been made against George II or any previous British king, and for none was George III personally responsible. But it suited Jefferson's purpose to lay the blame for the separation on one man, and that man the King: a distant figure, personally unknown in America, the symbol of British authority. George III became the scapegoat for the sins of the British Parliament and the British governing class.

It was not George III, but Parliament, who attempted to tax America; it was not George III, but the British governing class, who stood to gain by the Americans' contribution towards the costs of the empire. The most that can be alleged against the King is that he stood by Parliament in their quarrel with the American people. What else could he have done? He had received an excellent education, and had been taught that the Stuart dynasty fell because it opposed the rights and pretensions of Parliament. George III was resolved not to make that mistake. He would not attempt to play the tyrant as Charles I and James II had done. He would be a truly constitutional king, and defend the rights of Parliament. George III is a classic example of the danger of trusting to history as a guide to statesmanship.

'The sovereignty of the Crown I understand', wrote Benjamin Franklin. 'The sovereignty of Parliament I do not understand. . . . We have the same king but not the same legislature.' The Americans demanded independence of Parliament, not separation from the Crown. They were ready to acknowledge George III as their king, provided they were allowed to govern themselves. This Parliament was

facing page : item 122

determined they should not do. To quote Franklin again: 'Every man in England seems to consider himself as a piece of a sovereign over America; seems to jostle himself into the throne with the King, and talks of our subjects in the colonies.' The American rebellion was a nationalist revolt against imperialism, not a republican revolt against monarchy.

Unlike some people in British governing circles, the King did not believe it would be easy to subdue the rebellion. He never underestimated the Americans, and from the beginning pressed for an all-out effort. Nor was he daunted by defeat. Even Cornwallis's surrender at Yorktown in October 1781 did not cause him to despair, and he seriously contemplated abdication rather than recognition of the independence of the United States. He never regretted his conduct during the American war; and he told John Adams in 1785 that though he was the last man in England to consent to the separation, he would be the first to meet the friendship of the United States as an independent power.

King George's tenacity (or some would say, obstinacy) in supporting the cause of Parliament has led historians to neglect more attractive aspects of his character. He was a popular king, who could speak freely and easily to all ranks of his subjects from Dr Johnson to a farm labourer; and he had a great sense of humour. He was probably the most cultured monarch ever to sit on the throne of Great Britain. His library, now in the British Museum, was freely available to scholars and was for a long time the only national library. He collected works of art and scientific instruments, founded the Royal Academy of Arts, and was deeply interested in science. He commissioned the great telescope, with which Sir William Herschel discovered the existence of the *nebulae*. A lover of country life, he practised scientific farming and made it pay. He was interested in every aspect of culture – art, music, literature and science – and his people benefited from his interest.

Above all, he was a deeply religious man; and in an age when kings were the universal objects of flattery, he knew his own limitations. He left as an instruction to his biographer that 'the tongue of malice may not paint me in those colours she admires, nor the sycophant extoll me beyond what I deserve'. Perhaps the most revealing words about George III were those he wrote himself:

I do not pretend to any superior abilities, but will give place to no one in meaning to preserve the freedom, happiness, and glory of my dominions, and all their inhabitants, and to fulfil the duty to my God and my neighbour in the most extended sense. That I have erred is undoubted, otherwise I should not be human, but I flatter myself all unprejudiced persons will be convinced that whenever I have failed it has been from the head not the heart.

JOHN BROOKE

'I cannot say, but I wished some of my violent Countrymen could have such an opportunity as I have had. I think they would be convinced that George the third has not one grain of Tyrany in his Composition, and that he is not, he cannot be that bloody minded man they have so repeatedly and so illiberally called him. It is impossible; a man of his fine feelings, so good a husband, so kind a Father, cannot be a Tyrant.'

From the diary of Samuel Shoemaker, a Loyalist who left Philadelphia with the British in 1778, and arrived in London via New York in 1783. On 10 October 1784, he met the King.

111

109
George III, 1738–1820
Johann Zoffany

London, 1771. Oil on canvas
152 cm × 137 cm
The Marquess of Zetland, Richmond, Yorkshire

George III came to the throne in 1760 at the age of twenty-two. From the very first, until he outgrew his tutor, Lord Bute, he leaned heavily for advice on the man who had brought him up. He had, then, an education which kept him from general contact with children of his own age. It was an inhibiting experience which, given the King's own nature, was bound to produce a youth who was shy, somewhat introverted, and therefore ripe to be misinterpreted by many historians. Phrases like 'a clod of a boy', 'lazy, luckless', are no guide to the personality of a man whose later development was to make him a sensitive patron of literature, painting, botany, astronomy and other sciences.

As King, George III strove to break the power of the Whig politicians and thereby recover more direct political control for the throne. This battle was waged for twenty years or more and was a leading factor in his reaction to the American Revolution. Much of the Opposition's policy in those decades was devoted to defending Parliamentary rights, yet paradoxically it was Parliament the Colonies feared, not the King.

The King was severe with his nine sons and six daughters, for whom on behalf of Britain he tried to secure royal and Protestant marriages in a drastically restricted matrimonial world. And yet inside the walls of his own home he was to be seen carrying about in his arms 'by turns Princess Sophia and . . . Octavius'; or playing games on the floor with little Amelia.

George III reigned over a society whose very nature, with the advent of the Industrial Revolution, was about to undergo radical change. There were cleverer men than he who could not read the writing on the wall. It was not in him to perceive the political opportunities to be seized in the course of the American Revolution, as it was not in his advisers to be aware of the possibilities. It is sufficient to record that when it was all over he said he would 'never lay my head on my last pillow in peace and quiet so long as I remember the loss of my American colonies'.

This portrait is Zoffany's own contemporary copy of the picture which he hung in the Royal Academy in 1771.

110
A View of the Palace at Kew from the Lawn
London, 1763. Engraving, inscribed: 'Jos. Kirby delint., W. Woollett sculpt.'
30·6 cm × 46·9 cm
Library, Royal Botanical Gardens, Kew, Surrey

This particular palace in the gardens at Kew was known as the White House. Kew, largely the creation of George III's mother, was a favourite home of the King. Under his influence, the Gardens were first established as a botanical centre of international renown.

A visitor to London in 1774 recorded: 'Mr. Green the Gardener Said he gathers Some (roses, pinks and carnations) 3 Times a Week all the Year Rownd, there was Oranges and Lemons all in full Groath, also Tea Trees . . .'

George III appointed Kew's first gardener/administrator, on whose behalf botanists of the time searched other parts of the world, and later America, for seed specimens.

111
The plant 'Strelitzia Reginae Willd'
Francis Bauer

London, *c.* 1790. Pencil and watercolour
53·3 cm × 36·7 cm
Trustees of the British Museum (Natural History), London

Of the many plants introduced to Kew in George III's time, this *Strelitzia Reginae* was one of the more spectacular. It was named in honour of the Queen, Charlotte of Mecklenburg-Strelitz, and brought to Kew in 1773. 'Willd' stands for Willdenow, discoverer of the plant.

112
A palette set by Sir Joshua Reynolds
The Royal Academy of Arts, London

The King's interest in painting arrived at its fullest expression in December 1768, when 'for the purpose of cultivating and improving the arts of painting, sculpture and architecture' he founded the Royal Academy. Reynolds was its first President, a position he held until his death in 1792, when Benjamin West succeeded him. Reynolds and the art of the period are represented here by the palette the painter set up with colours for the Marchioness of Buckingham.

110

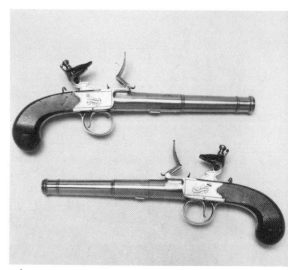

116

113

113
Mounted fan
London, 1781. Engraving
Trustees of the British Museum, London

George III and Queen Charlotte lived full musical lives. Both maintained their own small orchestras for entertainment at home, as this fan well demonstrates. The Queen sang and played the harpsichord. The King played the flute and the harpsichord, and sometimes the violin. The King was a fervent admirer of the music of Handel and of J. C. Bach, who settled in London in 1762 and soon became Music Master to the Queen.

114
Set of drawing instruments, a gift from George III
Public Archives, Halifax, Nova Scotia

At Kew, the King kept a very large collection of mathematical and other scientific instruments and models – some 2000 in all. A few he gave to his children as playthings. This set was a present from the King to Lord Bute, his former tutor.

115
Military sword of George III
87·5 cm overall length
Her Majesty the Queen

This is a regulation military sword of the late 18th century, worn on military duties by the King. Its grip is of wood spirally bound with copper wire.

116
Flintlock pistols of George III
17·7 cm barrel length
Her Majesty the Queen, by whose gracious permission they are reproduced

These were the King's own pistols and were made by one of the more distinguished gunmakers of the day, Tow of London, whose name is engraved on the lock. Tow went into partnership in 1775 and took over the business in 1783. He had a shop in Bond Street and provided sporting guns, among others, to the West End trade.

117
Study for a portrait of Queen Charlotte, 1744–1818
Benjamin West

London, *c.* 1776. Black and white chalk on blue paper
27·6 cm × 20·9 cm
Her Majesty the Queen, by whose gracious permission it is reproduced

From the limited selection of potential brides, George III eventually settled for Charlotte of Mecklenburg-Strelitz, whom he married in 1761. She suffered a stormy crossing of the North Sea and was married on the evening of her arrival in London. She bore the King fifteen children.

This study was made by West for a portrait in oils of the Queen and the Princess Royal.

118
Study for the crown of Queen Charlotte's Coronation portrait
Allan Ramsay

London, 1761. Black chalk heightened with white on blue paper
24·6 cm × 31 cm
National Gallery of Scotland, Edinburgh

119
Study for a portrait of the Prince of Wales
Allan Ramsay

London, c. 1765. Black chalk heightened with white on faded blue paper
41·2 cm × 27 cm
National Gallery of Scotland, Edinburgh

Before 1769 Ramsay painted a portrait of Queen Charlotte with her two eldest sons, Prince George and Prince Frederick. This is thought to be a study of Prince George, later the Prince Regent, and then George IV.

120
Princess Mary
Richard Cosway

London, c. 1781. Pencil, face in watercolour
20 cm × 15·2 cm
Courtauld Institute Galleries, London

Princess Mary was the King's fourth daughter. Many contemporary writers and subsequent historians have commented on Queen Charlotte's 'ugliness'. If they were right, one wonders how the Queen came to have so many good-looking children, even allowing for the flattery of Court painters.

117

119

118

120

121
The Apotheosis of the Princes
Benjamin West

London, *c.* 1783. Pen and ink, brown wash, blue wash in the sky. Squared in pencil for enlargement
19·2 cm × 14·6 cm
Courtauld Institute Galleries, London

Prince Octavius died in May 1783, and is seen here being received into heaven by an angel and his brother Alfred who had died the year before. At the bottom of the picture is Windsor Castle. George III was particularly fond of Octavius and mourned his loss bitterly. 'Heaven will be no Heaven to me,' he said, 'if Octavius is not there.' The study is part of the preparation West made for a complete version in oils exhibited at the Royal Academy in 1784 under the title 'The Apotheosis of Prince Octavius'.

122
George III as Commander-in-Chief of the Army
Benjamin West

London, 1779. Oil on canvas
255·3 cm × 182·9 cm
Her Majesty the Queen, by whose gracious permission it is reproduced

The King as Captain-General took his military duties seriously, for the most part putting army interests above political considerations. During the American Revolution George III retained his command until the French entered the war in 1778, when, because of the growing complexity of operations, Lord Amherst took control.

In West's portrait the King is seen in a military coat, wearing the ribbon and star of the Garter. In his hands he holds the plans of camps at Cox Heath and Warley, where militia and regular regiments practised manoeuvres. In the background the Royal George fires a salute, and a detachment of the 15th Light Dragoons is led by Lord Amherst, in the uniform of a general, and the Marquis of Lothian.

ten button holes. 11 - 11.

10 button holes

red yellow white

Kings arms in

Tyger Skinn.

A Shilling for a Redcoat

WITH A REGULAR ARMY of some 48,000 men, of whom only 8000 were stationed in North America, Britain had difficulty in assembling enough troops to quell the disturbances of April 1775, and was forced to call in the help of foreign auxiliaries. From the beginning of the war until Burgoyne's surrender of almost 5000 needed men at Saratoga, in October 1777, only one regiment was added to the army. After Saratoga fears of a French invasion, and reforms in the recruiting laws, improved the situation to such an extent that by the end of the war the army had increased to 110,000 men, of whom some 56,000 were serving in America.

The main battle line of the army consisted of the regiments of infantry, of one or two battalions of 477 men each. The service battalion was sub-divided into ten companies, one of which was the 'Grenadier', and another the 'Light Infantry' company. The former, whose original task had been to hurl hand grenades, consisted of 'the tallest and briskest fellows', and the latter of good marksmen of light build and active temperament. From their 'posts of honour' on the right and left flanks of the battalion these picked men became known as the 'Flank Companies', the remaining eight the 'Battalion Companies'. Only two cavalry regiments, the 16th and 17th Light Dragoons, served in America, but there were several companies of Royal Artillery in attendance to serve the guns that accompanied the army in the field.

The infantryman was armed with the famous Brown Bess flintlock musket, which had been in service since 1717. Reliable enough, except in bad weather, it was not much use beyond eighty yards' range. Twelve separate movements were needed to prime and load this cumbersome weapon; nevertheless a trained soldier could loose off five of the one-ounce lead balls in a minute. Officers and sergeants both carried swords and halberds or espontoons, but these made them too conspicuous to the American marksmen, and they were soon abandoned in favour of light muskets, or 'fusils', and bayonets. The cavalry were armed with flintlock carbines, pistols and swords.

At the beginning of the war the army was not very suitably dressed for the work in hand, but as time went on tactical needs and supply shortages changed the look of the average soldier from parade ground stiffness to improvised practicality. The battalion companies wore large black cocked hats, coarse red coats braided with coloured regimental lace, white waistcoats and breeches, long black gaiters and shoes. The knapsack, blanket, haversack containing four days' provisions, water flask, cartridge box containing sixty rounds, and other weapons completed a load of some sixty pounds. The grenadiers wore fur caps which, as they were without a brim, did not interfere with their throwing; and the light infantry wore small 'convenient' caps, short red jackets and waistcoats, white breeches, and calf-length gaiters copied from civilian shooting dress.

Life in the army was not a popular occupation. Pay was not enough to meet the rising living standards of the day, enlistment was usually for life, discipline was harsh, and rewards for gallantry and long service virtually unknown. Seamen used to say, 'A messmate before a shipmate, a shipmate before a stranger, a stranger before a dog, a dog before a soldier'. The thankless task of the recruiting officer was not eased by the two methods available for obtaining recruits. The first was persuading the gullible to enlist by pure salesmanship, aided by a small bounty and a shilling to drink the health of the King. The second was pardoning convicted criminals on condition that they enlisted. Physical requirements were low, 5 feet 6½ inches being the minimum acceptable height for a grown man, and, provided the recruit had the use of his limbs, the most superficial medical examination sufficed. After Saratoga new legislation increased the bounty to £3, limited the period of service to three years or the duration of the war, and permitted the enlistment of 'all able-bodied idle and disorderly Persons' and those convicted of 'running' goods up to the value of £40.

Once in the army, food accounted for the greater part of the private soldier's pay of four shillings a week. One newly-joined private of the 1st Foot Guards breakfasted in London on pea soup and bread, and dined on meat pie, bread, and sometimes small beer, which together with five pence a week for laundry, cost him three shillings and fourpence. Hairpowder, pipeclay, blacking, and the many stoppages to cover his clothing, medicines, repair of arms, and fees of various sorts, soon swallowed up the rest. Another recruit, William Cobbett, considered himself lucky if he could manage to save a halfpenny a week out of his pay; nevertheless, cold and half-starved, he managed to teach himself 'grammar', and rise to the rank of sergeant-major before he was twenty-five.

The officers did not fare much better, one complaining bitterly that the average tailor, weaver or mechanic lived more respectably on his pay. Each step in rank had to be bought for a large sum of money, and advancement was correspondingly blocked to men of moderate means. Thus most of the regimental officers came from the poorer rural aristocracy, and the senior and general officers, who owed at least a part of their promotion to the fact that they were also active politicians, from the nobility. The junior officers regarded the regiment as their home, and its efficiency and reputation was their main interest in life. Many were illiterate, others read avidly the military literature of earlier ages, while a few younger officers, like Wolfe and Howe, were leading innovators. With marked exceptions the officers showed consideration for the comfort and happiness of their men, in the paternalistic spirit of the country squire, and the bond with their N.C.O.s was often close. Most believed in the draconian discipline of the day, which punished major and minor offences alike with liberal doses of the cat o'nine tails. Others more humane, of whom Burgoyne was a typical example, abandoned flogging in favour of such lesser punishments as extra drill, making men wear their coats inside out as a mark of disgrace, confinement to barracks, imprisonment in the 'black-hole', and a diet of bread and water.

During the Seven Years War (1756–63), the typical 18th-century European soldier, drilled by blows and repetition into marching and firing like a machine, had proved to be a liability in the dense, Indian-infested forests of North America. A new system of warfare, that of the light infantry, based on a combination of European discipline and open-order Indian fighting, was soon devised by Wolfe, Howe, Amherst, Bouquet and Rogers, and was applied with notable success; but at the end of the war the light infantry was disbanded and their expertise thrown away, while the army turned once again to the rigid, linear tactics of Frederick the Great. Largely through the influence of Howe a light infantry company was, however, added to every battalion in 1770, and four years later he was allowed to assemble seven of these companies at Salisbury, for training in his own system of light infantry drill.

These innovations had made little impact by 1775, and when war came it was at first conducted in the old manner. The march to Concord and the murderous ascent of Bunker Hill were clumsy and costly operations which soon led to a change of command. Gage's successor, Howe, and his second-in-command, Clinton, nearly won the war in 1776 with their successful combined operation, the largest yet seen, against New York. Here, time and again, frontal assaults were used in conjunction with wide-ranging flank attacks, and the light infantry were much in evidence. The defeat of the dashing Burgoyne, successful cavalry leader but poor organiser, at Saratoga, was the turning point of the war, and from then on major operations were confined to the Southern states. Here a fierce guerrilla warfare was waged, Cornwallis's troops excelling themselves and on several occasions showing themselves the masters of the Americans at bush-fighting. By the end of the war the light troops and their leaders, Tarleton, Ferguson, who invented the first breech-loading rifle, and Simcoe, were as proficient as any in the history of the British army.

Britain's failure in America cannot justly be blamed on the lack of courage or skill of her soldiers. It was largely the result of inept generalship, of natural obstacles, and of maladministration. Supplies had to be brought 3000 miles by sea, and then carried immense distances, over bad roads, through a sparsely populated countryside. The absence of a centralised command, the lack of harmony between the services, the various government departments and boards, and the jealousies of high officials, all combined to reduce the chances of final victory.

JOHN MOLLO

123
View of an Army Camp
The view shows artillery, guards, layout of tents and recreation marquees during the Revolution.

The original impressions are with the National Army Museum, London, and the Anne S. K. Brown Military Collection, Providence, Rhode Island.

124
Life-size recruiting figure
Pre-1768. Painted wood
182·8 cm high
City of Kingston-upon-Hull Museums and Art Galleries, Humberside

Figures such as these were propped up outside recruiting centres to attract attention. This one dates from the decade before the American troubles.

125
Recruiting poster, 88th Keating's Regiment
1779. Printed paper
53 cm × 43 cm
National Army Museum, Chelsea, London

The poster was designed to raise a regiment specifically for the Revolution. Keating's, formed in 1779, fought in the West Indies and was disbanded in 1783.

126
Shoulder belt plate of the 88th Keating's Regiment
c. 1780. Brass
National Army Museum, Chelsea, London

127
Beating up for Recruits
London, 1781. Hand-coloured engraving, published by Sayer and Bennett
37 cm × 46 cm
Anne S. K. Brown Military Collection, Providence, Rhode Island

The drummer raises the emotional temperature while the officer shows potential recruits a purse of money.

128
Recrues Anglois partant pour l'Amérique
1780. Hand-coloured engraving, pirated version of English satire of H. W. Bunbury
29·2 cm × 33 cm
Anne S. K. Brown Military Collection, Providence, Rhode Island

The French used Bunbury's comment as propaganda.

ADVANCE THRE
OR THE MI

129

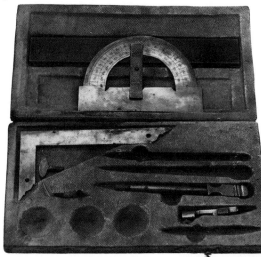

138

BACKWARDS. (...)

EROES

164

129
'Advance Three Steps Backwards. Or the militia heroes'
Inscribed: 'Peter Potgun'

London, 1779. Hand-coloured engraving
24·1 cm × 33·6 cm
Ref: BM Add. 585
Trustees of the British Museum, London

With the bulk of its army serving abroad, Britain was forced to recruit its militia, the 18th-century Home Guard, from the more deprived sections of the community – those, in fact, not at all physically suited for active combat. The problem became acute in 1779 when a French invasion threatened.

130
'The Terror of France, or the Westminster Volunteers, 1779'
London, 1779. Engraving
17·4 cm × 30·7 cm
Ref: BM 5552
Trustees of the British Museum, London

Its poem reads:
> Can we Invasions dread, when Volunteers
> Like these, propose to Fight the Gay Monseiurs?
> Certainly No! such Taylors, Coblers, Bakers,
> Always must Conquer, led by Engine Makers.

131
The Encampment on Blackheath
Paul Sandby

London, 1780. Watercolour
31·6 cm × 43·7 cm
Trustees of the British Museum, London

In June 1780, a mob of 50,000 with Lord George Gordon at its head marched on Parliament calling for the repeal of a recent act granting relief to Roman Catholics. During the next few days London was the scene of the worst riots in its history. Martial law was proclaimed and the army moved into Hyde Park, which was described as 'resembling the field of Malplaquet'. Other regiments were camped outside London at Blackheath. This Sandby painting reproduces a vivid scene of army camp life.

132
Colonel George John Cooke
Johann Zoffany

c. 1780. Oil on canvas
91·4 cm × 71 cm
Private collection

Cooke was Colonel of the West Middlesex Militia and typical of those country gentlemen who gave their services to the army on a part-time basis. He was also M.P. for Middlesex.

133
Album containing fifteen drawings of soldiers at Warley Camp
Philip de Loutherbourg(?)

1778. Pencil and ink on paper
Album: 34 cm × 23·4 cm
Anne S. K. Brown Military Collection, Providence, Rhode Island

There is strong internal evidence that these sketches were made by de Loutherbourg at the scene of the encampment and manoeuvres on Warley Common in 1778. Four of the sketches are annotated with the names of the companies the figures represent. Others are marked with the artist's notes on colours etc, as if he were sketching for a painting. Reference to the adjacent painting, 'The Review at Warley Camp', suggests that the grenadier in the bottom left-hand corner was taken from some of these sketches. They are the best examples of contemporary illustrations of military dress.

134
Warley Camp: the Review
Philip de Loutherbourg

1780. Oil on canvas
121·3 cm × 183·5 cm
Her Majesty the Queen

George III (with the group in the middle distance) reviews an artillery train during the exercises on Warley Common in Essex in October 1778. This picture is a companion piece to 'The Mock Attack', which shows the manoeuvres following the review.

Warley Camp that summer was the scene of joint exercises between regular units and the militia at a time when a French attack seemed imminent. The camp was not very popular: the troops complained that they were starved. Warley, and other similar camps, were an annual feature as long as the crisis persisted.

135
Six-pence a Day
'Exposed to the Horrors of War, Pestilence and Famine, for a Farthing an Hour'
W. Humphrey(?)

London, 1775. Engraving
22 cm × 34 cm
Ref: BM 5295
Trustees of the British Museum, London

This anti-recruiting satire shows 'the Hardship a Soldier and his Family endure on the bare Subsistence of Sixpence a Day while the lowest Trade earns sufficient to enjoy the Comforts of Life.' In contrast a sedan-chair carrier earned three shillings a day, a coachman two shillings and a sweep one shilling. The soldier is enduring '. . . Yankees. Fire and Water. Sword and Famine.'

[Beyond the infantry in battle lay vast numbers of specialists who supported the line troops: musicians, engineers, the physicians, and artillery. All were vital to the Revolutionary War.]

136
Chart of military architecture
Engraved plan. A 1790s reprint of a 1770s chart, printed by Bowles and Carver, London
46 cm × 64·4 cm
Fort Ticonderoga Museum, New York

Defence works wherever the British army operated were laid out according to well-defined regulations. That is why fortresses, whether in America, the West Indies or India, looked much the same.

137
Entrenching tools
Spade, stonemason's pick and shovel. Iron
New York State History Collections, Schenectady

To build the numerous fortifications and siege works, as demonstrated in the military architecture charts, each regiment carried a range of entrenching tools. These were excavated from sites once occupied by General Burgoyne's army.

138
Surveyor's equipment used on campaign
Bennington Museum, Vermont

- Theodolite and box made by James Simons of London, captured from the British at the Battle of Bennington.

- Leather-covered case of drawing instruments, containing brass protractor and square, wooden rule and parts of four other instruments.

- *The Practical Surveyor*, published by John Hammond, enlarged by Samuel Warner, 4th edition, London, 1765.

- Telescope by Adams of London, captured at Bennington.

- Surveyor's chain.

- Compass in mahogany case. Probably English, used by an American colonel at the Battle of Bennington.

139
Drummer's coat, 1st Foot Guards
c. 1780
Victoria and Albert Museum, London

Drummers and fifers wore coats more highly decorated than those worn by the infantryman. Their coats were laced (that is, distinguished by the colour of the braiding pertinent to their regiments) 'in such Manner as the Colonel shall think fit'. Their caps were bearskin with a metal badge on the front. This drummer, if he followed his regiment, went into battle at Brooklyn, New York, Brandywine, Germantown, Guilford Court House and Yorktown.

140
British army drum
Mr Crosby Milliman, Georgeville, Quebec

When newly issued the wooden drums would, according to regulations, be 'painted with the Colour of the Facing of the Regiment with the King's Cypher and Crown and Number of the Regiment under it'.

141
Pair of fifes with their cases
Scottish, late 18th century. Brass
38·4 cm and 35·5 cm long
Scottish United Services Museum, Edinburgh

Music was necessary to 18th-century armies. Besides raising morale and giving the beat to a march, the drum and the fife were used to issue orders in camp and in battle; to strike camp, sound reveille or charge into attack. Their shrill pitch and staccato rap carried further than the human voice.

Every company should have had a drummer and a fifer. A regiment could have had as many as twenty, plus a drum-major and a fife-major.

142
15th Foot Regimental March
c. 1778. Music sheet, printed
27 cm × 36 cm
East Yorkshire Regimental Museum, Beverley, Humberside

This march carried its regiment into action at Charleston, Brooklyn, New York, Brandywine, Germantown, Freehold and Florida.

143
Major McBean's Regimental March
1782. Contemporary sheet of music
60·9 cm × 40·6 cm
Royal Warwickshire Regiment Museum, Warwick

144
Surgical equipment
Amputation set in oak case, containing two saws, two amputation knives and one finger knife, forceps, tenaculum, shagreen case for surgical needles, and two tourniquets; second half of the 18th century. Scarificator (used for minor blood-letting); 1769. Lancets and cases, also for blood-letting; 18th century.
Wellcome Institute for the History of Medicine, London

145
Gunner's ammunition pouch and belt
with hammer and two spikes for clearing
artillery vents
1780. Leather
National Army Museum, Chelsea, London

The gunner's pouch was suspended from a shoulder belt. It was made of white leather to a special artillery pattern. Also attached to the belt were a small powder horn and, in special sockets, the equipment he needed for servicing the guns.

146
Portrait of an artillery officer
Thomas Gainsborough

Third quarter of the 18th century. Oil on canvas. Signed
19 cm × 16·8 cm
Private collection

The Royal Regiment of Artillery was organised into battalions of companies consisting of a captain, six officers, six non-commissioned officers and ninety-two other rank and file. They operated six cannon, as

well as howitzers and mortars. At the beginning of
the Revolution, Howe's army had about 2000 artillerymen in its ranks. The officer in this portrait holds
in his right hand a gauge for measuring the size of
shot.

147
Grenadier rank and file fur cap
British, 1768 pattern. Brown fur with white metal
japanned plate
31·6 cm high
*Wallis and Wallis Military Heritage Museum,
Lewes, Sussex*

The die-struck plate of a grenadier was decorated
with a Royal crest within the letters 'GR', and a motto
scroll 'Nec Aspera Terrent' – 'not even difficulties
deter us'. This was the motto of the House of Hanover and appeared on all grenadier caps during the
reigns of George I, George II and George III.

148
Grenadier fur cap front plate
British, 1768 pattern. White metal with japanning
20 cm high
East Yorkshire Regiment Museum, Beverley, Humberside

The plate is original; the fur is a reproduction.

149
Soldier's coat of the 1st Foot Guards
British, 1773. Red wool
National Army Museum, Chelsea, London

A battalion of Foot Guards which included men of
the 1st was reviewed by George III on Wimbledon
Common in March 1776, before it sailed for America.
It fought at New York, Brandywine, Germantown,
in the Southern Campaign, and surrendered at Yorktown.

150
Officer's coat of the 49th Foot
British, 1775. Red wool
National Army Museum, Chelsea, London

The 49th Foot served in the Colonies between 1775
and 1778 at the battles of Bunker Hill, New York and
Brandywine. From there they went to the West
Indies.

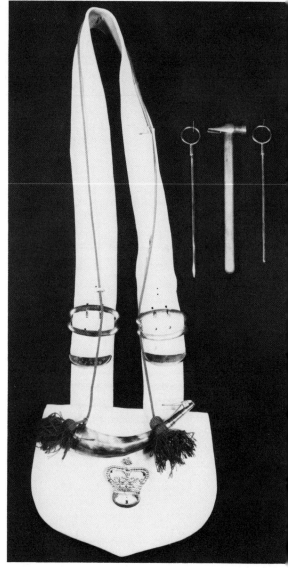

145

46

44

151
Waist cartridge box with Royal Cipher and Crown
British, leather and wood, with holes for eighteen cartridges
Mr Edward Charol, Stamford, Connecticut

The loading of a musket was developing from the powder horn stage to the cartridge, a roll of cartridge paper which contained a lead ball and the right measure of gunpowder. These were prepared in advance and carried in the cartridge box – a block of wood drilled to take a dozen or more cartridges.

152
Long Land Pattern musket
Mr A. B. MacNab, Stowmarket, Suffolk

The British musket used in the American Revolution was called the Brown Bess, a name first recorded in print in 1785 and whose origins are still obscure. The Long Land Service Musket of the British Army (its official name) was first made in 1717 and remained regular issue until 1768. In that year, in keeping with attempts to lessen the weight of the soldier's equipment and clothing, the Short Land Service Musket (New Pattern) was introduced. This was 42 inches (106·6 cm), as opposed to 46 inches (116·8 cm), long, and it weighed 10 pounds 8 ounces.

153
Short Land Pattern musket
Mr A. B. MacNab, Stowmarket, Suffolk

154
Two Militia Pattern muskets
(42-inch simplified version of Land Pattern musket)
Mr A. B. MacNab, Stowmarket, Suffolk

155
Short Land Pattern musket
Mr Francis A. Lord, Columbia, South Carolina

156
Long Land Pattern musket
Regimental Museum of the Cameronians, Hamilton, Lanarkshire

157
Infantry officer's sword and scabbard
1768–1820. Gilt, brass, steel and leather
96·7 cm long
Scottish United Services Museum, Edinburgh

Swords varied greatly in length and design according to the wishes and taste of the officer. At the outbreak of the Revolution rank and file soldiers found swords cumbersome and relied more on their bayonets.

158
Glamorgan Militia sword
Mr Francis A. Lord, Columbia, South Carolina

159
British short sword
Mr Francis A. Lord, Columbia, South Carolina

160
Military blunderbuss made at the
Tower Armouries
Mr Francis A. Lord, Columbia, South Carolina

The blunderbuss was used at close range and fired ten to twelve round balls at each discharge.

161
Officer's folding lantern
Tin lantern, six pointed sections, with isinglass panels
Fort Ticonderoga Museum, New York

162
Officer's folding cooking stove
Iron
New York State History Collections, Schenectady

When filled with burning wood, this stove could be used for grilling meat or fish, or for boiling a kettle (pot) of beans balanced on the corner supports.

163
Wooden document trunk
English, 1776. Embossed leather on wood
19.6 cm high; 46·3 cm long; 25·4 cm wide
Bennington Museum, Vermont

This trunk, captured by the Rebels at the Battle of Saratoga, was used to carry official despatches and maps.

164
British officer's document box
English. Leather-covered wood
12·7 cm high; 33 cm long; 18·4 cm wide
Guthman Collection, Westport, Connecticut

165
Powder horn of Jonathan Webb
1758, with later inscription by James Cameron of the 42nd Highlanders. Carried with an Indian bead belt
Scottish United Services Museum, Edinburgh

Horns decorated with maps were made in England by professional engravers for British officers sent to America. These horns served a dual purpose, as the work followed contemporary maps and provided a guide to a man's whereabouts as well as carrying his powder. Others were engraved by their owners with primitive images of scenes and inscriptions.

166
Horn of the 26th Foot Light Company
1771–84. Inscribed: 'MD 26'
Scottish United Services Museum, Edinburgh

167
Priming horn
Late 18th century. Horn and brass with spring-loaded lever
Scottish United Services Museum, Edinburgh

168
Horn of the 40th Foot (or the 2nd Somersetshire Regiment)
Belonging to: 'Serj^t W. Lidford'
Queen's Lancashire Regiment, Warrington, Lancashire

169
British officer's two-ounce pistol powder measure
Brass
Mr Francis A. Lord, Columbia, South Carolina

170
Light Company officer's cap
1770–83. Leather, with metal chain and metal embroidery
15·2 cm high
Scottish United Services Museum, Edinburgh

An extremely rare example of the cap worn by British élite troops and their officers during the Revolution.

171
A Brown Bess of the 23rd Foot
Tower Armouries, London, pre-1768
46-inch (116·8 cm)
Long Land Service Musket
Private collection

At the beginning of the Revolution the British army was equipped with a great number of the 46-inch musket. It took twelve movements to load, but a trained soldier could fire five balls a minute. This musket belonged to the regiment, known also as the Royal Welch Fusiliers, which fought in America throughout the war.

172
Officer's fusil and bayonet
1780. Made by G. Innes. Steel, wood and brass
139·7 cm long, plus bayonet 30·4 cm
Scottish United Services Museum, Edinburgh

Officers' guns were lighter, finer and more ornate than the arms of their men. The fusil, a word borrowed from the French, was purchased by the officer just as he bought his pistols from a favourite gunsmith and therefore varied according to taste and wealth.

173
Rifled musket carried by the Reverend James McLagen, chaplain to the 42nd Foot
1775–85
137·1 cm long
Scottish United Services Museum, Edinburgh

This musket, carried by the regiment's chaplain, was converted to a percussion rifle at a later date.

174
Steel grenade cup for use with flintlock musket
Scottish United Services Museum, Edinburgh

The grenade cup slotted on to the musket in the same manner as the bayonet. One man held the gun while another lit the fuse of a grenade and dropped it in the cup.

175
Flintlock pistol of Highland type
Made by Isaac Bissell. All steel
31·6 cm long overall
Scottish United Services Museum, Edinburgh

This pistol was carried by a Redcoat of the Royal Highland Regiment, or 42nd Foot (the Black Watch). It was made by Isaac Bissell of Birmingham, who made military weapons for the British army between 1775 and 1785.

176
Infantry officer's sword and scabbard
1730–96 pattern. Steel and leather
101·6 cm long overall
Scottish United Services Museum, Edinburgh

The sword blade is inscribed with a Royal Coat of Arms and 'FOR MY COUNTRY AND KING'.

177
Officer's dirk of the 42nd Foot
c. 1780. With silver mounts
45·7 cm long
Scottish United Services Museum, Edinburgh

[With the army run down in numbers since the victories of the Seven Years War, the outbreak of hostilities in America created a sudden manpower crisis. George III plugged the gaps with mercenaries. Calling on family ties with Germany, the King concluded a series of treaties with Hanover, Brunswick, Hesse-Cassel and other smaller German states, which produced in all an extra 30,000 men. These became known as the Hessians.]

178
Hessian fusilier cap
German, *c.* 1776. Brass, with leather, felt and burlap
22·8 cm high
Essex Institute, Salem, Massachusetts

A Hessian helmet said to be of the Fusilier Regiment von Knyphausen. The brass front is embossed with a lion, trophies and a monogram, 'FL', for Frederick the Second, the Landgrave of Hesse-Cassel. Traditionally, the helmet was taken from a Hessian soldier killed at Trenton, New Jersey, in January 1776.

179
Belt buckle plate inscribed P.R.
Mr Francis A. Lord, Columbia, South Carolina

This belt buckle plate is said to have been part of the accoutrements of a German soldier fighting with the British in the Revolution.

180
Coat of a Brunswick officer
German, 1789. Blue wool
National Army Museum, Chelsea, London

Although of a slightly later date, this coat is of the same pattern as those worn by officers in the Brunswick Infantry Corps in America.

181
Cartridge box and belt of the Brunswick Infantry Regiment Prinz Friedrich
English made, 1776. Leather with brass fittings
Bennington Museum, Vermont

Probably a grenadier's cartridge box. Although the rest of the Prinz Friedrich Regiment stayed at

Ticonderoga, its grenadiers formed part of General Burgoyne's forces on the Hudson. They fought at Bennington and at Saratoga.

182
Powder horn belonging to Hessian soldier Christopher Raborg
Inscribed: 'Febry Ann D. 1779', with an eagle
Mr Crosby Milliman, Georgeville, Quebec

183
Hessian officer's snuff box
German, late 18th century. Inlaid metal
Mr Francis A. Lord, Columbia, South Carolina

184
Hessian shaving kit
English razor, late 18th century. Wood, metal and leather
Bennington Museum, Vermont

Taken from the body of a German soldier at the Battle of Bennington. The kit includes a leather-covered wooden case, bottle and sharpening stone.

185
Camp stove used by Colonel Baum
Iron
66 cm high overall
Bennington Museum, Vermont

Lieutenant-Colonel Friedrich Baum, Commander of the Brunswick Dragoons, led a supply raid for horses and cattle on Bennington during Burgoyne's move south down the Hudson to Saratoga. It was a disaster. The 800 men unexpectedly ran into superior Rebel forces. Very few escaped death or capture. Baum, a brave leader who could speak no English, was himself killed.

186
Drum taken at the Battle of Bennington
1757. Painted wood
38·7 cm high; 50·8 cm in diameter
Bennington Museum, Vermont

The wooden drum carries the painted figures of three soldiers mounted on black horses.

168

178

88

70

153

187
A Hessian Grenadier
London, 1778. Coloured engraving,
inscribed: 'MD sc.'
Published by M. Darly
23 cm × 16 cm
Ref: BM 5483
Trustees of the British Museum, London

The point of the satire is the amount of loot the
German carries on his back. The Hessians were in-
corrigible plunderers of friend and foe alike in
America.

188
**Printed textile: 'Lord Charlemont at the
Provincial Review in Phoenix Park, Dublin'**
Irish, 1782. Printed cotton and linen
105 cm × 76·7 cm
Museum of Fine Arts, Boston, Massachusetts

This, one of the earliest known pieces of Irish linen,
illustrates the military life and its environment in this
period. The range of soldiers it depicts is rare –
infantry, grenadiers, light company, fifer and drummer, standard-bearer and cavalrymen. Troops like
these were raised to replace the regular regiments
which had left their garrison towns in Ireland for
America.

Twenty-five days to New York

GENERAL HOWE LEFT BOSTON with troops and supplies in such confusion on his evacuation fleet that there could be little thought of sailing south to take New York while Washington was still unprepared for a major confrontation. It was a highly desirable move, but the fleet sailed north to Halifax and a winter of reorganisation. Supply lines 3000 miles long presented problems.

The possession of New York was of the highest strategic importance. It was a known area of widespread Loyalist sympathies. Along a 1500-mile coastline there was at that moment only one harbour that could provide the Royal Navy with the facilities it needed, and that – Halifax – was at the most northern point of the combat area. Once entrenched in New York, the British would hold the southern gateway to the Hudson Valley-Lake Champlain route into Canada, and be able to operate a naval base capable of easy defence.

On 11 June 1776, General Howe sailed from Halifax for New York with 9000 men. Eighteen days later the fleet arrived off Sandy Hook, the peninsula guarding the entrance to New York Harbour. Once inside, the Redcoats, facing no resistance, landed on Staten Island, where the army set up camp half a mile across the Narrows from Long Island, and five miles south of New York city.

The General was to wait seven weeks before launching his expected attack. Why so long? Was he still suffering from the effects of his Bunker Hill losses? Had they made him ultra-cautious? Was the European military concept of conserving one's forces so strong in him that he could not adapt to new circumstances? (Lord Percy wrote that summer, '. . . our army is so small that we cannot even afford a victory'.) Or was it that at the back of William Howe's mind, as evidence will show, there lurked the feeling that perhaps the conflict could be resolved by peaceful negotiation? If that were true, more fighting would only push a cherished ambition further away from fulfilment.

From the middle of July the logistical support which had been engineered in London the previous winter began to drop into place with heartening regularity. On 12 July, Admiral Lord Howe, the General's elder brother, arrived on the *Eagle*. On 1 August Henry Clinton sailed in from South Carolina, with sizeable reinforcements, after an abortive attack on Charleston. Eleven days later, Commodore William Hotham appeared in New York Harbour with a brigade of guards and Hessians. Howe was now supported by something like 25,000 men.

facing page: item 191

While waiting, the Howes had already played the game of peacemakers. Admiral Lord Howe had arrived in the Colonies with a brief from the Government to investigate the possibilities of a peaceful settlement. While the brief limited the Admiral's field of operations, it is clear that the man himself was always attempting to step beyond the boundaries of what he had been entitled to achieve. From New York Harbour he issued a printed proclamation which promised all sorts of pardons for those who accepted the peaceful route to a solution. A copy was delivered to George Washington, which addressed him not by his assumed rank but by his civil title. The General refused to accept the letter. Courtesies aside, the Declaration of Independence had already been signed.

On 22 August, the British army attacked. Beginning at 8 a.m., landing craft brought out from England put 4000 men under Clinton and Cornwallis on the beaches of Long Island in the first wave. With them were von Donop's German corps of jägers and grenadiers. The boats were rowed back to Staten Island and returned with 5000 more troops. By noon 15,000 men, forty cannon and the horses of the dragoons had been put ashore. It was the largest combined operation ever executed until that moment.

The build-up went on. Three days later General von Heister, with two brigades of German mercenaries, crossed to Long Island. By then Cornwallis and von Donop's corps were camped four miles inshore at Flatbush. Washington, on Manhattan with 16,000 effective troops spread through Long Island, New York and its environs, looked for the first move from the British. Was it likely to be another frontal attack as at Bunker Hill? One of his generals, Putnam, marched up and down repeating to his Rebel troops the lesson he had enforced at Boston: 'Don't shoot till you see the whites of their eyes!'

From just north of where the British landed on Long Island there stretched eastwards a line of hills called the Heights of Guian. They presented a sharp slope to the British between forty and eighty feet high. The hills were thickly wooded and overlooked the plain on which the Redcoats set out their line of battle. There were four ways through those hills: the coastal road along the harbour shore, the Flatbush Pass, the Bedford Pass, and the Jamaica Pass on the eastern extremity.

On 27 August, just after midnight, General James Grant with 5000 men began to advance along the Long Island shore road as the main attack against the Rebels' last line of defence on Brooklyn Heights. During the fighting, Grant was reinforced with 2000 extra men, and the Rebels had to throw in reserves to prevent a British breakthrough. At the Flatbush Pass the Hessian forces were keeping up pressure with a constant bombardment. This entire operation was a feint.

With Cornwallis and Clinton, 10,000 men with twenty-eight guns had marched nine miles in just over five hours in a right-flanking movement through the Jamaica Pass, which was to have been under observation by a Rebel patrol. The British were undetected. At nine o'clock in the morning the right wing of the British army fired two signal guns for an advance on all fronts. The Redcoats were behind the Heights of Guian with a clear run to Brooklyn.

The Rebels scampered back to Brooklyn Heights as fast as they could go.

American General John Sullivan was captured; the Rebels lost 1047 men – killed, wounded or captured. That night of the 27th, Howe's army lay in front of the Rebel redoubts at Brooklyn. Many of the General's officers were for attacking at once (Washington had now crossed the East River from Manhattan), but Howe reckoned he had time in hand. The Royal Navy with its frigates would intercede in any Rebel retreat from the island. Unfortunately, the wind did not co-operate.

On the night of 29 August, a north wind was blowing down the East River and British ships could not get up. In six hours of darkness Washington evacuated nearly 10,000 men and supplies across the river to Manhattan. And while General Howe, facing New York, planned his next advance, his brother, Admiral Lord Howe, used the captured Sullivan as a messenger to Congress with a proposal that a delegation should meet him to discover the extent of his brief. On 11 September, Benjamin Franklin, Edward Routledge and John Adams arrived on Staten Island only to discover that the Admiral had no powers to offer negotiable terms for peace without reference back to London. The Rebel commission returned home, and on 15 September William Howe, with 13,000 troops, landed a third of the way up the island of Manhattan at Kip's Bay.

There again, delay prevented Howe from trapping a large Rebel army in New York itself. Most of these troops escaped up the Hudson shore to join Washington at a new line of defence on Harlem Heights. The British followed through with a series of brilliant manoeuvres at White Plains on the New York mainland, at Fort Washington, and at Fort Lee on the Jersey side of the Hudson. By 20 November, British generals had captured a total of 4400 rebel prisoners.

It was a time for congratulation, but for two things: Washington was retreating south into territories of passionate Rebel support; and the British army had only what it could hold.

KENNETH PEARSON

189
The Narrows
Photo-mural of the view of the Narrows between
Staten Island and Long Island with General Howe's
fleet at anchor. Admiral Lord Howe in the *Eagle* ap-
proaches his brother's anchorage, 12 July 1776.

The original drawing by Archibald Robertson is in
the New York Public Library.

190
A Plan of the City of New York & its Environs
John Montresor

1775. Manuscript map
78·7 cm × 59·6 cm
The Viscount Gage, Lewes, Sussex

This map of New York, giving details of its streets,
buildings, docks, etc., was dedicated to General Gage,
Commander-in-Chief of the British Army in America,
early in 1775.

191
**Sir William Howe, Commander-in-Chief of the
British Forces in America**
Unidentified engraver

Probably English, 1777. Mezzotint
35·5 cm × 24·7 cm
*Anne S. K. Brown Military Collection,
Providence, Rhode Island*

General Howe (1729–1814) had arrived in Boston in
May 1775. He commanded at Bunker Hill and, having
taken over from General Gage, ordered the withdrawal from Boston in March 1776 to Halifax, Nova
Scotia. Howe arrived in New York harbour on
25 June 1776, with three ships, the vanguard of his
forces. Within five days he had a fleet of 130 ships
with him, and on 2 July (two days before the American Declaration of Independence) he landed un-
opposed on Staten Island. Ten days later he was
joined by his brother Richard, Admiral Lord Howe,
with 150 ships and reinforcements from England.

By mid-August Howe had assembled 31,625 men
of all ranks (24,464 of them fit for duty) for the attack
on Washington and the Rebel army. It was the first
time that two brothers had ever commanded naval
and army forces in combined operations, and was the
largest amphibious attack yet in military history.

On the morning of 22 August, after a night of
'thunder, lightening, and prodigious heavy rain',
Howe led the assault across the Narrows on to Long
Island and the eventual capture of New York.

192

202

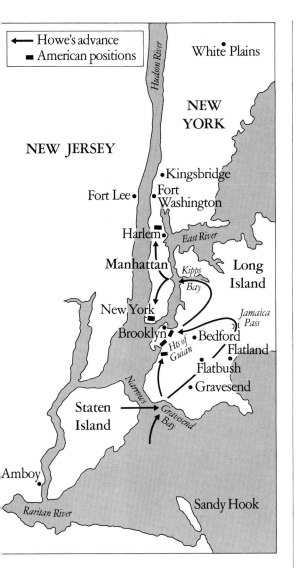

Map legend:
← Howe's advance
■ American positions

White Plains

Hudson River

NEW YORK

NEW JERSEY

Kingsbridge

Fort Lee • • Fort Washington

Harlem •   East River

Manhattan   Kipps Bay   Long Island

New York   Jamaica Pass

Brooklyn • Bedford
Hts of Guian   Flatland

Flatbush

• Gravesend

Staten Island   Gravesend Bay

Narrows

Amboy

Raritan River   Sandy Hook

192
Admiral Lord Howe
J. S. Copley

London, 1793–4. Oil on canvas
76·2 cm square
National Maritime Museum, Greenwich, London

Richard, Admiral Lord Howe (1726–99), seen here as Admiral of the Fleet in a portrait painted a little later than the Revolutionary war, joined his brother, General William Howe, at New York in August 1776. He arrived with a commission permitting him and his brother 'to treat with the revolted Americans, and to take measures for the restoration of peace with the colonies'. This dual role of war-making officers and peace commissioners would have played an important part in determining the overall conduct of their operations. If neither brother appeared ever to press early victories to their full advantage, it is clear other thoughts were on their minds.

Without, at this point, an enemy fleet to engage, Admiral Howe found his primary duties to be those of blockade and transport. In the summer of 1777 he moved with the army up the Chesapeake for the capture of Philadelphia (see item 402). It was with the entry into the war of France in 1778 that the admiral was once again to be involved in full-scale conflict (see item 505). Having offered his resignation earlier because, it is thought, he took umbrage at the appointment of another peace commission which he was not to lead, he returned to England in October 1778.

Admiral Howe still had an important role to play in connection with the relief of Gibraltar (see item 559).

[An admiral's cabin, centre of operations and a second home for months on end, was, given obvious restrictions, a relatively capacious area, to be furnished with many personal belongings. This recreated corner of Admiral Lord Howe's cabin resembles most closely those quarters he inhabited in his flagship, *Eagle*, in New York harbour in 1776. Almost all the objects belonged to the admiral. They have been brought together for the first time since then.]

193
The Admiral's sea-chest
91·4 cm wide; 121·9 cm long; 76·2 cm high
The Earl Howe, Amersham, Buckinghamshire

194
The medicine chest
The Earl Howe, Amersham, Buckinghamshire

195
The sword
99 cm overall length, steel, engraved with roses. Hilt decorated with steel wire. Leather scabbard
The Earl Howe, Amersham, Buckinghamshire

196
Book: 'Contemplations Moral and Divine', 1676
The Earl Howe, Amersham, Buckinghamshire

197
Two of the Admiral's ship decanters
The Lord Brabourne, Ashford, Kent

198
Lord Howe's telescope
72·3 cm long (open)
The Lord Brabourne, Ashford, Kent

199
Port bottle
National Maritime Museum, Greenwich, London

200
Captain Thomas Aubrey
Nathaniel Hone

1772. Oil on canvas
91·4 cm × 71·1 cm
National Museum of Wales, Cardiff

Captain Aubrey is seen here in the uniform of the 4th Foot, but in 1771 (presumably before the painting was finished and dated by Hone) he joined the 47th. The regiment fought at Lexington, Concord, and Bunker Hill in the third assault, then joined in the evacuation of Boston to Halifax. In Canada, Captain Aubrey formed part of the army assembled for Burgoyne's offensive down the Hudson, attacking New York State from the north. In September 1777 Aubrey was detached from the main force, leading two companies of the 47th to guard Diamond Island at the head of Lake George. He fought off a strong enemy assault, earning himself creditable mentions in Burgoyne's despatches home, and escaped capture, unlike the 47th and the rest of the army, at Saratoga.

201
Captain William Gardiner
Sir Joshua Reynolds

1773. Oil on wood
74·8 cm × 62·1 cm
The Lord Egremont, Petworth, Sussex

Gardiner sailed from Cork for America with his regiment, the 45th, on 6 May 1775. They arrived in Boston after Bunker Hill, but were present during the siege and withdrawal to Halifax. In the battle for New York, Gardiner, a grenadier, served as one of Sir William Howe's aides and in that capacity brought home the despatches reporting the Battle of Long Island. He was promoted to major in the 10th, and back in America joined the army in Philadelphia. He was wounded at Freehold during the city's evacuation in June 1778 and returned to England, rejoining his old regiment, the 45th, as a leiutenant-colonel.

202
Major Patrick Campbell
Attributed to J. S. Copley

Undated. Oil on canvas
74·3 cm × 62 cm
Mrs M. W. Guild, Edinburgh

Traditionally this portrait has always been associated with the subject and artist given above. Patrick Campbell was a major in the 71st Fraser's Highlanders, a regiment which served throughout the war from New York to Yorktown. However, the subject of this painting is not wearing the uniform coat of that regiment, which would have had buff facings, so he is perhaps not Campbell; and Professor Jules Prown of Yale University, the leading authority on the work of John Singleton Copley, questions the attribution. However, it is an outstanding portrait of an officer of the time seen with a howitzer, an artillery piece used in America during the war.

203
Captain John Peebles
Artist unknown

c. 1778. Miniature watercolour
4·1 cm × 3·1 cm
Scottish United Services Museum, Edinburgh

Peebles commanded the grenadier company of the 42nd, Royal Highland, Regiment throughout the war. He saw action at New York and in the Pennsylvania and Southern campaigns.

204
Pocket pistol by Robert Harvey of London
c. 1760. Cannon barrel, apple-wood butt, without trigger guard
17·7 cm long
City of Kingston-upon-Hull Museums and Art Galleries, Humberside

205
Blunderbuss pistol by Grice of London
1740–80
Brass body with screw-off wooden butt and turn-off iron barrel
43·1 cm long
Although marked 'London', Grice was the name of a gunmaking family based in Birmingham.
City of Kingston-upon-Hull Museums and
Art Galleries, Humberside

206
Flintlock military pistol made at the Tower Armouries, London
Ramrod fitted with a swivel
40·6 cm long
City of Kingston-upon-Hull Museums and
Art Galleries, Humberside

207
All-metal flintlock pistol
Steel with brass stock
30·4 cm long
Scottish United Services Museum, Edinburgh

Pistols like this were issued to all rank and file members of Highland regiments until 1789, and would have been carried in America by Scottish soldiers.

208
Bullet mould
Forged iron mould casting twelve different sized balls
48·8 cm long
Bennington Museum, Vermont

209
Brass bullet mould for making sixty pieces of buckshot
Mr Francis A. Lord, Columbia, South Carolina

Most bullets were cast at ammunition factories, but some soldiers carried bullet moulds in the field.

210
Officer's shoulder belt plate of the 3rd Foot Guards
1776–1800 pattern; gilt, brass, silver and enamel
Scottish United Services Museum, Edinburgh

Equipment was carried by both officers and men suspended from leather belts either round the waist or over the shoulder. Gradually buckles were replaced by plates inscribed with Royal insignia or regimental numbers.

211
Shoulder belt plate of the 42nd Regiment
1780–86 pattern; brass
Scottish United Services Museum, Edinburgh

212
Officer's shoulder belt plate, the 17th Foot
1780; silver
National Army Museum, Chelsea, London

213
Officer's belt plate, the 26th Foot
c. 1780; silver
National Army Museum, Chelsea, London

214
Rank and file belt plate, the 48th Foot
1780; brass
National Army Museum, Chelsea, London

215
Private's heart-shaped finial from a shoulder belt, 42nd Foot
Scottish United Services Museum, Edinburgh

216
Cartridge pouch badge, 26th Foot
Brass on leather
Scottish United Services Museum, Edinburgh

217
Ice creeper
Iron
New York State History Collections, Schenectady

Tied under the arch of the shoe, the four-pronged ice creeper projected just far enough to provide a footing on an icy surface.

218
The Hon. Sir Charles Stuart Lieutenant-Colonel of the 26th Foot
George Romney

c. 1779. Oil on canvas
127 cm by 101·6 cm
Glasgow Museums and Art Galleries

The fourth son of Lord Bute (George III's tutor), Sir Charles Stuart fought at New York as major in the 45th. The year after, 1777, he was promoted to lieutenant-colonel of the 26th, and commanded the regiment on its campaign in America until 1779. Described in the regimental history as 'one of the most famous soldiers that have ever been in the regiment', Stuart probably had his portrait painted when he arrived back in London from his war duties.

219
Lieutenant Sir Thomas Wallace
Artist unknown

1778. Oil on canvas
138·3 cm × 113 cm
Mr J. M. A. Wallace, Stranraer, Wigtownshire

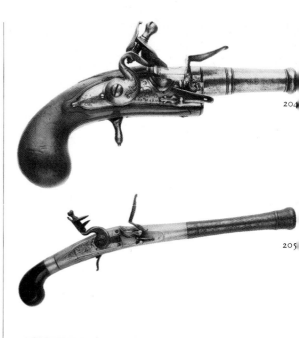

204

205

Sir Thomas Wallace joined the 82nd Regiment in 1778 when it was raised by the Duke of Hamilton. Several such 'loyalty' regiments were raised at this time specifically to support the war in America, and were disbanded when it was over. Wallace, a grenadier as his fur cap shows, went to America with his unit, but in 1779 was promoted to captain in the 44th and served in New York until he was posted to Canada towards the end of hostilities.

220
Lieutenant James Stewart
Artist unknown

c. 1780. Oil on canvas
74·8 cm × 62·8 cm
Scottish United Services Museum, Edinburgh

James Stewart was ensign in the 5th Foot in 1775 when he served at Lexington, Bunker Hill, and the battle for New York. In 1777 he transferred to the 42nd, or Royal Highland Regiment, as lieutenant, but not before being mentioned in General Howe's returns to Germain of those officers wounded at Germantown, outside Philadelphia, in October 1777. In the 42nd he was stationed in New York and Rhode Island, and took part in the Southern Campaign in Florida and Charleston, before the evacuation to Halifax in 1783.

This portrait was almost certainly painted in America. As the war progressed the 42nd Regiment 'disposed of their plaids etc . . . to purchase a more commodious dress for the American service', and Stewart is seen wearing the new uniform.

221
An Officer of the 35th Foot
Artist unknown

c. 1776. Oil on canvas
68·8 cm × 52·7 cm
Anne S. K. Brown Military Collection,
Providence, Rhode Island

224

218

Although this officer has not been identified, his regiment, the 35th, fought at Bunker Hill and New York. The regimentals are typical of the war period. Some authorities suggest the painting was executed in America.

222
Lieutenant-Colonel Henry Knight Erskine of Pittodrie
Henry Raeburn

1781–4. Oil on canvas
74·8 cm × 62·1 cm
Sir Andrew Forbes-Leith, Fyvie, Aberdeenshire

Before a change of name (through marriage), regiment and rank, the sitter served in America as Captain Henry Knight of the 43rd. He was at Lexington, Concord and Bunker Hill, and at New York as an aide-de-camp to General Howe. He returned to England in 1778 and was promoted to major in the 45th. He was at Warley Camp in 1781 in that capacity.

223
Captain Henry Barry
J. S. Copley

c. 1785. Oil on canvas
77·4 cm × 64·1 cm
Private collection

Captain Barry of the 52nd (whose uniform he is wearing in the painting) sailed with his regiment to Boston in 1774. The regiment served at Lexington, Concord and Bunker Hill, then in the campaign for New York and the capture of Rhode Island, 1776. Barry served as aide-de-camp and private secretary to Lord Rawdon until 1778; then he returned home with his regiment. Barry also wrote books and pamphlets on the troubles, which were published by the army in New York.

224
Captain and Lieutenant-Colonel The Hon. Cosmo Gordon
Attributed to Francis Wheatley

c. 1773. Oil on canvas
74·8 cm × 62·1 cm
Trustees of the Goodwood Collections, Chichester, Sussex

The Hon. Cosmo Gordon, second son of the Earl of Aberdeen, served in America as a grenadier of the 3rd Foot Guards. He was promoted to captain and lieutenant-colonel in 1773, and this portrait, showing

227

him in the uniform he would have worn in the war, may have been painted to mark the event. After New York, Gordon fought in the Pennsylvania and New Jersey campaigns under Howe, and in 1779 was involved in raids on Virginia. In 1780, he was accused of bad conduct during a raid on Springfield, New Jersey, by Lieutenant-Colonel Thomas of the First Foot Guards. Gordon was acquitted at a court martial, but in 1783, back in London, he challenged Thomas to a duel in Hyde Park and killed him. He was tried for murder but was cleared.

225
Silver gorget worn by the Hon. Cosmo Gordon of the 3rd Foot Guards (see item 224)
Trustees of the Goodwood Collections, Chichester, Sussex

Officers wore brass or silver gorgets at the neck as insignia of rank. They were inscribed with the Royal coat of arms and often the regimental number. They were vestigial remains of earlier breastplates.

226
Brass and gilt gorget with the Royal coat of arms
Guthman Collection, Westport, Connecticut

227
Silver gorget of the 21st Foot
With coat of arms and inscription: '21 Fuzil^{rs}'
Scottish United Services Museum, Edinburgh

228
Silver gorget of the 25th Foot
With coat of arms and inscription: 'XXV REG^{T}'
Scottish United Services Museum, Edinburgh

229
Three brass gorgets
Two with George III's cipher, one with coat of arms
McCord Museum, Montreal, Quebec

230
Two brass gorgets
One plain, one with the Royal coat of arms
Mr Francis A. Lord, Columbia, South Carolina

231
Silver gorget of the 6th Foot
1770–90 pattern, with coat of arms, cipher and inscription: 'VI'
Royal Warwickshire Regiment Museum, Warwick

232
Silver gorget of the 3rd Foot
Royal coat of arms, crest and motto
National Army Museum, Chelsea, London

233
Gilt copper gorget of the 20th Foot
with the Royal coat of arms
National Army Museum, Chelsea, London

234
Grenadier's bearskin cap frontlet
1768 pattern. White metal with black japanning
12·7 cm high
Scottish United Services Museum, Edinburgh

Until the uniform changes of 1768, grenadiers wore cloth mitre caps with embroidered decoration (see item 44); after that time they were issued with fur caps with decorated metal front plates.

235
2 buttons, gilt on bone, 21st Foot
Scottish United Services Museum, Edinburgh

Before 1767 uniform buttons were decorated with patterns or designs of a non-military nature, but following instructions of that year, each regiment had to have its number embossed on its buttons. All buttons were made of a wood or bone base which was covered with a metal disc, turned at the edges. Officers' buttons were gold or silver to match their lace; rank and file buttons were pewter or lead.

236
1 button, gilt on bone, 3rd Foot Guards
Scottish United Services Museum, Edinburgh

237
Cast buttons of the 23rd, 30th, 37th, 63rd Foot
University of South Carolina, Columbia

238
Button of the 23rd Foot
Greensboro Historical Museum, North Carolina

239
Pewter buttons of the 21st (2) and 26th Foot
Scottish United Services Museum, Edinburgh

240
Two brass buttons of the 26th Foot
Regimental Museum of the Cameronians, Hamilton, Lanarkshire

241
Bone button bases, and the matrices from which they were cut
University of South Carolina, Columbia

242
Sample of lace of the 40th Regiment of Foot
1768
The Queen's Lancashire Regiment, Warrington, Lancashire

Each regiment could be distinguished by the facing-colour of its uniform coats, on lapels and cuffs. The braid, or lace, round the button-holes was also distinctive, the pattern varying from regiment to regiment. Officers wore gold or silver lace; that of the rank and file was made of white worsted with a contrasting design. This sample of an ordinary soldier's lace was submitted to George III for approval in 1768, when the uniforms of the army were being regularised.

243
Two British snuff boxes
Mr Francis A. Lord, Columbia, South Carolina

244
Officer's folding fork with walnut handle and pocket knife
Mr Francis A. Lord, Columbia, South Carolina

Both officers and men had to carry their personal equipment with them when the army was in the field.

245
Man-of-war Boat
Paul Sandby

Undated. Pencil drawing
27·9 cm × 50·8 cm
Trustees of the British Museum, London

One type of vessel used in the Battle of New York.

246
A British Gunboat
Joseph Wright of Derby

c. 1770. Pencil on paper
31·6 cm × 33·3 cm
Derby Museum and Art Gallery, Derbyshire

Wright shows a British gunboat in action and has added a plan of the boat. Such a vessel as this would have supported troops in the landing on Long Island.
The drawing is inscribed: '¼ of Inch Scale to a foot'.

On the diagram of the boat is written in the appropriate places: 'Seats for the Rowers', 'Platform wherin the Gun Works', 'Magazine under this platform'.

247
A View of Gravesend in Kent with Troops passing the Thames to Tilbury Fort
Artist unknown

Undated hand-coloured engraving
30·4 cm × 44·3 cm
Anne S. K. Brown Military Collection, Providence, Rhode Island

This is probably the best view of troop-transport vessels for the period. The landing barges are equipped with drop-fronts for the easier loading and unloading of men and equipment.

248
The Battle for New York
The diorama shows British landing barges unloading grenadiers, etc., and artillery on the beaches of Long Island on the morning of 22 August 1776, as the opening move in the capture of New York.
The map illustrates the British army routes to the total occupation of the New York area: through Long Island, Brooklyn Heights, New York City (with its Broadway, Wall Street and the Bowery), Manhattan and the East and Hudson rivers. The two groups of figures represent the respective sizes of the two armies: the Rebel, led by Washington on horseback, numbering 19,000; and the British, with Howe and Clinton on horseback, numbering some 24,000.

249
British troops landing in the Jerseys
Photo-mural of the British troops landing in the Jerseys in November 1776, under Lord Cornwallis. The sketch is attributed to Thomas Davies, who served with Cornwallis's forces. The original is in the New York Public Library.

250
Forcing Hudson River Passage 1776
Dominic Serres

1779. Oil on canvas
71·1 cm × 114·3 cm
United States Naval Academy Museum, Annapolis, Maryland

On the morning of 9 October 1776, the 'Roebuck, Phoenix, and Tartar Ships of War pass'd up the North (Hudson) River, under a very heavy cannonade from the Rebel works, but made the Signal of receiving no damage.' (Diary entry of Archibald Robertson, an eminent British military engineer.)

The Royal Navy now controlled the Hudson along its Manhattan length. Howe had captured New York town, and left Washington holding Harlem Heights and Fort Washington (seen firing on the right of the picture). The Navy's new move up the river was the prelude to the next battle. Three days after the event recorded in the painting, Howe outflanked the Rebels, made Harlem Heights untenable, and Fort Washington fell on 16 November.

In control of the Hudson, British troops were able to take Fort Lee (firing on the left of the picture) and to drive Washington on the retreat into New Jersey and Pennsylvania.

Dominic Serres's painting was probably created from sketches and eye-witness accounts. The canvas is signed lower left: 'D. Serres 1779'. He made three versions of the subject for each of the frigate captains. This version was handed down from Captain Sir Andrew Hamond of the *Roebuck*.

251
A view of the City of New York from Long Island
John Montresor (?)

Undated. Ink and watercolour drawing
25 cm × 42·4 cm
Ref: LC-USZ62-20492
Library of Congress, Washington, D.C.

The artist was looking across the East river to the southernmost tip of Manhattan. His position was to the north of the area where the British troops made their first landings.

252
View of the Hudson River from Fort Knyphausen
Thomas Davies

New York, 1779. Watercolour on paper
34·5 cm × 52·7 cm
Sigmund Samuel Canadiana Collection,
Royal Ontario Museum, Toronto

This painting is described on the verso, 'A View on the Hudson River looking down towards New York from Fort Knyphausen 1779'.

Thomas Davies, a British captain with his own artillery company at the Battle of New York, commanded the guns at this fort after its capture in November 1776, before which it had been called Fort Washington (see item 250). The little town of New

247

252 (detail)

York lies hidden by the hills of Manhattan in the middle distance on the left. On the horizon is Staten Island, and to the right are the New Jersey shores.

253
New York after the Fire
C. J. Sauthier

1776. Manuscript map, scale 1:5376 approx.
80 cm × 59 cm
The Duke of Northumberland, Alnwick

The map reads: 'Plan of the City of New York as it was when His Majesty's Forces took possession of it in 1776 . . . Survey'd in October 1776 by C. J. Sauthier.'

The Rebels' works are shown in yellow, and the section of the city which was burnt shows up in pale red and dotted lines. The fire began shortly after midnight on 21 September 1776. It was confined to an area between Broadway and the Hudson; 493 houses were destroyed, denying good billets to the British.

254
Lieutenant-Colonel Alured Clarke, 1745 ?–1832
Tilly Kettle

1767–70. Oil on canvas
254 cm × 165 cm
Major Basil Heaton, Mold, Clwyd

Alured Clarke was promoted lieutenant-colonel in the 54th Foot in 1775, from major in the same regiment, and sailed with his men from Ireland to America in spring 1776. They arrived at South Carolina, off Charleston, and were involved in a disastrous attack on Sullivan's Island, and then withdrew to New York. Clarke led his unit at the Battle of New York and the occupation of Rhode Island in late 1776. The following year he moved, with the same rank, to the 7th Foot, the Royal Fusiliers, and commanded them during the Southern Campaign in Georgia and the Carolinas. By now he had risen to brigadier-general.

In 1782 Clarke was appointed muster-master-general of the Hessian troops by George III, and returned to New York to organise them.

In the painting Clarke is wearing the uniform of the 5th Foot, with whom he served as captain from 1767–71. As the artist left England for India in 1770, the work must have been executed before that date.

255
Soldiers at Warley Camp
These enlarged figures of soldiers are taken from the pencil and ink sketches, probably by de Loutherbourg, in the Warley Camp album (see item 133).

General Washington's Army

THE AMERICAN COLONISTS had guns. No fact is more important in explaining the success of the rebellion than the almost universal possession of firearms. By law (except in Quaker Pennsylvania), adult white males, with few exceptions (clergymen, college students and public officials), were required to take part in military exercises several times each year. Although the colonial militia was never an efficient military force, it was from this large pool of armed and at least partially-trained manpower that a Rebel army quickly emerged in 1775.

Within a few days after the first fighting at Lexington and Concord, about 20,000 New England militiamen had surrounded the much smaller British garrison of Boston. Beaten at Bunker Hill in June, the rag-tag Rebel force fought well enough to inflict 1150 casualties on their red-coated enemies. The Continental Congress in Philadelphia adopted the New England soldiers and appointed George Washington from Virginia to lead them, giving substance to the idea that there was to be a 'Continental' army, and not a disconnected war of guerrilla resistance.

Guerrilla war was the last thing contemplated or advocated by Washington, a gentlemanly planter with conventional European ideas about raising an army and waging a war. Washington spent much of the next seven years trying to turn his Continental army into a disciplined and trained fighting force, capable of standing up to British and German regulars in the open field. He never wholly succeeded, in spite of von Steuben's strenuous efforts to introduce Prussian drill and proper discipline. After the first flush of enthusiasm, most Rebel soldiers returned to their farms and families. Few Americans were willing to enlist for three years or the duration of the war, which was the term set by Congress – at Washington's insistence – for Continental recruits in 1776. By the end of that year, when the Revolution seemed on the brink of collapse, Washington had only 3000 Continentals under his command, and at Valley Forge the following winter his army shrank again to a mere 5000 men in fighting condition, although separate Continental forces existed to the north, on the frontier, and in the south. Thereafter, the effective strength of the Continental army hovered around 15,000, rising every spring on the eve of a new campaign, falling every autumn with the first snow.

Even less impressive, from some points of view, including Washington's, was the mass of armed men who only occasionally performed active service: the Revolutionary militia. Poorly trained as the colonial militia had been, badly disci-

facing page: item 282

plined and undependable under fire, the citizen-soldiers of the Revolution were ten times as numerous as the Continentals, but were frequently described as worse than useless because they consumed rations, pay, and precious supplies with little to show for the investment. But perhaps opponents of the Revolution had the clearest appreciation of the value of the Rebel militia, for they saw how quickly the Continental army could swell its numbers or replace its losses by short-term drafts from the militia, and how pervasively the militia controlled every part of the Colonies not actually occupied in force by the British. Washington was only the first of many to underestimate the value of these part-time unsoldierly soldiers.

The two major parts of the Rebel army – the part-time militia, and the more professional Continentals – in fact played essentially complementary roles in the war. While the militia held much of the countryside, even a small force of Continentals kept their enemy concentrated and wary, unable to extend Royal authority much more than a day's march from British headquarters. When the militia ran away, the Continentals stood and fought. When the Continentals were beaten, as they were, badly, in the south in 1780, bolder militiamen would fight on in the guerrilla fashion deplored by Washington but so effective in keeping alive the flame of resistance. Evidence was everywhere of Rebel inefficiency, cowardice, corruption, and even demoralisation, yet early in the war observers concluded that such an army could never be defeated, at least not without a war of terror and extermination for which the British had neither the means nor, perhaps, the stomach.

Historians continue to argue about whether the Rebel army could have won without French intervention in 1778. The real question is whether the British would have given up in disgust before the Rebels gave up in exhaustion, and is unanswerable. What is clearer are some of the revolutionary effects of keeping a Rebel army in the field from 1775 to 1783. In a population of less than three millions, several hundred thousand men performed active service for up to a year or more, many of them seeing other parts of America for the first time; the rolls of the Rebel army, small as it may have been at a given time, show that its turnover rate was high, with a large proportion of the white, and a sizeable part of the black population serving at one time or another. Officers of that army, men like Washington, Hamilton, Knox, and Greene, emerged from the war with a degree of national 'fame' that only Benjamin Franklin and a few clergymen had achieved in pre-Revolutionary America; these military heroes would become an important part of the post-war political leadership. Finally, the desperate effort to keep a Rebel army in the field, to feed it, arm and clothe it, pay it, and otherwise maintain it as a fighting force, came near to wrecking the economic and political structure of the new United States. The air of crisis created by the long struggle of the Rebel army, both with its British enemy and with its own unruly supporters, created the atmosphere for a second, equally crucial struggle. That was the struggle to turn the fine rhetoric of the Declaration of Independence of 1776, when the war was new, into the hard-bitten reality of the Federal Constitution of 1787, when Americans had fully experienced the disruptive effects of a long, difficult war.

JOHN SHY

256

256
General David Forman, 1745–97
Charles Willson Peale

c. 1784. Oil on canvas
129·5 cm × 99·6 cm
Berkshire Museum, Pittsfield, Massachusetts

Rebel General Forman, born in Monmouth County, New Jersey, was appointed in June 1776 to command a New Jersey regiment, and sent to reinforce Washington in New York. He arrived to join the forces then defeated by the British. For much of the war that followed Forman was the scourge of New Jersey Loyalists; he was known as 'Devil David'.

Forman's uniform of blue with buff facings is representative of the colours adopted by the American Continental army.

257
Colonel Marinus Willett, 1740–1830
Ralph Earl

c. 1790. Oil on canvas
231·7 cm × 142·2 cm
Metropolitan Museum of Art, New York

Colonel Marinus Willett began his service as a captain in the 1st New York Regiment. With this unit he joined the American invasion of Canada in 1775. Returning to New York, he was commissioned a lieutenant-colonel in the 3rd New York Regiment and was there during the New York battles. In 1777 he was sent to Fort Stanwix, a key post in the Mohawk Valley (see page 147), where he lead a successful sortie from the fort against the British. Of this sally Willett wrote: 'We totally routed two of the enemy's encampments, destroyed all their provisions that was in them, brought off upwards of 50 brass kettles, and more than a hundred blankets . . . with a number of muskets, tomahawks, spears, ammunition, clothing, deer skins, a variety of Indian affairs, and 5 colours which . . . were desplayed on our flagstaff under the Continental Flag.' For this act of bravery, Congress voted, on 4 October 1777, to present him with an 'elegant sword'. In this portrait Willett is wearing it.

258
The sword of Colonel Marinus Willett
French, 18th century. Presentation dress sword; blade of blued steel, gilt-edged; hilt is silver gilt
100 cm long
Metropolitan Museum of Art, New York

This was the sword Congress voted to present to Willett for bravery at Fort Stanwix.

299

259
The Blue Ball Inn sign
Pennsylvania, *c.* 1769. Paint on wood
148·5 cm × 109·2 cm
Historical Society of York County, York, Pennsylvania

[Along with the church hall, the American tavern
was the most popular meeting place for a local community. While the first may have fed the spirit, the
second could offer a warm fire in winter, plenty of
rum and ale, and food of another kind. As with the
Green Dragon in Boston (see item 23) and the Royal
Oak at Medford (see item 30), the Blue Ball Inn of
York County, Pennsylvania, was a centre of great
activity for Rebel regular soldiers and the district
militia. Besides a bar and a kitchen for serving the
traveller, the local tavern had small rooms and a
dormitory for those staying longer than just for a
meal.

The Blue Ball, built in 1769, was a staging post on
the fifty-mile route between York and Baltimore. The
scene in this interior reconstruction is set in a fierce
Pennsylvania winter during the Revolution.]

260
Royal American Regiment musket
1747. 46-inch Brown Bess, with Tower Armouries
lock; European walnut stock; butt plate marked
'R. AM. REG.'
New York State History Collections, Schenectady

The 60th Foot, or Royal American Regiment, fought
in the Seven Years War, and when it was over, stayed
behind to garrison the Colonies. Many of the guns
with which the men were issued would have been
absorbed into general use during their long period of
service in America and would have been turned
against the British army when the Revolution broke
out.

261
Fish-belly (club butt) musket
New England
57½ inches (146·6 cm) overall length
New York State History Collections, Schenectady

A typical hunting weapon, the lock, barrel and brass
furniture of which were salvaged from a Brown Bess.
The re-use of precious parts of old guns was a common feature of colonial gunsmithing.

270

265

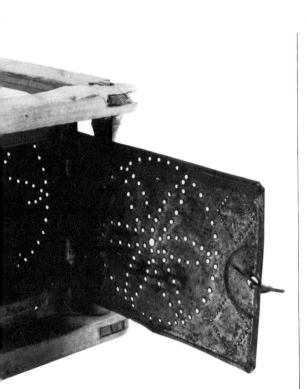

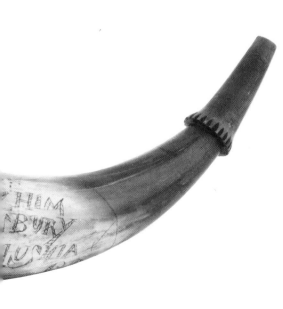

262
American-made musket
61¾ inches (156·8 cm) overall length
Mr Edward Charol, Stamford, Connecticut

This musket, pieced together from American, English and Hessian parts, was surcharged 'u.s.' and 'u.states' on lock, stock and barrel.

263
Equipment of the Continental army
Mr Francis A. Lord, Columbia, South Carolina
• **Bayonet,** made in Massachusetts
• **Bayonet scabbard frog,** made of leather
• **American leather cartridge box** for 24 cartridges
• **Sabre** used by the cavalry
• **A sword**
• **Militia sword** from South Carolina
• **Wooden canteen,** once the property of Captain E. V. Collins
• **Oak canteen** from North Carolina, with strap and stopper
• **Wooden, barrel-shaped rum canteen**
• **Wooden canteen** used by a squad of eight men under General Gates at Saratoga

264
Wooden canteen with two holes
Greensboro Historical Museum, North Carolina

265
Continental army equipment
Bennington Museum, Vermont
• **Oak barrel canteen** with iron handle and pewter drinking spout, carried by a Rebel at Bennington
• **Barrel canteen,** painted grey
• **Powder horn** of Peleg Matteson, with a turned plug and brass tacks
• **Powder horn** made by Jabez Fairbanks in 1756, and decorated by pricks of an awl. Used in the Seven Years War, it was brought out for the Battle of Bennington twenty-one years later
• **Powder horn** made by Asahel Wright in 1777

266
Camp stove, made of iron
Mr Crosby Milliman, Georgeville, Quebec

267
Soldier's Bible, bound in leather
with brass fittings
Ross E. Beard Jr Collection, Camden Historical Commission, South Carolina

268
'Rules for the Better Government of the Troops'
Philadelphia, 1776. 36-page pamphlet printed by
John Dunlap
19 cm × 12·3 cm
Maryland Historical Society, Baltimore

269
Tin candle mould
New England, *c.* 1770
Mr Francis A. Lord, Columbia, South Carolina

270
**Foot warmer used in the
Catamount Tavern in Vermont**
Wooden frame, with tinned iron, pierced box,
enclosing an iron coal container
Bennington Museum, Vermont

271
A trapunto ('stuffed work') quilt
Blue taffeta on a brown wool backing, with
floral motifs
242·6 cm square
*Independence National Historical Park,
Philadelphia, Pennsylvania*

The quilt was made in Philadelphia in 1761 by
Hannah Callender and Catherine Smith 'in testimony
of their friendship', and is typical of the needlework
of colonial America.

272
Light Dragoon helmet
American, *c.* 1778–81. Leather, brass and horsehair
20·3 cm high
Guthman Collection, Westport, Connecticut

Heavy leather jockey caps like these were adopted by
the Light Dragoons in their combat against the
British and Provincial (Loyalist) light cavalry companies which patrolled the southern colonies in the
second half of the war. With its brass comb holding a
horsehair plume, the helmet was a necessary protection against sabre slashes.

273
Pair of flintlock pistols
Scottish, 18th century
Metropolitan Museum of Art, New York

These pistols belonged to Jonathan Porter, owner of
the Royal Oak Tavern in Medford, Massachusetts
(see item 30), who served as a lieutenant in the militia.

274
Spur of Captain Michael Smyser
American, *c.* 1776
Historical Society of York County, York, Pennsylvania

Captain Smyser of the York County Militia was captured at the surrender of Fort Washington by the
Hessians in 1776.

275
Committee of Safety musket
Pennsylvania, *c.* 1775
Historical Society of York County, York, Pennsylvania

When the Revolution began the Colonists had very
few military guns, and went to war with hunting and
fowling weapons (see item 49). But early in 1775
local Committees of Safety were contracting gunsmiths to produce muskets, based on the Brown Bess,
to arm their local soldiers. Very few have survived.
This is the first American example of a manufactured
product with interchangeable parts.

276
Flintlock sporting rifle
Pennsylvania, *c.* 1760
45 inches (114·3 cm) barrel length; ·45 bore
The Armouries, H.M. Tower of London

The American soldiers also used a gun with a rifled
barrel. Developed by Pennsylvania-German gunsmiths, it became known as the Pennsylvania or
Kentucky rifle. This example, with its brass mounted,
maple-wood stock, and barrel with seven grooves
which gave the ball a three-quarters turn as it fired,
is the sporting prototype of the military weapon.

Slow to reload, and unreliable in bad weather, the
rifle was only a formidable weapon in skilled hands.
However, the frontiersmen of Pennsylvania, Kentucky and Virginia were experienced riflemen, and
could pick off a Redcoat at 300 yards, four or five
times the range of a smooth-bore musket. In general,
150 yards may have been a more realistic effective
range. The American rifle companies in their fringed
buckskin jackets, particularly that led by Daniel
Morgan, earned a considerable reputation against the
British who were unused to their woodland, Indian-
style fighting techniques. However, by 1781, largely
as a result of Washington's ambition to make the
Continental army resemble its European counterpart,
the rifle had been abandoned as a military weapon.

277
Wooden canteen of Noah Allen
American
19 cm diameter
Fort Ticonderoga Museum, New York

One of the most important personal items of equipment for the Rebel soldier was the canteen which held his liquid refreshment. The Continental army authorities tried to provide one for each man, not always successfully. Once issued with one, a soldier like Noah Allen would mark it to be sure he kept it.

278
Powder horn engraved with ships, fish and birds
Cornelius Van Wormer

Inscribed: 'Skeensborough, May the 12th 1777'
Fort Ticonderoga Museum, New York

Skenesboro, as it was properly spelt, was an important ship-building centre at the southernmost tip of Lake Champlain. Burgoyne captured it on his strike south towards Saratoga less than two months after Van Wormer carved his horn there.

279
Powder horn
1783. Inscribed: 'Success to the United States of America Made for the Reverend William Hill by Jo. Cloud'
Greensboro Historical Museum, North Carolina

280
Powder horn of Nathaniel Sunsamun
Inscribed: 'his horn made in the year 1777 in February the 24 My Liberty Ile have or death'
Mr Crosby Milliman, Georgeville, Quebec

Sunsamun was a Mohegan Indian from Preston, Connecticut, fighting for the Rebels.

281
Sketch of an American soldier
Valley Forge, 1778. Pen and ink
16 cm × 16·7 cm
North Carolina State Archives, Raleigh

When Private John Massey was discharged from the Continental army at Valley Forge on 28 February 1778, he doodled on the back of his discharge papers. He drew some geometric designs, and the figure of a soldier, with cocked hat, frock-coat and pigtail. Such a contemporary view of an American soldier is almost unknown in the iconography of the Revolution.

282
Painted wooden drum
Decorated with an eagle holding a banner in its beak inscribed 'Sons of Liberty', a shaft of arrows in one claw and a flag in the other; dark green with gold
34·9 cm high
Fort Ticonderoga Museum, New York

283
Wooden fife
Mr Crosby Milliman, Georgeville, Quebec

284
Wooden fife carried by a member of the 7th Pennsylvania Line Regiment
Historical Society of York County, York, Pennsylvania

Music was as important to the Continental army as it was to the British. Most of the tunes were traditional airs from the British Isles which had been sung as ballads or marched to by soldiers for many years. With new titles and patriotic words, the songs took on new meanings.

285
Giles Gibbs's Book for the Fife
East Windsor (now Ellington), Connecticut, 1777.
Manuscript
10·1 cm × 16·5 cm (closed)
Connecticut Historical Society, Hartford

In this small manuscript book of music scores, Giles Gibbs, a Connecticut fifer, noted down the tunes he needed to remember. He probably copied them from a printed fife tutor, perhaps a London publication. The air titled 'Thehos Gendar' is the earliest known version of 'Yankee Doodle', though what Gibbs's title means is unclear. After three years' service in the Continental army, Gibbs was killed by a British raiding party in Vermont in 1780, aged just twenty.

286
Ballad broadside entitled 'The Yankey's return from Camp'
Printed verse with woodcut
26·3 cm × 21·9 cm
American Antiquarian Society, Worcester, Massachusetts

Probably published in Boston, these words were sung to the tune of 'Yankee Doodle'. Under a rare contemporary scene of American soldiers and a drummer, they were possibly inspired by a visit to the Rebel camp in Cambridge, Massachusetts, in 1775.

287
'An American General and An American Rifleman'
London, 1789. Hand-coloured engraving
22·2 cm × 33·2 cm
Anne S. K. Brown Military Collection,
Providence, Rhode Island

Published in Barnard's *New Complete & Authentic History of England*, this was a contemporary British view of what the enemy wore.

288
A pair of prints
German, 1783–4. Hand-coloured engravings by Berger, from designs by Chodowiecki
Each 9·2 cm × 5·5 cm
Anne S. K. Brown Military Collection,
Providence, Rhode Island

Continental army uniforms, a rifleman and a Pennsylvania infantryman, and uniforms of two members of Washington's staff. Taken from a yearbook of 1784 (see item 28), these were contemporary German impressions of the Continental army.

289
The American Rebels' armaments
Charles Blaskowitz

Boston, 1775. Pen, ink and watercolour
29·2 cm × 42·5 cm
Ref: LC-USZ62-45565
Library of Congress, Washington, D.C.

This illustration by army surveyor and mapmaker Charles Blaskowitz is a contemporary British impression of the defence works and batteries which the Rebels were capable of building.

290
Broadside ordering the purchase of grain for the army
'Supply Chamber, Watertown, Massachusetts'
25 May 1775
20 cm × 15·5 cm
Massachusetts Historical Society, Boston

291
Broadside stipulating army rations
'Provincial Congress, Watertown, Massachusetts'
10 June 1775
23 cm × 16·5 cm
Massachusetts Historical Society, Boston

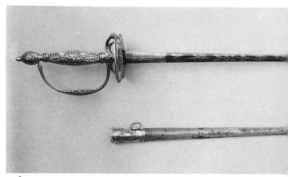

258

1. Americanischer Scharffschütz oder Jäger. (Rifleman
2. reguläre Infanterie von Pensilvanien.

288

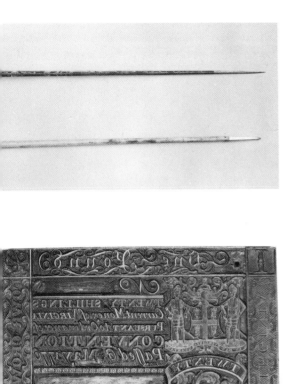

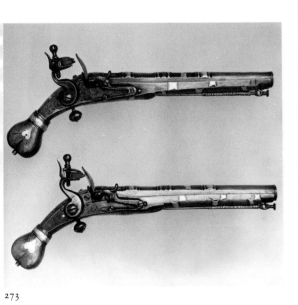

In the weeks after the first confrontation at Lexington and Concord the Rebels were faced with creating an organised army out of a body of militia. Supplies to feed the huge number of men suddenly camped outside Boston in the days before Bunker Hill proved one of the chief problems for the commissariat of the Massachusetts forces.

292
Three Continental army buttons, inscribed 'USA'
American, *c.* 1779. Pewter
1·5 cm diameter
Guthman Collection, Westport, Connecticut

After 1779 all regiments were ordered to wear buttons marked 'USA' on their uniform coats, while carrying buttons with State symbols on their hats.

293
Cup and spoon of William Bemis
American, 1779. Horn
Mr Crosby Milliman, Georgeville, Quebec

294
Officer's snuff box
American. Decorated leather
Mr Francis A. Lord, Columbia, South Carolina

295
Brass powder flask, with motto 'E Pluribus Unum'
American, 1777–91 pattern
11·4 cm long
The Queen's Lancashire Regiment, Warrington, Lancashire

296
Pair of camp cups
Boston(?), 1750–70. American coin silver
8 cm high
The Society of the Cincinnati, Washington, D.C.

These silver camp cups belonged to Lieutenant John Maynard, Third Regiment of the Massachusetts Continental Line. He was captured by the British at White Plains in 1776 and held in military prison in Halifax. A British officer – and fellow Mason – befriended him there and when Maynard was exchanged the officer gave the cups to him.

The quality of the work indicates that the cups were made by a master silversmith, probably a member of the Tyler family, who worked in Boston between 1690 and 1800.

297

273

297
Engraved plate for printing 20-shilling Continental currency bill
Virginia, 1776. Copper plate on wood block
6·9 cm × 9·2 cm
Virginia Historical Society, Richmond

298
Engraved plate for printing £3 bill
Virginia. Copper
10·6 cm × 20·1 cm
Virginia Historical Society, Richmond

British coins rarely reached the Colonies, and trade was conducted with foreign currency brought in by shipmasters. Businessmen and shopkeepers used currency balances to weigh coins for their relative value, which varied from one colony to another.

To alleviate the problem the Continental Congress authorised the issue of a Continental currency in 1775, and each colony brought out its own paper bills of varying denominations, usually decorated with Rebel slogans and insignia. Much of the cost of the war was met by the issue of this money – $250 million by Congress and $200 million by state governments. The paper bills depreciated so quickly that they inspired the saying 'not worth a Continental'.

299
General George Washington, 1732–99
The great-grandson of an Englishman, Washington, a Virginian planter, was appointed Commander-in-Chief of the Continental army in June 1775. He was at that time the most experienced native-born soldier in the Colonies. He had fought alongside the British on the western frontiers of the colonies in the Seven Years War. Despite the reputation he earned then as a military tactician against the French and the Indians, he showed no great flair. Nevertheless, his decision to cross the Delaware at Christmas 1776, only eight weeks after his final retreat from New York, and then to defeat the Hessians at Trenton and the British at Princeton in swift running battles was an imaginative stroke which fired Rebel morale.

George Washington demonstrated two great virtues as a leader. He always chose to stay with his men, a principle exemplified by his presence at the cruel winter camps of Morristown, New Jersey, and Valley Forge, Pennsylvania. And, though a harsh disciplinarian, his imposing presence and consummate diplomacy enabled him to rise above the squabblings of his officers and hold together the conflicting tensions in his army.

Detail from the painting 'George Washington at Princeton' by Charles Willson Peale, at the Pennsylvania Academy of Fine Arts, Philadelphia.

300
Four volumes from George Washington's library
The Boston Athenaeum, Massachusetts

For those who have concentrated on the military and political aspects of Washington's life, his library holds many surprises – some illustrated here.
1. *Seneca's Morals*, by Sir Roger L'Estrange, London, 1746
   16·5 cm × 8·8 cm
2. *A Complete View of the British Customs*, by Henry Crouch, of the Custom-House, London, 1731 Octavo
3. *The Hot-House Gardener on the General Culture of the Pine-Apple* . . . by John Abercrombie, London, 1789. Octavo
4. *The Compleat Tutor For the Violin*, London, of the period. Octavo

301
George Washington's campaign trunk
Leather-covered, iron-bound trunk; oval brass plate reads 'GEN^L WASHINGTON No 3'
85·7 cm long; 48·2 cm wide; 38·1 cm high
Collection of the Mount Vernon Ladies' Association, Virginia

The trunk is one of a number of pieces of military equipage which Washington used during the Revolution; in this instance, for clothing and documents.

302
George Washington's medicine chest
24·1 cm long; 20·9 cm wide; 22·8 cm high
Wellcome Institute for the History of Medicine, London

This medicine chest was inherited by Washington's nephew and retained in the family until it was bought at a sale in the United States earlier this century. The lid bears a plate with the initials 'GW'.

303
Decanter belonging to George Washington
Two reeded rings at neck, with wheel stopper. Specially designed for travelling case
18·4 cm high without stopper; 24·1 cm wide; 7·6 cm diameter at base
National Society of Colonial Dames of America, Wethersfield, Connecticut

304
Henry Knox, 1750–1806

General and chief of artillery. In 1775 Knox of Massachusetts was proprietor of 'The London Book Store' in Boston, where he spent a great deal of time reading European books on artillery. Steadily loyal to Washington, he possessed much administrative ability. His greatest exploit was the 300-mile trek he organised in the winter of 1775–6, when he and his team dragged some sixty guns from the newly-captured Fort Ticonderoga to Boston. It was the setting up of those guns on Dorchester Heights overlooking Boston that finally persuaded the British to evacuate the town.

Knox, it is said, was 'forceful, often profane', and had a 'pompous, self-complacent walk'. He commanded the guns at New York, Brandywine, Germantown and Yorktown.

The original Charles Willson Peale portrait is at Independence National Historical Park, Philadelphia.

305
Books from Henry Knox's library

The Boston Athenaeum, Massachusetts

1. *Essay on the Art of War*,
   London, 1761
   Octavo
2. *The Cadet, a military treatise*, by an Officer,
   London, 1756
   Octavo
3. *The Field Engineer of M. le Chevalier de Clairac*,
   translated from the French by John Muller,
   Master of the Royal Academy at Woolwich,
   London, 1773
   Octavo
4. *A Philosophical Enquiry into the Origin of our Ideas of
   the Sublime and Beautiful*, by Edmund Burke
   6th edition, London, 1770
   Octavo

306
Henry Knox trade card
Nathaniel Hurd

Engraving
9·8 cm × 12·7 cm
American Antiquarian Society, Worcester, Massachusetts

'. . . and Sciences', says Knox's trade card. Into this category fell those books on guns which Knox, soon to be chief of artillery in the Continental army, studied in his own store.

307
Henry Knox gorget
Brass with gilt
Fort Ticonderoga Museum, New York

This strange gorget was once British. Someone, if not Knox, defaced the Royal Coat of Arms and superimposed 'US', an arm with a sword, and the motto 'Inimica Tyrannis' – 'hostile to tyrants'.

308
Richard Montgomery, 1738–75

Montgomery was the son of an Irish M.P., educated at St Andrew's and Trinity College, Dublin. At 18 he became an ensign in the 17th Foot and enjoyed a distinguished military career during the Seven Years War in Canada, upper New York, and the West Indies. Back in England he was considerably influenced by the ideas of Burke and Fox, and sold his commission to settle on a farm at King's Bridge, New York, in 1773.

In June 1775, Richard Montgomery was made a brigadier-general in the Continental army and he set out for the invasion of Canada under General Philip Schuyler. When Schuyler became ill, Montgomery led the Rebel forces to Quebec, taking St Johns (now St Jean) and Montreal. At Quebec he joined up with the second prong of the American attack under Benedict Arnold. When the combined forces launched their offensive against the city on 31 December 1775, Montgomery was killed.

The original portrait by Charles Willson Peale is at Independence National Historical Park, Philadelphia, Pennsylvania.

309
Richard Montgomery's sword
Officer's private hanger, horn grip set in silver hilt, pommel in the form of satyr's head, lion mask at bottom of hilt; hallmarked, London, 1774, 'LB', or possibly 'HB'
84 cm long
Royal Ontario Museum, Toronto

This sword formed part of the effects of Rebel General Richard Montgomery who was killed leading the attack on Quebec.

310
Richard Montgomery's powder horn
1770–76. Horn
Royal Ontario Museum, Toronto

This horn belonged to General Montgomery and is

decorated with the Royal coat of arms surmounting cannon, flags and drums. The map shows New York and the Hudson River, Lake George, the Lake Champlain route to Montreal, the Mohawk River, and the Lake Oneida route to Lake Ontario.

311
Alexander Hamilton, 1757–1804

The son of a Scottish merchant and born in the West Indies, Alexander Hamilton showed great promise as a scholar and got himself to college in New York in 1773. He threw his studies to one side in 1775 to form a volunteer company and was commissioned as captain in the Provincial Company of New York Artillery in March 1776. He commanded his guns at Long Island, White Plains, and saw action at Trenton and Princeton.

In March 1777, Hamilton became secretary and aide-de-camp to Washington, who was much impressed by his qualities as a writer. He was promoted to lieutenant-colonel at the age of twenty. He held his secretarial post for almost four and a half years, when, after a quarrel with Washington, he claimed a command in the field. At Yorktown Hamilton led the crucial attack into redoubt No. 10 (see item 536).

The original portrait by John Trumbull is at the National Gallery of Art, Washington, D.C.

312
Alexander Hamilton's field desk

Mahogany with brass trim. The plate reads: 'Alexander Hamilton Yorktown Oct 19th 1781' 49·5 cm long; 27·9 cm wide; 20·3 cm high *Fort Ticonderoga Museum, New York*

The field desk had great importance for the man who, as a lieutenant-colonel, acted as secretary to Washington for almost four and a half years.

313
Nathanael Greene, 1742–86

A Rhode Island man descended from English immigrants, Nathanael Greene emerged from the Revolution as one of its more formidable generals. His early days, however, were none too successful: a fever prevented him from directing the defence of Long Island, and he was involved in the loss of Fort Washington.

It was in the Southern Campaign (see page 191) that his reputation grew. Though Greene never produced any spectacular victories over Lord Cornwallis in the southern Colonies, his use of guerrilla tactics forced the British general into a campaign of move-

ment, which, while it covered a great deal of territory, diminished the number under British command.

The original painting by Charles Willson Peale is at Independence National Historical Park, Philadelphia, Pennsylvania.

314
Message pouch originally belonging to Nathanael Greene

Canvas and leather, with buttons *Historical Society of York County, York, Pennsylvania*

Officers needed pouches for carrying written orders or maps, couriers for taking despatches, often in code, from commander to commander. This pouch was first used by General Nathanael Greene, then by his aide, Major John Clark (who fought at Boston, Long Island, Trenton, Brandywine, Germantown and Monmouth) to whom Greene gave it.

315
Friedrich von Steuben, 1730–94

Since it lacked expertise in the early days of its existence, the Rebel army was not long in employing the services of volunteer foreigners. Von Steuben, born in Magdeburg and trained in the Prussian army, introduced himself to Washington at Valley Forge in February 1778, through contact with Benjamin Franklin in Paris.

At Valley Forge, with 100 picked men, he began to instil in the American army the military virtues of discipline and order through countless drill sequences. In May 1778, Congress recognised his contribution by confirming his appointment as major-general, inspector-general of the Continental army. His ideals were published in a book, a kind of European-bred training manual, in the following year.

The original painting by Charles Willson Peale is at Independence National Historical Park, Philadelphia, Pennsylvania.

316
The von Steuben drill manual

Entitled: 'Regulations for the Order and Discipline of the Troops of the United States' 1779. Restored quarter leather binding 17·1 cm × 11·1 cm *United States Military Academy Library, West Point, New York*

It was with this book that von Steuben, foreign volunteer and inspector-general to the Rebel army, codified his drill techniques.

317
Horatio Gates, 1728–1806
Horatio Gates was, it is said, the son of the Duke of Leeds' housekeeper. Described once as a 'little ruddy-faced Englishman, peering through his thick spectacles', Gates suffered much in his competition for recognition. He first served in the British army in the Seven Years War, where he began his friendship with Washington. In June 1775, he was appointed adjutant-general to General Washington.

Gates's greatest success was his defeat of Burgoyne at Saratoga (a victory which many attribute to a colleague, Benedict Arnold), as a result of which many American Congressmen thought him the right man to replace Washington. His inadequacies as a commander, however, showed themselves when he was sent to the southern colonies to face Cornwallis. His defeat at the Battle of Camden in effect ended his career in the field.

The original painting by Charles Willson Peale is at Independence National Historical Park, Philadelphia, Pennsylvania.

318
Daniel Morgan, 1736–1802
General Morgan, grandson of a Welsh immigrant to Pennsylvania and first cousin to Daniel Boone, first worked in the British army in the Seven Years War as a teamster with horses. In 1756 he struck a British officer and was sentenced to 500 lashes. Later in life, 'Old Wagoner', six foot tall and bulkily built, still bore the mental and physical scars, and was ripe to join the Revolution.

First in command of a corps of Virginian riflemen, Morgan scored very early successes at the Battle of Saratoga. Later, thwarted in his ambitions, he resigned from the army, but resumed when disaster threatened the Rebels in the south. His greatest coup was his defeat of Banastre Tarleton at the Battle of Cowpens, South Carolina, in January 1781.

The original painting by Charles Willson Peale is at Independence National Historical Park, Philadelphia, Pennsylvania.

319
Henry Lee, 1756–1818
Born of the Lee family of Virginia, Henry Lee graduated from Princeton at the age of seventeen and was admitted to read law at the Middle Temple in London when the outbreak of the Revolution blocked his plans. From service as a captain with the Virginia cavalry he was soon promoted to Continen-

tal status. After many successful skirmishes (one of which earned him a Congressional medal – only eight were awarded during the war), 'Light-Horse Harry' Lee joined General Greene in the Southern Campaign. There, as a lieutenant-colonel, Lee (aged twenty-four) fought many cavalry engagements in the manner of his rival adversary, Banastre Tarleton.

The original painting by Charles Willson Peale is at Independence National Historical Park, Philadelphia, Pennsylvania.

320
Benjamin Lincoln, 1733–1810
A Continental army general from Massachusetts, Benjamin Lincoln rose through militia ranks to the Continental army commission of major-general. He commanded the American defences at Saratoga and two years later surrendered Charleston in South Carolina to Cornwallis. He was paroled until exchanged for two British generals. Lincoln's greatest moment of glory was his acceptance of the sword of surrender at Yorktown.

The original painting by Charles Willson Peale is at Independence National Historical Park, Philadelphia, Pennsylvania.

321
Thaddeus Kosciuszko, 1746–1817
Trained as a military engineer in France, Kosciuszko found little to help his career in Poland, and as he was sympathetic with French philosophical ideas of liberty, he borrowed money to reach Philadelphia in August 1776. Within the next three months he had been appointed colonel of engineers in the Continental army. Kosciuszko's role as an engineer of fortifications was best exemplified by his work at the Delaware River forts, at Saratoga, on the defences of West Point, and in the Southern Campaign.

The original bust by H. D. Saunders is the property of the Architect of the Capitol, Washington, D.C.

322
Casimir Pulaski, c. 1748–79
A Continental dragoon leader, Pulaski had fought for the Poles against Russia and fled to Turkey on the partition of his homeland. Through Benjamin Franklin in Paris the Polish cavalryman was directed to Washington, for whom he fought as a commander of dragoons at Brandywine and elsewhere.

The original portrait is at Fort Pulaski National Monument, Georgia, the property of the United States National Parks Service.

Red, White and Black Loyalists

AT THE OUTBREAK OF WAR, most Americans acknowledged the sovereignty of George III. John Adams' view was that one-third of the American people were Patriot, one-third Tory and one-third neutral, but this was a superficial view. It now seems more likely that the proportion was one-fifth rather than one-third Loyalist. New York was, as the British headquarters throughout the war, a Loyalist centre; and there were strong pockets of loyalism in Pennsylvania, Georgia and in the Carolinas. Clearly, wherever the British army appeared, there were waves of Loyalist sentiment, though these were as often out of self-interest as from conviction.

The Loyalist role in the war has been analysed by Dr Paul Smith of the Library of Congress. In his study *Loyalists and Redcoats* and from his analysis of the War Office papers in the Public Record Office he lists forty-one Loyalist regiments and concludes that 19,000 men fought on the Loyalist side. Other estimates go higher, to as many as 50,000, but this is unlikely; it has to be remembered that some enrolled more than once to obtain bounty money, or served in different places. There were in all some 300 companies – at one time or another – in some fifty provincial corps. Alongside the familiar regiments – the Royal Americans, Butler's Rangers, the Royal Greens and the King's Royal Regiment – are more exotic titles: the Roman Catholic Volunteers (who had a number of Irish volunteers among them), Skinner's Greens, the Royal American Reformers, the Black Pioneers and, not least, the Ethiopian Regiment. Two Loyal regiments became regular units of British infantry – the Royal Highland Emigrants and the Volunteers of Ireland – and in the last two years of the war in the south they at least came into their own. But, though their major role in battle was slight, they played a key part in the underground world of the spy and the informer.

The Loyalists included many from the Colonial establishment – ex-governors and ex-lieutenant-governors, lawyers and Anglican ministers, customs officers and 'friends of government', but they represented also a wide cross-section of American society and were by no means exclusively drawn from the Establishment. When, in June 1776, a number of people were arrested in New York on suspicion of plotting to kill George Washington, they included the Mayor of New York and some officials, but also farmers, tavern-keepers, two gunsmiths, two tanners, two doctors, one saddler, one silversmith, one shoemaker, 'a pensioner with one arm' and an unfortunate described only as 'a damned rascal'. When an Act of Banishment was passed against 300 Loyalists in Massachusetts in 1778, one-third were described as merchants or professional men, but another one-third were farmers, and the rest artisans, labourers and small shopkeepers.

Many important families were split: the Fairfaxes and the Randolphs of Virginia, the Bulls of South Carolina, the Curwens of Massachusetts, the Pells of New York. For this was not only a guerrilla war, but a war inside families. Divided, Tory in sentiment and upper class in tone, they produced few natural leaders and no outstanding military figure, unless one counts Benedict Arnold, the traitor who plotted to sell West Point to the British in 1780. Traitor or not, he was an able battle commander.

William Franklin, Benjamin Franklin's illegitimate son, lacked his father's finesse and capacity for leadership. He was arrested in 1776 while serving as Royal Governor of New Jersey and was handed over to the British in 1778. He served from 1780 to 1782 as president of the Board of Associated Loyalists, seeking feebly to organise guerrilla campaigns in the middle states.

Perhaps the most prominent Loyalist family was that of Beverley Robinson, born in Virginia but identifying with New York where he had married the wealthy Suzannah Philipse. He raised the Royal American Regiment and served with Clinton in 1777. Benjamin Thompson served for a time as a Loyalist commander and saw some action around Charleston in 1782, but his main service was as Germain's Under-Secretary of State at the Northern Department in the middle years of the war. He was knighted in 1784.

One group of Loyalists could be disturbingly and clearly identified from the outset: the Iroquois. The Mohawk Valley had been administered for the previous twenty years by Sir William Johnson in his role of Superintendent of the Northern Indians. His skill kept at least four of the six nations firmly on the British side until his death in 1774. His son Sir John and his nephew Guy continued that tradition, and throughout the war Joseph Brant and his Mohawks were active on the British side. Brant led the Indians on St Leger's expedition to support Burgoyne in 1777; and with 400 savages, supported by a number of whites, he set up the effective ambush at Oriskany in August 1777.

But the Indians were troublesome allies; the advisability of such alliances was hotly debated in London. Their use of the tomahawk and the scalping knife was savage; and they were hard to control. There was a great loss of goodwill towards the British along the frontier after Indian raids. It has nevertheless to be said that the Mohawks in their barbarous way were active fighters on the frontier and that they stood by Britain throughout the war. And to them Britain, after the war, was generous in turn.

With American victory in 1783, however, those still loyal to the King faced a dilemma. Some 40,000 were driven from home, and in all 100,000 (one in thirty of all white families) had chosen to go by 1783; many of them lost their property for ever. The majority, with no place to go, took the oath of allegiance to the United States, accepting exclusion from public office and from the professions. New York made $3,600,000 from the sale of confiscated Loyalist property, Maryland $2 million. The peace treaty stipulated that the states return the property, but little was in fact done by way of restitution. But in a personal sense, they were rarely met with violence. Of Pennsylvania's Loyalist 'blacklist' of 490 names, only a few were punished, and only two were hanged.

Many Loyalists, however, became exiles. In the end some 8000 settled in Britain and 5000 (1300 from Canada) claimed for compensation from the British Government. By 1790, when the final report of their claims was published, the Government had distributed over £3 million in doles as well as offering Government posts and appointments of ministers to parishes, against a total claim of over £10 million. This was of course the saddest part of the American story. Thomas Hutchinson, American-born, businessman, colonial historian and good servant of Massachusetts, went into exile in 1775 and died in London in 1780 with his heart still aching for Boston. He lived for most of these years in Brompton Row and in the houses alongside him were some twenty-five fellow Bostonians, a lost and broken colony of exiles. Nor were he and his colleagues adequately consulted by the home Government; after meeting the King on his first night in London, he never had a close personal conversation with him again. The British Government during the war, as before it, neglected its friends. But it did reward those who removed to the bleak wastes of Nova Scotia with Government land to the extent of three million acres and, given the conditions there, treated them well. One million dollars was spent on resettling them.

Perhaps in conclusion two points should be made. If the story of the Loyalists is seen first and last as the record of a failure, the failure was only in the North American colonies south of what is now the state of Maine. If they failed in the United States, they succeeded overseas: 40,000 of them settled in Canada and they are essentially its founding fathers. They were important in Nova Scotia, New Brunswick and Prince Edward Island and they created Ontario. Without them Canada would hardly have been strong enough to survive ultimate American annexation. The promise of the Quebec Act was made real by the fact of Loyalist influx, and Canadian nationalism was built on Loyalist foundations.

ESMOND WRIGHT

323
A Prospective View of Old Newgate
Connecticut's State Prison
Richard Brunton

Granby, Connecticut, 1799–1801. Line engraving
52 cm × 52 cm
Connecticut Historical Society, Hartford

Simsbury, or Granby, copper mines fell into disuse
by 1773 and became Connecticut's gaol. Renamed
Newgate, after the London prison, the mines soon
acquired a worse reputation than those of their name-
sake. In the Revolution, both Loyalists and prisoners
of war were incarcerated there in appalling conditions
in subterranean cells.

   Little is known about Brunton. He first advertised
in 1781, and was noted for his bookplates. This print
was made when Brunton was himself serving a two-
year term for counterfeiting, but, although a little
later than the war, the scene of the prison life – the
price a man often paid for loyalty to George III –
would not have changed.

324
Map of the Great River St John with
Negro settlements
Printed map of 1788, based on surveys of 1784–7,
marking Loyalist communities
53·3 cm × 43·1 cm
Ref: PRO CO700
Public Record Office, London

Around the lower reaches of the St John river cluster
the first of the Negro settlements. At the top of the
map stands York County (see next item).

325
Land petition of William Fisher,
a black, York County
'To His Excellency Thomas Carleton, Governor and
Captain General in and over the Province of
New Brunswick', 14 March 1785
30·5 cm × 19 cm
Provincial Archives, Fredericton, New Brunswick

When the British armies left the United States at the
end of the war they took with them at least 14,000
black Loyalists. The numbers were made up of those
slaves who had escaped and joined the British forces
and of those who still worked for emigrating
Loyalists. Fisher describes himself as a 'black man . . .
that having left New York in the year 1783 and come
in the ship Peggy . . .'

323

332

326

Lord Dunmore, the Royal Governor of Virginia, had put the American interpretation of the word 'freedom' to the test when he offered liberty to the slaves of Rebels in his colony if they would go over to the British side. Within a week 500 blacks had answered his call. By December, the Governor had a troop of 300 blacks in uniform with the words 'Liberty to Slaves' across their chests. They were the first members of 'Lord Dunmore's Ethiopian Regiment'. In later years, escaping slaves in their hundreds joined the British Company of Black Pioneers, or worked behind the lines as blacksmiths, waggoners, cooks, carpenters or mechanics.

With the war over, the 14,000 departing blacks left for the West Indies, the Bahamas and for Canada, where many of them settled in New Brunswick and Nova Scotia. William Fisher, forced to leave New York, was making a new home as a freeman in New Brunswick.

326
Colonel Sir William Johnson, 1715–74
Attributed to Sir Joshua Reynolds

Undated. Oil on canvas
88·9 cm × 71·1 cm
The Trustees of the late Mrs Leavett-Shenley

In the long history of Britain's foreign relations, some of her representatives discovered a strange affinity between themselves and the native population among which they chose to live. William Johnson was one of this tradition.

Born in Ireland, Johnson reached the Mohawk Valley in upper New York about 1738, and by the time he was appointed Superintendent of Indian Affairs in 1756, he had acquired a large estate, several Indian liaisons through which a number of bastards were born, and a talent for communicating with the Indians in their own languages which kept most of them faithful to George III.

Johnson's influence stretched from upper New York down past the Ohio River, through Pennsylvania into Virginia. His greatest act of diplomacy was to persuade most of the Six Nations (the Mohawk, Oneida, Tuscarora, Onondaga, Cayuga and Seneca tribes) to remain allies of the British against the Rebels, though a great many of the Oneida fought with the Americans.

The Superintendent's most abiding friendship was with Chief Joseph Brant, to whose sister Johnson was 'married'. His death in 1774 was a blow both to the British and to the hundreds of Indians who loved

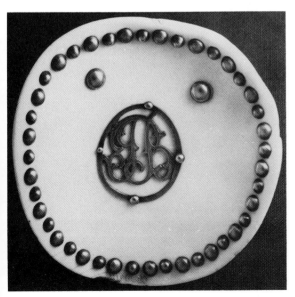

331

and trusted him. Had he lived, many historians argue, the course of the Revolution in upper New York might have followed a different line.

Traditionally, this portrait is held to be by Sir Joshua Reynolds.

327
Re-strike of a certificate given to loyal Indians
1770. Taken from an engraving by Henry Dawkins
25·4 cm × 23·8 cm
New York Historical Society, New York City

For their loyalty to the Crown many Indians were given either silver medals or certificates to reward their act of faith. This certificate is a modern impression taken from the original plate engraved for Sir William Johnson.

328
Sir John Caldwell, Lieutenant-Colonel of the 8th Foot, in the dress of an Indian Chief
Artist unknown

c. 1780. Oil on canvas
128·3 cm × 102·9 cm
Major F. E. G. Bagshawe, Matlock, Derbyshire

Sir John Caldwell was commander of the 8th Foot which served in Quebec from 1768 to 1785. During his period of service he was elected an Indian chief by the Ojibways and given an Indian name which meant 'The Runner'. In this picture he is dressed as he appeared at a grand war council at the Wakeetomike village of the tribe in January 1780. Many of the articles he is wearing have survived (see next item).

329
Indian items belonging to Sir John Caldwell
1. Pipe, East Sioux style
   Bowl of catlinite; stem of wood, paint and skin
   Bowl: 4·5 cm high; stem and bowl: 23 cm long
2. Pouch, Eastern Great Lakes
   Tanned, smoked skin, quillwork and hair
   27·5 cm × 28 cm; strap: 87 cm long
3. Garters, Ojibway type
   Beads, yarn and metal cones
   59 cm long, including fringe
4. Knife and sheath, Eastern Great Lakes
   Tanned skin, quillwork and metal cones
   Sheath: 22·5 cm without fringe; knife: 21·5 cm; strap: 64 cm
National Museum of Man, Ottawa

These articles, seen in Sir John's portrait, are in almost mint condition and are very rare.

330
Joseph Brant, Chief of the Mohawks, 1742–1807
George Romney

c. 1776. Oil on canvas
127 cm × 101·6 cm
National Gallery of Canada, Ottawa

The subject of this portrait, who was called Thayendanegea, travelled, when only thirteen, with the Indian Superintendent, Sir William Johnson, into the frontier fighting of the Seven Years War. At the Battle of Crown Point he took his first scalp. Impressed with the abilities of the boy, physical and intellectual, Johnson sent him to school at Lebanon, Connecticut, where he refined his English and learnt Latin, Greek and agriculture.

Called Joseph Brant by Sir William Johnson, the young brave, an Anglican convert, fought alongside the British throughout the Revolution and was particularly effective on his raids into the far western regions of New York. At the same time, not the least of his accomplishments were his translations of the New Testament and the Prayer Book into his native language.

In 1776, Brant visited London, where he was presented at Court. He mixed with Boswell's society, was painted by Romney, and was an outstanding success at any soirée where he appeared in full chieftain dress. After the Revolution Brant and his tribes, known collectively and generically as the Iroquois, were granted land in Canada close to lakes Erie and Ontario; and there he died.

331
The tomahawk, war club and shell gorget of Chief Joseph Brant
1. Tomahawk
   Wood, iron and brass
   37 cm long; 17 cm wide
2. War club
   Wood
   51 cm long; 12·5 cm wide
3. Shell gorget
   Shell and silver
   9 cm diameter
Royal Ontario Museum, Toronto

This gorget, inscribed with silver lettering 'JB', is loosely based on the British officer's insignia of rank, but made from materials more familiar to Brant.

332
Two False Face masks and a Corn Husk mask of the Iroquois
1. Wood with horsehair
   67 cm, including hair-length
2. Wood with horsehair
   56 cm long, including hair-length
3. Corn husks
   36 cm high, 33 cm wide
Royal Ontario Museum, Toronto

The False Face and Corn Husk masks are symbolic of the highly sophisticated nature of Iroquois society. The calendar of its year was deeply committed to religious ceremonies related to the seasons. In spring, autumn and mid-winter the False Face Society, sometimes accompanied by the Husk Face Society, danced, wearing these wooden and straw faces to drive away sickness. The wooden masks were carved first on the tree and then cut out of the tree itself so that the spirit of the tree entered the mask.

Tradition ensures that these three masks, although dated later than the Revolutionary period, convey the image of the tribal ritual of the late 18th-century Iroquois. Though grotesque, they were benevolent spirits, working their magic among tribes who practised settled agriculture in summer, and who hunted in winter.

333
Ceremonial outfit of Red Jacket
Buckskin, beadwork, cloth-lined
Jacket 97·8 cm long; trousers 101·6 cm long
Woodland Indian Centre, Brantford, Ontario

Red Jacket (c. 1758–1830), a Seneca Indian chief, fought reluctantly with the British. He was accused of being a coward by Brant and acted during the Revolution more as a despatch carrier than a warrior. His Indian name, Sagoyewatha, was less used in English circles than Red Jacket, a name derived from the first coat a British officer gave him.

334
Indian treaty medal
Silver, with wampum necklet
7·6 cm diameter
McCord Museum, Montreal, Quebec

These original silver medals were given to Indian chiefs by George III in recognition of their loyalty, and to mark treaties of friendship.

335
Four George III medals presented to Indian Chiefs
Silver
Diameters: 6·1 cm, 6·1 cm, 7·7 cm, 7·9 cm
Private collection

336
The Cricketers
Benjamin West

London, 1763. Oil on canvas
101·6 cm × 127 cm
Private collection

This painting, of five young Americans during their education in England, is the quintessence of the way in which the Revolution divided friends and split loyalties. Each young man came from a wealthy colonial home, yet twenty years from the day the picture was painted, one had lost all and fled back to England, one had died a Loyalist, two had thrown in their lots as members of the United States Government, and one was 'a marked Tory'. From left to right, the friends relaxing over their cricket bats, epitomising the Loyalist-Patriot confrontation that was to come, are:

ANDREW ALLEN of Philadelphia, twenty-one. In England 1761–5, at the Middle Temple. He played an active part for the Rebels in the early days of the conflict, but could not support the Declaration of Independence and joined the British army. His property was confiscated and he moved to London.

JAMES ALLEN, twenty-one, Andrew's younger brother. Educated in precisely the same way, but he took a less active part in politics once home. When war broke out he retired to the country and died in 1778 still 'very obnoxious to the independents . . . and determined to oppose them vehemently'.

ARTHUR MIDDLETON of South Carolina, twenty-one. Educated in Hackney, St John's College, Cambridge, and the Middle Temple, he became instrumental in independence moves in South Carolina, and signed the Declaration. A member of the Continental Congress throughout the war, Middleton spent a year, 1780–1, as a British prisoner in Florida.

RALPH IZARD of South Carolina, twenty-one. Enjoyed twelve years' schooling in England, finishing at Trinity College, Cambridge, and finally decided, in 1771, to settle in London. His birth, wealth and temperament bore the marks of a Tory, but, a true patriot, he could not stay once Britain and America were at war. In 1776 he went to Paris and eventually, in 1779, arrived home, where he became a member of the Continental Congress.

RALPH WORMELEY of Virginia, eighteen. After Eton and Trinity Hall, Cambridge, he returned to America to hold British Government posts. Little is known of him after 1776 but his reputation as 'a marked Tory'.

337
Benjamin Thompson, 1753–1814
Thomas Gainsborough

1783. Oil on canvas
74·5 cm × 62·4 cm
Fogg Art Museum, Harvard University, Cambridge, Massachusetts
(Bequest of Edmund C. Converse)

Benjamin Thompson was one of very few Loyalists to achieve success in England. He arrived from his native Massachusetts in 1776, carrying despatches for Germain from Gage, and was given a post in the Colonial Office. Once in London he concentrated on a hobby he had developed in America, experiments in gunpowder, and he became a Fellow of the Royal Society. In 1780 Thompson was appointed Under-Secretary for the Colonies, but was 'disgusted by the want of talent displayed by his principal' (Germain) and after thirteen months went to America as lieutenant-colonel of the King's American Dragoons, a Loyalist regiment. Arriving too late to see any real action, he was involved in skirmishes in the south, returning to London after the peace, where he was knighted by George III.

In later years Thompson spent much time in Germany, calling himself Count von Rumford (after Rumford, Massachusetts), but was best known as a scientist, inventor and founder of the Royal Institution of Great Britain.

338
Peter Oliver, 1713–91
Richard Wilson

Birmingham, 1778–82. Oil on canvas
Signed: 'R. Wilson Pix.'
76·2 cm × 53·3 cm
Museum of Fine Arts, Boston, Massachusetts
(Gift of Mrs W. Austin Wadsworth)

Peter Oliver, brother of Lieutenant-Governor Andrew Oliver (see item 15), was Chief Justice for the colony until he left Boston with the British in 1776. When he arrived in London, via Halifax, he was received by the King and granted an honorary degree by the University of Oxford.

The high cost of London life forced many poverty-stricken Loyalist refugees to leave the city, particularly after Saratoga, when they realised their plight might not be as short-lived as they had anticipated. In 1778, Loyalist Thomas Hutchinson commented, 'the very few Americans that are left in London wear pretty long faces . . . it is now become a rare thing to meet a Yankee even in the Park.'

That same year Peter Oliver moved to Birmingham, followed by many of his relatives, where he lived the rest of his life.

339
Letter from Peter Oliver to Lord George Germain
London, 23 May 1777. Manuscript
Ref: PRO AO.13/75
Public Record Office, London

In 1783 the British Government established a commission to assess the claims made by Loyalists for compensation for loss of property and position caused by the Revolution. It examined over 4000 such claims before 1790, when it ceased to function.

The Americans in London had been pressing for just recompense since their arrival, as the pensions that were granted were less than adequate. In this letter Oliver describes how he has been 'divested of my Property by the Rage of Rebellion', complains that he had to pay his fare from America to Britain, and points out that anything that he 'snatched from the Jaws of Rebellion' had been long since spent. Oliver was granted an annuity of £400, which was reduced to £300 in 1783, a cut which he considered an insult.

340
Basting spoon of Lieutenant-Governor Andrew Oliver
Silver
35·5 cm long
Mr Andrew Oliver, Boston, Massachusetts

When Rebel mobs attacked the homes of British Government officials and Loyalists, forcing the owners to flee, the most precious portable family treasures were often the only things to survive. When Andrew Oliver's house was vandalised by a Boston crowd, he managed to save some of the silver, which has been in the family ever since (see item 15).

341
Political tracts, from the library of the Reverend Jonathan Odell
Leather-bound volume, including copies of 'Taxation no Tyranny' and 'The Patriot'
Provincial Archives, Fredericton, New Brunswick

Odell served as chaplain to the Pennsylvania Loyalists and the King's American Dragoons during the Revolution. He was also secretary to Sir Guy Carleton (see item 586). When he moved to New Brunswick after the war with other Loyalists, copies of well-known Tory tracts were included in his library, notably these milestones in anti-American propaganda by Dr Johnson.

342
Set of eighteen plans showing the estates of Georgia Loyalists
1769–73. Coloured manuscript
Each plan: 30·4 cm × 40·6 cm
Ref: PRO MPI/61
Public Record Office, London

Many Loyalists were concentrated in the southern colonies and suffered badly during the latter part of the war at the hands of small bands of 'patriot' skirmishers. When peace came, most Georgia Loyalists fled to the Bahamas or other West Indian islands. These plans were submitted to London as part of their claims for compensation.

343
Colonel John Murray
J. S. Copley

Boston, 1762. Oil on canvas
124·4 cm × 99 cm
New Brunswick Museum, St John

Murray, a leading citizen in his community, was an active supporter of the Crown in pre-Revolutionary Massachusetts. He antagonised local Rebels to such an extent that they attacked his house and stabbed his portrait with a bayonet when they found he was out. The hole can still be seen.

Murray fled to Boston and then to Britain, where he settled in Wales in considerable poverty, his £26,000-worth of estates and £1000 annual income having been confiscated by the Rebels in 1779. In 1783 he was granted an annuity of £250 by the Government, and a year later moved again, this time to St John, New Brunswick, a newly-established settlement for Loyalist American emigrants.

344
Waistcoat belonging to Colonel John Murray
Light blue satin trimmed with edging and buttons of gold thread, sequins and beads
New Brunswick Museum, St John

345
Murray's sabre
Leather-bound grip, and metal scabbard
96·5 cm overall length
New Brunswick Museum, St John

346
Silver cutlery belonging to Colonel Murray
Pistol-handled knife and fork, made by William Adley of London, 1767
Knife: 27 cm long; fork: 21·5 cm long; blade and tines of steel
Spoon by T. & N. Chawner of London, 1765
20 cm long
New Brunswick Museum, St John

When Murray fled from America he took with him only a few precious possessions. He told a friend that his pocket-watch alone represented almost half his total worth. When he arrived in Canada these few mementoes of his past life were still with him.

347
Oval drop-leaf table, made with a penknife by Colonel Beverley Robinson
Top of bird's eye maple, on a tripod pedestal
38·1 cm long; 27·9 cm wide; 54·5 cm high
New Brunswick Museum, St John

Beverley Robinson (1722–92) a wealthy, land-owning Loyalist, joined the British and offered his services to the army. He raised the Loyal American Regiment almost entirely from his tenants, and distinguished himself throughout the war, serving on various committees. Perhaps his greatest contribution was to the secret service, directing spies, providing information and persuading defectors. He accompanied Major André some way up the Hudson to the fatal meeting with Arnold (see items 366 to 374).

348
Blue enamel ring
The initials 'S.P.', for Suzannah Philipse, inset in chip diamonds
Major Basil Heaton, Mold, Clwyd

349
A Communion Beaker
Tapered sides and hand engraved; part of the
Philipse family silver
8·8 cm high
Major Basil Heaton, Mold, Clwyd

350
Six octagonal pistol-handled silver knives
Made by Thomas Hammersley of New York,
who worked between 1727 and 1781
Major Basil Heaton, Mold, Clwyd

In 1748, Beverley Robinson of Virginia married
Suzannah Philipse, a rich New York heiress, with
vast estates on the Hudson. By 1776, the Robinsons
were one of the wealthiest families in New York, but
all their assets were seized by the Rebels during the
Revolution. When they came to England, however,
they managed to bring the family silver and jewels,
which were used in their new home outside Bath.

351
Wafer-iron
Charles Oliver Bruff

Nova Scotia, 1785–1800. Wrought iron,
painted black
87 cm long; diameter of face 16 cm
Nova Scotia Museum, Halifax

Bruff (1735–1817) was a New York silversmith before
the Revolution. In 1775 he advertised swords in the
New York Mercury 'for those Gentlemen who are
forming 'themselves into companies in defense of
their liberties'. However, he stayed on in the city
during the British occupation and in 1784 he was
granted a tract of land in Nova Scotia, having been
among the first wave of Loyalist emigrants to reach
Canada.

Once there, Bruff turned his hand to more practical
work, turning out the household items in demand in
an infant community. This wafer-iron, with its cross-
hatched engraving, and Bruff's name inscribed round
the edge, may have been used for Communion bread.
It is the only example of his work in Nova Scotia
ever to have come to light.

352
Cadwallader Colden and Warren De Lancey
Matthew Pratt

1774–5. Oil on canvas
127 cm × 101·6 cm
Metropolitan Museum of Art, New York

336

Cadwallader Colden (1688–1776) was born in Ireland, and went to America when he was twenty-two. Moving to New York, he rose rapidly in position until in 1761 he was appointed lieutenant-governor, a position he held until his death three months after independence had been declared. A staunch supporter of the King, he weathered the Stamp Act troubles despite being burned in effigy and losing his home to the mob.

If Colden himself was a leading New York Loyalist, the De Lancey family, into which Colden's daughter married, constituted one of the most influential blocks of Loyal sympathy. At least four members fought for the King, two in Loyalist regiments and two in the regular army. Warren De Lancey, seen here with his grandfather, joined the 17th Light Dragoons as a cornet in 1780, serving under his cousin, Oliver, who was major in the same regiment.

353
John Singleton Copley
Gilbert Stuart

London, *c.* 1784. Oil on canvas
Oval, 67·2 cm × 56·2 cm
National Portrait Gallery, London

Copley established a reputation as a portrait painter at home in Massachusetts in the 1760s, which spread to London when his 'Boy with the Squirrel' was exhibited in 1766. His sympathies lay, if anywhere, with the Rebels. But all his in-laws were Loyalists (his father-in-law, Richard Clarke, was the consignee to whom the Boston Tea Party tea was directed), so Copley became involved with politics despite his inclinations to shun them for the sake of his art.

In 1774 he left America, overcoming an irrational fear of travel, to tour Europe and visit London. He arrived in England in 1775 and was fêted by society and artists alike, and when his wife and children reached London they settled into a permanent home in Hanover Square. Copley soon became established as one of the leading portraitists of the age.

354
Journal kept by Prudence Punderson, November 1778 to March 1783
114 pages, 33 cm × 15·2 cm
Connecticut Historical Society, Hartford

355
'The First, Second, and Last Scene of Mortality'
Needlework picture by Prudence Punderson
(1758–84)
New England, *c.* 1775. Crimped floss silks on silk
31·9 cm × 42·3 cm
Connecticut Historical Society, Hartford

Prudence Punderson, member of a Loyalist family from Preston, Connecticut, was typical of many young girls of her day. She was skilled in needlework at an early age, here using silks which were widely used in the Colonies at the time but seldom in England. Her life in New England was disrupted when she was forced to flee to New York with her family because of their Loyalist sympathies. The journal contains eye-witness accounts of events on Long Island, poems, letters, stories and needlework patterns. Despite her Tory leanings, she married a Rebel soldier.

356
Lieutenant-Colonel John Graves Simcoe
1752–1806
Jean Laurent Mosnier

c. 1798. Oil on canvas
76 cm × 63 cm
Metropolitan Toronto Central Library, Ontario

Simcoe served in the British army during the early part of the Revolution. He was wounded at Brandy-wine while a captain in the 40th, and was then pro-moted to command the Loyalist Queen's Rangers, a unit raised in 1776 by Robert Rogers from New York and Connecticut Loyalists.

Simcoe's men, eight companies of riflemen, one of grenadiers, a light company and a Highland com-pany, were based at New York and Philadelphia. Later, with a cavalry troop added, the Queen's Rangers fought vigorously in the south and were interned at Yorktown. Simcoe is wearing his Queen's Rangers uniform in the painting.

357
A Journal of the Operations of the Queen's Rangers, From the End of the Year 1777, to the Conclusion of the Late American War
Lieutenant-Colonel John Graves Simcoe,
Commander of that Corps
Exeter, 1781. Printed for the author
Trustees of the British Library, London

Simcoe wrote the history of the corps he had com-manded and presented this copy to George III. Manuscript maps and watercolour illustrations of members of the unit are among several items bound into the volume. They provide valuable information about the uniform of this particularly distinguished Loyalist regiment. In 1779, when five provincial units were granted places on a newly-created Ameri-can army establishment, the Queen's Rangers be-came the First American Regiment.

358
Uniform coat of William Jarvis of the Queen's Rangers
Late 1780s. Green wool with velvet facings
Fort York Museum, Toronto, Ontario

By 1778 some 10,000 suits of green regimentals had been shipped from England to America to clothe the provincial troops. But later that year it was decided to kit them out in red, like the regular soldiers, so red coats were despatched. Simcoe, however, was un-willing to change and the Queen's Rangers continued to wear green. Three Philadelphia units which were attached to the Queen's Rangers were also equipped with green uniforms.

This coat is slightly later than the Revolution, as the high-cut collar reveals, but is fundamentally the same as would have been worn by Simcoe and his fellow officers.

359
Uniform coat worn by Captain John Leggett, Loyalist officer
Red wool, with buttons inscribed 'RP' for Royal Provincial
Public Archives of Nova Scotia, Halifax

Leggett served in the Royal North Carolina Volun-teers during the Revolution, afterwards settling in Nova Scotia. Little is known of the regiment's ser-vice, except that 114 of its men were with Cornwallis at Yorktown.

360
Uniform coat worn by Captain Alexander Fraser of the 84th Foot
Red wool, blue facings, with buttons inscribed '84'
McCord Museum, Montreal, Quebec

In 1775 Colonel Allan Maclean raised a regiment in Canada of Scottish veterans who had settled there after the Seven Years War. It was further augmented by Scots from New York and North Carolina, and took the name Royal Highland Emigrants. In 1779 the regiment was one of only two provincial units to be added to the British army establishment, and was numbered the 84th.

The 1st Battalion served throughout the Revolution in Canada, the 2nd fought in the southern colonies and part of that was interned at Yorktown. The regiment, which wore a uniform similar to that of the 42nd, Royal Highland Regiment, including the plaid, was disbanded in 1784.

361
Lieutenant-Colonel John Small, 1726–96
Artist unknown

Miniature of unknown date. Painted on ivory
Oval, 5.7 cm × 4.4 cm
Private collection

John Small was one of the Scottish veterans living in Canada who were called on to rally opposition to the Rebels. In 1775 he received a major's commission to raise a Highland company in Nova Scotia. He fought at Bunker Hill, then was appointed commander of the 2nd Battalion Royal Highland Emigrants (see item 360), and served with them in New York and the south. He is pictured in their uniform, with a highland bonnet.

362
Lieutenant-Colonel Edmund Fanning, 1739–1818
Thomas Goddard

Date unknown. Watercolour on ivory
Oval, 7.3 cm × 6 cm
Captain W. C. Wickham, Ashland, Virginia

A North Carolina Loyalist, Fanning crossed the Rebels early in the troubles. His house was burned down in 1770. In the winter of 1776–7 he raised a Loyal regiment, the King's American Regiment, which soon acquired a reputation for cruelty. Fanning, seen here as commander of his corps, was in active service throughout the war and was wounded twice.

In 1779, the King's American Regiment was placed on the new American establishment and became the 4th American Regiment. In that same year Fanning lost his extensive estates in North Carolina, and after the war he moved to Nova Scotia, where he was appointed lieutenant-governor.

Thomas Goddard was an American miniaturist active between 1779 and 1788.

363
Gorget of the King's American Regiment
Brass with gilt
Fort Ticonderoga Museum, New York

The gorget is engraved with the name of the Loyalist regiment, with, underneath, '4', indicating the title of 4th American Regiment granted in 1779.

364
Drum of a Loyalist Regiment
c. 1776. Painted wood
38.1 cm high; 40.6 cm diameter
King's Landing Historical Settlement, Fredericton, New Brunswick

After the war, the remnants of fourteen provincial regiments and some Germans arrived to settle in New Brunswick. The men brought with them their equipment and accoutrements, many of which have survived in this part of Canada. This drum probably belonged to a member of the British Legion (Tarleton's troop) and apparently dates from very early in the war.

365
Brown Bess musket
Made at the Tower Armouries, with bayonet. Short Land pattern
Lock, with flint, engraved 'Tower', crowned 'GR'
Barrel length: 42 inches
Musée de l'Empéri, Salon-de-Provence, Bouches du Rhône

The provincial regiments were equipped by the Board of Ordnance just like the regulars. They were issued with standard Brown Bess muskets; in some cases these were surplus stock Long Land pattern (46-inch) while in others, they were given the new Short Land pattern (42-inch) muskets.

'TREASON OF THE BLACKEST DYE...'
The secret service played a vital role in the management of the American war. It operated on all levels, from the high-powered agents in Paris and London, to the Loyalist courier carrying messages through Rebel lines, to the defector playing informant. Bizarre relics of the spies' activities have survived to this day: hollow bullets, templates to fit over coded letters, even a parchment note with spittle and teethmarks where the unfortunate spy tried to swallow the incriminating evidence.

The army commanders in America relied heavily on a well-developed underground network to provide up-to-the-minute information about terrain, position of Rebel forces and strength of opposition. Leading Loyalists, such as Beverley Robinson (see item 347) played a key role in this. The army adjutant-general (the general's right-hand staff officer) was in charge of organising the secret service.

The outstanding spy story of the American Revolution was the defection of Benedict Arnold to the British, and the subsequent execution of Clinton's adjutant-general, John André, who had been caught by the Rebels with damning papers in his boot.

Arnold's and André's paths had crossed several times during the war and they had friends and acquaintances in common. The American general was therefore familiar to André when he began to handle the highly secret correspondence between Arnold and Clinton in 1780. Under the guise of a commercial treaty, Arnold was planning to 'sell' the key Hudson River fort at West Point, of which he was commander, to the British.

In September 1780 André travelled up the Hudson in the sloop *Vulture* to meet Arnold. Secretly, Arnold handed over details of the defences of West Point. André, unable to get back to his boat because of American fire, was forced to abandon his uniform and attempted to travel overland in civilian clothes to the British lines. He was caught by three American militiamen.

Arnold heard of this just before Washington himself arrived, managed to get aboard *Vulture*, and arrived safely in New York. André, on the other hand, was tried by a military board which included Nathanael Greene, Henry Knox, von Steuben and Lafayette, found guilty, and, despite every possible effort by the British to treat for his life, was hanged.

365 (detail)

366

366
Colonel Benedict Arnold, 1741–1801
1776. Hand-coloured mezzotint, published by
Thomas Hart of London
36·4 cm × 26·3 cm
Anne S. K. Brown Military Collection,
Providence, Rhode Island

This mezzotint commemorated one of Arnold's most daring exploits of the Revolution, a trek with 1100 men for 350 miles up the Kennebec river in the midwinter of 1775–6 to attack Quebec from the south. As a project it failed (the city and Canada stayed British), but as an exploit it marked Arnold out as one of the finest Rebel leaders.

Arnold organised the American evacuation of Montreal; he commanded the flotilla on Lake

367

Champlain (having organised its construction) which halted the British advance south for a year (see item 378), and he played an important role in the Rebels' victory at Saratoga, although seriously wounded in one leg.

In 1778, after the British evacuation of Philadelphia, Arnold was appointed Governor of the city and quickly married his second wife, Peggy Shippen, a society belle from a Loyalist family who had been fêted by British officers, notably John André, during the occupation. Accused of extortion and embezzlement, Arnold resigned his position, but after an inquiry he was reinstated and given the command at West Point. He now made overtures to the British.

Once on the King's side, Arnold's fortunes fared badly. He was mistrusted by British officers, who blamed him for the death of André, and although he led numerous raids in Virginia and Connecticut he was never given high command.

Back in England, Arnold was consulted by George III, and granted a considerable sum in compensation for his losses, but he lived the rest of his life in New Brunswick and the West Indies.

The reasons for Arnold's defection will probably always remain uncertain, despite many explanations suggested by historians. He was a brilliant soldier and leader, a favourite of Washington, and a considerable force in the Rebels' successes up to Saratoga. But he was temperamental, quick to make enemies of fellow officers and was in constant dispute with Congress over his promotion (or lack of it) and finances.

Some have suggested that the alliance with the French in 1778 was so abhorrent to him (he could not tolerate Roman Catholicism) that he found it impossible to fight alongside them. Others have postulated that Peggy Shippen married him (perhaps at André's suggestion) to secure his alliance. Whatever the precise truth, it is known that Arnold was thoroughly disgusted at the treatment he had received from the Americans and thought that perhaps the British would deal better. He was a rich prize, but one that the British army never really enjoyed.

367
Major John André, 1751–80
Attributed to Sir Joshua Reynolds

Date unknown. Oil on canvas
74·8 cm × 62·1 cm
Major-General Sir Allan Shafto Adair, London

André, of Genevese extraction, travelled to America in 1774 as a lieutenant in the 7th Foot, was captured at St Johns in November 1775, during the Rebel attack on Canada, and spent a year on parole in Pennsylvania. He was then promoted to captain in the 26th, and became aide to General Grey in Philadelphia. During the British stay in the city, André, a sociable and dashing young officer, organised many functions, including the Meschianza, a great week-long extravaganza, fête and ball which bade farewell to Sir William Howe as commander of the British forces in North America. It was at this time he became a close friend of Peggy Shippen.

André's successful handling of army life in Philadelphia recommended him for the job of aide-de-camp to Clinton, and subsequent promotion – his last – to major and adjutant-general. André was one of the most able and popular staff officers in the army and his loss was felt deeply.

Sir Joshua Reynolds is known to have painted a portrait of André, and it has traditionally been held that this is the one.

368
Leather pocket-book said to have belonged to Major André
Connecticut Historical Society, Hartford

This pocket-book was donated to the Connecticut Historical Society in the 19th century by the grandson of Joshua Barrell, of Massachusetts, who had acquired it while serving in the Continental army.

369
Three documents found in Major André's boot on 23 September 1780, which led to his execution as a spy

- Pass, signed by Benedict Arnold, for Mr John Anderson (André's alias) to pass through the Rebel lines
  Manuscript in ink, dated 22 September 1780
  10·1 cm × 16·5 cm

- List of artillery orders at West Point, in case of attack, written in Arnold's hand
  Manuscript in ink, dated 5 September 1780
  33·8 cm × 20·3 cm

- Return of Ordnance in the different Forts, Batteries etc at West Point and its dependencies, signed by G. Bauman, Major commanding Artillery
  Manuscript in ink, dated 5 September 1780
  33·8 cm × 41·8 cm
New York State Library, Albany

374

At nine o'clock on the morning of 23 September 1780, already in sight of the British lines, André was stopped by three militiamen. Had he produced his pass, there would have been no problem. As it was, he enquired if the men were English and, misunderstanding their reply, revealed who he really was. When Washington saw the papers he had hidden in his boot, revealing all the defences of the forts on the Hudson, André's situation was hopeless.

370
Major John André: self-portrait

1835. Engraving, from a sketch done the night before his execution, 1 October 1780
15·8 cm × 18·3cm
New York State Library, Albany

André's skill as an artist can be seen in this self-portrait. The original pen and ink sketch is at Yale University Art Gallery.

371
Major André being rowed from the sloop 'Vulture' to the shore of Havershaw's Bay, on the Hudson, 23 September 1780, to meet Arnold
John André

c. 1783. Engraving, from a sketch by André done about 1 October 1780
18·7cm × 28·8cm
New York State Library, Albany

The original sketch for this was found on the table in André's prison, with other papers, after his execution. They were all taken to New York by his servant and given to Lieutenant-Colonel Crosbie of the 22nd. When Crosbie returned home he had the sketch engraved and a limited number of prints made for distribution among his friends 'as a small mark of Friendship for that very valuable and unfortunate man'. This particular copy was given to the Earl of Lincoln.

372
Orderly book, kept by Captain William Popham, aide-de-camp to General James Clinton of the Continental army

1776–83
Society of the Cincinnati, Washington, D.C., by permission of Rear-Admiral William Sherbrooke Popham, U.S. Navy Ret., Charleston, South Carolina

Captain Popham was serving at West Point when Arnold was commander. His orderly book for 26

September 1780 recounts the story of Arnold's defection: 'Treason of the blackest dye was yesterday discovered . . .'.

373
Autograph letter from Edward Shippen Jr to Jasper Yeates, Philadelphia, datelined 'Cottage 1st Novr 1780'

23 cm × 19 cm
Historical Society of Pennsylvania, Philadelphia

After Benedict Arnold had defected to the British, his wife Peggy was ordered to leave Philadelphia and join him in New York. Her father, Edward Shippen Jr, was a respected lawyer in the city and although a Loyalist, managed to get on with both British and American officials during their sojourns there. Writing here to Jasper Yeates, a fellow lawyer but supporter of independence, he bewails the loss of his daughter, whose continued presence in Philadelphia would not be in the 'public safety'.

374
The Unfortunate Death of Major André

André met his death with fortitude. All American witnesses describe it with great respect for the British spy. His wish was to be shot as an army officer, but because he was disguised as a civilian, Washington argued, he would die a civilian spy's death on the gallows. On this point the commander was adamant – an obstinacy for which he has subsequently been heavily criticised. British high command did everything it could, short of actually handing Arnold back, to save André, but to no avail.

In 1821 André's remains were exhumed from their burial place in Tappan, New York, and re-interred in Westminster Abbey.

This engraving was made for Barnard's *New Complete and Authentic History of England*, published soon after the war. Drawn by Hamilton and engraved by Goldar, the print from which this is taken is in the Anne S. K. Brown Military Collection, Providence, Rhode Island.

Showdown on The Hudson

ON 6 MAY 1777 GENERAL JOHN BURGOYNE stepped ashore at Quebec after a six-week Atlantic crossing from England. He carried a letter which effectively changed the whole course of the American Revolution. The letter, from Germain to Sir Guy Carleton, Governor of Quebec and Commander-in-Chief of the British forces in Canada, gave instructions for Burgoyne to lead an offensive south into New York.

Carleton, the letter said, was to hold Canada with 3770 men, while Burgoyne advanced with some 7000 troops through Lake Champlain to Ticonderoga, which he would capture from the Rebels, and then on to Albany. A diversionary force, 2000 strong, under Lieutenant-Colonel Barry St Leger, would move east from Lake Ontario, gaining control of the Mohawk valley (a tributary which joined the Hudson at Albany) while a third group, detached from Howe's New York army, would move north up the Hudson for a tripartite rendezvous in that city.

The plan was simple. For centuries the Hudson River-Lake Champlain waterway had been the main thoroughfare of the north-east. When no roads existed, this almost continuous chain of lakes and rivers was the only overland route from New York to Canada. In war, it became a line of vital strategic importance, for by controlling it the British could cleave the colonies in two, cutting New England off completely from Pennsylvania and the south.

And the plan was not new. After the Rebels' brazen capture of Fort Ticonderoga in 1775, it soon became clear that a British offensive on that axis was vital. In the summer of 1776 Carleton himself had been attempting just such a move, but through delays and bad timing his advance south down Lake Champlain came so late that the Rebels had time to build a fleet to harrass him. After the Battle of Valcour Island, 11–13 October 1776, Carleton withdrew into Canada, and another year was lost.

This time things were different, however. The strategy had been devised and presented to Germain and the King in London by Burgoyne himself, hoping for promotion. When he received approval, he wasted no time in setting things in motion. And once he was back in Canada, excellent preparations having been made by Carleton during the 1776–7 winter, Burgoyne was ready to start operations six weeks later.

The expedition set out south with panache, like a 'splendid regatta', as a witness

facing page: item 388
(detail)

described it. At the end of June Burgoyne arrived at Ticonderoga with 9500 fighting men – British regulars, Germans, Indians, Canadians and Tories – and 1000 camp followers. By 5 July, the fort was his.

But at this point things began to go wrong. Burgoyne's first mistake was to overestimate the American opposition on Lake George, and he opted to move south to Fort Edward (just before linking up with the Hudson) on a parallel route which took him to the tip of Lake Champlain, and then twenty-two miles overland. In a scheme in which speed was essential this move was disastrous. He took twenty days to cover the land distance, was constantly harrassed by Rebel obstructions and failed to gain control of the critical waterway which would guarantee his supply lines back to Montreal.

Suddenly these supplies, on which his army was totally dependent, seemed in jeopardy. Now 185 miles from base, Burgoyne had to rely on land transport, and both horses and wagons were seriously lacking. Forage was scarce in the woods and anyway the Rebels had already picked the country clean. The local Loyalist support, on which Burgoyne was relying, had failed to materialise. In a desperate attempt to reinforce supplies, an expedition was despatched to Bennington, southwest of Fort Edward. Nearly 1000 men were lost (killed or captured) with large numbers of drums, muskets, swords, ammunition wagons and four brass cannon.

When, in mid-August, Burgoyne heard of this major setback he still had time to save the situation and retreat. But, an inveterate gambler and a vain man, he was reluctant to abandon the plan which he believed would bring him glory. True to say, he was still expecting to meet a victorious St Leger at Albany, and Howe's support force, but with dwindling numbers and supplies the chances of his own expedition getting there were rapidly diminishing.

The long delay at Fort Edward – over a month – gave the Rebels time to gather in force. Gates, now in charge of the Continental army on the Hudson, had between six and seven thousand men by mid-September, with militia flocking to the cause from all sides. Burgoyne had to cross the Hudson to reach Albany, but knew that by doing so he would risk severing his supply line to the north completely. However, having collected supplies for thirty days, he decided to chance it at Saratoga. On 13 September the crossing began. Behind, the enemy fell on the British communications links and cut them; ahead, Gates's army sat on Bemis Heights overlooking the river. The road south was closed to Burgoyne.

The encounter at Saratoga comprised two episodes. In the first, Burgoyne chose direct attack. Ignorant of the land and of the Rebels' dispositions, his Indian scouts having mostly deserted, he tried to outflank the Americans, but was checked and counter-attacked by Benedict Arnold. The British army that day, 19 September, lost 600 men. If Burgoyne had pursued the attack next day he might have won. As it was, receiving a message that Howe's detachment under Clinton was about to leave New York to help, he dug in.

For eighteen days Burgoyne sat tight. He knew now that the Mohawk expedition had failed, the crucial Fort Stanwix at the valley head having been rescued for the Rebels by that ubiquitous saviour, Benedict Arnold. Clinton was his only hope. But as days passed Gates's forces grew to 11,000, while the British shrivelled to less than 5000. On 7 October he launched a final attack, but again it was a disaster, and the British were forced to withdraw, leaving 500 sick and wounded along with their 600 dead. For yet another week they tried to hold out, surrounded on all sides by cannon, snipers and marauding militiamen. On 14 October, Burgoyne, having lost all hope of Clinton, surrendered.

The Rebels' victory at Saratoga was a national disaster for Britain. When news arrived of Burgoyne's surrender, London was deeply shocked. Within three months France seized the opportunity to enter the conflict and a colonial revolution had, for Great Britain, escalated into world war.

Burgoyne himself was soundly disgraced and an account of his conduct was demanded in the House of Commons. Historians have never been sure whether to place the blame squarely on Burgoyne's shoulders, or how much he had been let down by officials in London or by fellow commanders in America. At one time, after the event, he claimed that he had been abandoned by Howe. Yet it is clear that Burgoyne could never have expected a full thrust north by Howe's army, as the orders for Howe's expedition into Pennsylvania had been seen by Burgoyne before he left London in the spring.

Whatever the causes – over-extended supply lines, endless time-lags in long-distance communications, over-ambitious officers – Burgoyne's collapse epitomised the problems that were eventually to overwhelm the British army in North America. But not just yet. As Burgoyne was assembling on the banks of the Hudson to cross at Saratoga, Howe was thrashing the Rebels at Brandywine. And as Burgoyne sat at the foot of Bemis Heights, his men dying, his supplies vanishing, praying for help from Howe, another British army was marching victorious into Philadelphia. General Sir William Howe was busy winning battles of his own.

PATRICIA CONNOR

375
Blunderbuss, said to have been given to Benedict Arnold by Ethan Allen
Fort Ticonderoga Museum, New York

In May 1775 a Rebel force of between two and three hundred men, under the joint leadership of Ethan Allen and Benedict Arnold, attacked and captured British-held Fort Ticonderoga on Lake Champlain. Although the commander there, Captain William Delaplace, had been warned of the likelihood of an attack, when the onslaught occurred at dawn on 10 May he was surprised and the fort fell without a shot fired. The garrison of two officers and forty-eight men, mostly invalids, was captured.

The importance to the Rebels of this escapade was twofold. As a morale booster, coming less than three weeks after Lexington and Concord, it was very significant. And in practical terms, the artillery taken at Ticonderoga and Crown Point, a fort ten miles north which fell at the same time, included some seventy-eight serviceable guns, six mortars, three howitzers, thousands of cannon balls and flints, and other stores. This enormous hoard was taken by Henry Knox to Boston six months later (see item 304) and gave the Rebels strength to chase the British out.

This blunderbuss was supposedly given by Allen to Benedict Arnold, his fellow commander at the time.

376
Ledger from the Catamount Tavern, Vermont, showing accounts for Ethan Allen's stay there
Manuscript book, 32 pages in cardboard cover
Bennington Museum, Vermont

377
Brass-framed spectacles worn by Ethan Allen
Bennington Museum, Vermont

Ethan Allen (1738–89), who led the attack on Ticonderoga, was one of the most colourful Rebel leaders of the Revolution. He was already outlawed by the Crown for stirring up trouble, in the region of what is now Vermont, during the discontent before the beginning of the war. The Green Mountain Boys, of which Allen was commander, were also at Ticonderoga. A group of backwoodsmen formed into a company to defend territorial rights in the early 1770s, they were an active force during the early part of the war in the highlands overlooking the Hudson.

It was in New England taverns like the Catamount that revolutionary talk, over a dish of beans and a glass of rum punch, was most easily spread.

A View of TICONDEROGA from

380

. *North Shore of Lake Champlain.*

378
The Naval Engagement on Lake Champlain, 11 October 1776
Henry Gilder

Watercolour on paper
25 cm × 36 cm
Her Majesty the Queen

When the British offensive from Canada began in the summer of 1776 Sir Guy Carleton's greatest need was for boats. He needed a fleet to carry the army south down Lake Champlain to the Hudson, and it would have to fight off the American flotilla which had been hastily constructed, under the supervision of Benedict Arnold, at the southern end of the lake, 125 miles away.

A large number of ships was assembled at St Johns, at the lake's northern extremity. Many of them were prefabricated and carried over the Richelieu river rapids for reassembly on the lake. There were twenty gunboats, 680 flat-bottomed boats, two schooners, a captured gundalow, a sixteen-gun 'radeau' and a three-master with eighteen guns. It was a fine achievement, but it took time. The fleet did not sail until 4 October.

On 11 October the British, sailing rapidly south, passed the Americans who were hiding between Valcour Island and the west bank of the lake. They dared not sail on, leaving Arnold's fleet of fifteen ships behind, as this would endanger their supply lines. Turning, they tacked into a strong northerly wind to join battle. The superior British guns trounced the Rebel fleet, but during a foggy night Arnold managed to slip his ships out of the bottleneck and escaped quickly to the south with his flotilla battered, but its morale high.

The day belonged to Britain, but the glory was the Rebels'. By building from scratch, in a few weeks, a fleet competent to tackle the British Lake Champlain squadron, they managed to force a British withdrawal and delay the offensive from Canada for a whole year. That breathing-space for the Rebels contributed much to Burgoyne's downfall.

Gilder's view of the battle, looking north up Lake Champlain, shows the position at about 12.30 p.m., with the British schooner *Carleton* (*g*) broadside to the advancing American fleet (*f*) backed up by a line of between fifteen and twenty British gunboats (*i*). Grounded alongside is the American schooner *Royal Savage* (*h*) and in the foreground are the larger British vessels which are trying, in a strong wind, to move up to support the *Carleton*.

Gilder's key, which has recently come to light, identifies the following by letter:

a Cumberland Head
b Cumberland Bay
c Valcour Island
d Petite Isle
e Grand Isle
f Rebel fleet
g British schooner *Carleton*
h American schooner *Royal Savage* (grounded)
i Line of British gun boats
k Three-masted British sloop *Inflexible*
l British schooner *Maria*
m British gundalow *Loyal Convert*
n British 'radeau' *Thunderer*

379
Objects recovered from the Philadelphia

The *Philadelphia* was one of eight gundalows built to Benedict Arnold's design on Lake Champlain by the Rebels in 1776. These flat-bottomed boats were pointed at each end, had two square sails on a single mast and were essentially rowing-boats, although in a favourable wind they were very fast under sail.

The *Philadelphia* sank at the Battle of Valcour Island. In 1935 she was raised, and is exhibited today at the Smithsonian Institution in Washington, D.C. When she came up, many small everyday objects and relics of the battle were recovered. These items included shoes, buttons, cannon and musket balls, bar shot, spoons and axe-heads, a kettle and other cooking equipment, and a cannon.

380
A View of Ticonderoga from a Point on the North Shore of Lake Champlain
James Hunter

1777. Watercolour on paper
34 cm × 42 cm
Trustees of the British Library, London

When Burgoyne and his 9500 troops arrived at Ticonderoga, it was held by a garrison of 2500 Rebels under General Arthur St Clair. Swiftly, in the first days of July 1777, the British surrounded the fort and cut off the Americans' land retreat. On 4 July engineers began to build a path up Mount Defiance, a steep hill which loomed over the fort but which had never been defended as it was thought insurmountable. By noon on the 6th four British cannon were ready at the top to blast their shot into the fortress.

Unfortunately for Burgoyne, St Clair saw the works on Mount Defiance in progress and managed to engineer a withdrawal on the night of the 5th, by boat, down the lake. The British awoke on the 6th to find that they had captured the fort without firing a shot. Burgoyne's army gave chase and scored some victories, but failed to annihilate this large Rebel force as it should have. George III, however, was delighted at the news and exclaimed, 'I have beat them! I have beat all the Americans!'

Hunter's painting shows the advance defence lines of the fort (middle distance, slightly right) with the boom and boat-bridge which cut the lake at its narrowest point, sheltering the American ships in its lee. It was apparently painted in the week before the attack while Burgoyne's forces were mustering on both sides of the lake.

381
Major-General William Phillips, 1731 ?–81
Artist unknown

Undated miniature in oils
6·7 cm × 5·5 cm
Mr Peter Sonerville-Large, Delgany, County Wicklow

William Phillips, an artillery officer, was Burgoyne's second-in-command during the 1777 campaign. At Ticonderoga he was in charge of constructing the road to the top of Mount Defiance and dragging the guns into position. He distinguished himself for gallantry at Saratoga, where he commanded the left flank of Burgoyne's army, and personally conducted the retreat when the British surrendered.

After more than three years as a prisoner of the Americans, Phillips was exchanged for General Benjamin Lincoln and led several expeditions into Virginia with some distinction. In May 1781, while manoeuvring around Richmond, Virginia, with Benedict Arnold against Lafayette, Phillips went down with fever and died within a day.

382
Pocket watch carried by
Major-General William Phillips
c. 1750. Gold
Mrs Rosamond Phillips, Dublin

383
Major-General John Burgoyne, 1722–92

When Burgoyne arrived in Boston with Howe and Clinton to reinforce Gage in May 1775, he had a distinguished career behind him. He had married a rich heiress; he had fought in the Seven Years War and had raised, at his own suggestion, the first light cavalry regiment in England; he had become an M.P. An eloquent speaker in the House of Commons, Burgoyne was a friend of Dr Johnson, a member of all the fashionable clubs, a playwright whose work had been produced by Garrick at Drury Lane, and an amateur actor. He was also a spendthrift and gambler.

Burgoyne was popular at Court and his proposals regarding policy in America fell on receptive ears. Until Saratoga, almost everything had gone according to his wishes.

Once his army had been surrendered, Burgoyne obtained permission from Washington to return to England, where he faced a torrent of criticism. He answered his opponents skilfully, blaming Germain, Howe, even his own soldiers, for his disasters. He did himself little good. He was ordered, as a prisoner of war, to return to America and join his fellow officers in confinement, but refused to go, and was finally stripped of all honorary rank and position. As the dust settled Burgoyne found friends in the Opposition, and in the last ten years of his life his career began to burgeon again.

This picture is taken from the portrait of 'Gentleman Johnny', as his soldiers called him on account of the humane treatment he handed out to them, painted by Sir Joshua Reynolds in 1766, when Burgoyne's reputation was at its zenith. It hangs in the Frick Collection in New York.

384
Alexander Lindsay
6th Earl of Balcarres, 1752–1825
Attributed to Alexander Nasmyth

c. 1782. Oil on canvas
76·2 cm × 63·5 cm
Private collection

Balcarres was in command of a battalion at Ticonderoga in 1777, and led the flank companies under General Simon Fraser during the pursuit of the Americans after their evacuation of the fort. At Hubbardton on 7 July, although thirteen bullets actually passed through his clothing, he was wounded only in the left thigh.

At the second battle of Saratoga, on 7 October, Balcarres gained promotion to brigadier-general when Simon Fraser was killed. He had strongly fortified his own position and, reinforced by members of other units who had retreated into Balcarres's redoubt, he was able to repulse a daring attack by Benedict Arnold.

After two years' imprisonment with the army in America, he returned home and was appointed lieutenant-colonel of the 2nd battalion, 71st Foot, in which uniform he was painted.

385
The Burial of Brigadier-General Simon Fraser
John Graham

Undated. Oil on canvas, laid on a wood panel
70 cm × 92 cm
National Army Museum, Chelsea, London

After distinguishing himself as leader of one of Burgoyne's advance corps during the fighting following Ticonderoga, Fraser was mortally wounded by a rifle ball during the second Saratoga battle. He was nursed through the night of 7 October by the wife of the Brunswick general, von Riedesel, but died next morning. According to his own wishes he was buried in one of the British redoubts at sunset. The Americans let off a constant bombardment during the ceremony, for which they were heavily criticised afterwards.

Graham's painting of the event was engraved in 1794 and became a popular scene of the Revolution. It shows some interesting details, particularly to a student of uniforms. The figure on the right with a fur hat is apparently a member of a Loyalist regiment.

386
Major John Dyke Acland, 1746–78
Sir Joshua Reynolds

1771. Oil on canvas
125·7 cm × 100·2 cm
Lady Acland, Broadclyst, Devon

In the story of the American Revolution, very few women emerged in significant roles. The few that did were extremely brave and we find them among those who chose to follow their husbands to the battlefield. The supreme example on the British side was Lady Harriet Acland.

Major Acland of the 20th Foot served with General Burgoyne in the Hudson Valley campaigns where he was wounded at Ticonderoga and nursed by Lady Harriet. At the second Battle of Saratoga, on 7 October 1777, Major Acland was wounded again. The major, in charge of the Grenadiers, had ordered his Redcoats: 'Fix bayonets and charge the damned Rebels'. A murderous American volley stopped the Grenadiers. Acland lay helpless with bullet-holes through both legs, and he was captured.

Lady Harriet was distraught. She pleaded with Burgoyne to be allowed to join her husband on the enemy side. Moved by her pleas, the general gave her a *laissez-passer* (see item 389) to cover her journey up the Hudson. That night she took a boat and, with two servants and an artillery chaplain, she was rowed up the river to the Rebel position (see item 388). Suspicious sentries kept her boat off-shore until daylight, when Lady Harriet was allowed to land, and she was taken to General Horatio Gates.

The Rebel general was equally moved by her plight and agreed to let her stay. Lady Harriet nursed her husband back to health at Albany until he was fully recovered, when General Gates agreed to the major's return to British lines in exchange for Ethan Allen, who had been captured, or an American officer of equal rank. To ensure Acland's safe journey through Rebel-held territory to the British in New York City, Gates gave the major a letter (see item 390) explaining the exchange role he was expected to play and thereby making it clear he was to be given safe-conduct.

Back in England, and now warmly disposed towards Americans for their treatment of him, Acland resumed his seat in Parliament. But his fierce disposition led him to a duel in Devonshire in October 1778, where, though he escaped injury, he caught cold and died.

387
Lady Harriet Acland, 1750–1815
Sir Joshua Reynolds

1771. Oil on canvas
125·7 cm × 100·2 cm
Lady Acland, Broadclyst, Devon

Lady Harriet married John Dyke Acland in November 1770. Her devotion to her husband when he was captured, and the trials she had to suffer before she returned to England, are made more poignant by the fact that she was bearing her first child when she crossed to the Rebel lines. The Baroness von Riedesel wrote of the Aclands at the time, 'She loved him dearly, although he was a rough fellow who was drunk almost every day, but, nevertheless, a brave officer.'

388
Lady Harriet travelling up the Hudson
R. Pollard

Undated. Oil on canvas
48·3 cm × 63·5 cm
Executors of the late Mr Auberon Herbert

In this primitive painting Lady Harriet is seen approaching the Rebel lines. Her chaplain holds a flag of truce. Lady Harriet has in her right hand the *laissez-passer* from Burgoyne.

389
General Burgoyne's laissez-passer given to Lady Harriet Acland
9 October 1777. Ink on paper
29·2 cm × 17·8 cm
New York Historical Society, New York City

This is the letter that General Burgoyne gave to Lady Harriet to ensure her safe conduct to the Rebel lines where her husband lay wounded. She is seen carrying it in the painting of her Hudson trip. The letter reads:

Sir   Lady Harriot Ackland, a Lady of the first distinction by family rank & by personal virtues, is under such concern on account of Major Ackland her husband, wounded & a prisoner in your hands, that I cannot refuse her request to commit her to your protection.

Whatever general impropriety there may be in persons acting in your situation & mine to solicit favours, I cannot see the uncommon perseverance (?) in every female grace, & exaltation of character of this Lady, & her very hard fortune without testifying that your attentions to her will lay (?) me under obligation.

I am Sir
Your obedient Servant
J. Burgoyne
Oct^{ber} 9 1777
M.G: Gates.

390
Letter from General Horatio Gates to Major John Dyke Acland
25 December 1777. Ink on paper
37·7 cm × 20 cm
Mr Mervyn Herbert, Taunton, Somerset

Gates's letter was written from 'Kings Bridge Lines, Albany' on Christmas Day, 1777. It explained to Major Acland that he was being released in exchange for Ethan Allen or an officer of equal rank (Allen was later exchanged for someone else); and that Gates expected one American soldier and two civilians for the three Acland menservants he was freeing.

391
Letter from George III to Lord North
24 May 1778
22·8 cm × 18·1 cm
Her Majesty the Queen

The King was eager to hear from Major Acland himself the story of his adventures. His letter to the Prime Minister reads:

Lord North – Yesterday when Major Ackland was presented I told him I should wish to hear his account of the different scenes he had been engaged in since he quitted the Island before he goes into the Country, and he having said he should go in two or three days, I desire you will appoint him to come tomorrow morning at half past Eleven; the zeal he has shewn made me think him deserving of this distinction, I find he is very sensible of it, by his having mentioned my intentions with pleasure

Queens House
May 14th 1778,
m/40pt. 10 p.m.

392
General Horatio Gates at Saratoga
James Peale

c. 1799. Oil on canvas
91·6 cm × 68·9 cm
Maryland Historical Society, Baltimore

When Burgoyne surrendered his army, he handed over 4991 men (2139 British, 2022 Germans and 830 Canadians). These became known as the Convention army, named after the convention that was signed to mark the surrender. Under its terms, the troops were to be shipped home on condition that they did not return to fight in America. Congress, however, spotted that even if they themselves did not come back, they could relieve other troops to fight in their stead. After lengthy wrangles, both sides picking holes in the agreement, the men were marched off to spend the war as prisoners.

After a year in Massachusetts, the army was taken south on a twelve-week mid-winter trek to Virginia. Most of the Hessian prisoners escaped into Pennsylvania en route to join compatriot settlers there. At the end of the war the prisoners were dragged back north again to avoid rescue by Tarleton and Simcoe, by which time their numbers had been reduced to half by death, desertion and exchanges.

In this painting, Gates is seen reviewing his Redcoat prisoners after Saratoga. Their muskets are stacked and the colour lowered. Although the picture

was painted some time after the Revolution, the artist James Peale, younger brother of Charles Willson Peale, had himself served in the Continental army and would have reproduced the scene with great accuracy.

393
Cannon surrendered by Burgoyne at Saratoga
1776. Brass, three-pounder; made at the Royal Brass Foundry, Woolwich
Barrel: 101·6 cm long, 7·6 cm diameter;
carriage: 177 cm long; wheels: 91·4 cm diameter
Fort Ticonderoga Museum, New York

In January 1776 the Board of Ordnance gave instructions to the Royal Brass Foundry at Woolwich to cast twenty cannon of a new type for use in America. Germain realised that for an offensive southwards from Canada to succeed, the artillery would have to be light enough to travel easily over rough country, transportable on horseback and quickly manoeuvrable. The new light three-pounder, designed by Captain William Congreve of the Royal Artillery, seemed the answer.

The Dutch master gun-founders, Jan and Pieter Verbruggen (father and son), who were then in charge of the foundry, responded quickly to the Board's call for urgency. They had cast twenty brass guns only two months after the original order was placed, and by August had completed a total of seventy-three light three-pound cannon.

This cannon (the carriage is partly original), one of those produced at Woolwich for Burgoyne's expedition, was handed over to the Rebels on 17 October 1777.

394
Drum used by the Continental army at Saratoga
Painted wood
Georgia Historical Society, Savannah

This drum has an inscription painted on it at some later date stating that it was beaten at Saratoga and, later, in the Southern Campaign, at Cowpens and Eutaw Springs in 1781.

395
Map of the first Battle of Saratoga
Full title: 'A Plan of the encampment and position of Burgoyne's army at Sword's House on the Hudson River near Stillwater on 17 September 1777, with the positions of that part of the army engaged in the battle on 19 September'
Lieutenant William Cumberland Wilkinson

1777. Manuscript map
35 cm × 36 cm
Ref: Faden Collection 69
Library of Congress, Washington, D.C.

Wilkinson was a lieutenant in the 62nd Foot and, as assistant engineer, accompanied his regiment on Burgoyne's expedition down the Hudson. His map of the positions at the first battle of Saratoga shows clearly the Rebel stronghold on Bemis Heights, with Burgoyne's forces spread out in a line ready for the frontal attack. The road to Albany, heading south off the top of the map, on the banks of the river, is guarded by enemy artillery on the heights.

396
Powder horn, engraved with a map of the Hudson River-Lake Champlain waterway
c. 1763
McCord Museum, Montreal, Quebec

Whereas many powder horns were engraved in idle moments by their owners, others were supplied to the army already engraved by professional artists. The vital routeway between New York and Canada was a favourite subject, both in the Seven Years War and in the Revolution, providing important information about the intricate geography of land and water in this much contested area.

397
Manuscript copies of papers laid before the House of Commons relating to General Burgoyne's expedition
May 1778
The Earl of Derby, Prescot, Merseyside

398
'A State of the Expedition from Canada, as laid before the House of Commons by Lieutenant-general Burgoyne and verified by Evidence'
Published 1779
The Earl of Derby, Prescot, Merseyside

On 26 May 1778 Burgoyne was called upon to answer in the House a motion set forward by a Mr Vyner, 'to condemn the state and condition of the army which surrendered at Saratoga'. Vyner also asked why Burgoyne had been allowed to return home. Burgoyne parried his critics skilfully. A select committee was established to examine the state of the army under Burgoyne, and the following year the lieutenant-general published his own account, in which he set out to prove that the army he had been given was half the size promised and badly equipped.

383

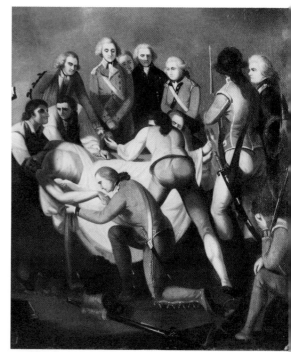

385 (detail)

99
Proposal for the Exchange of Lieut. General Burgoyne for an equivalent of American prisoners of War. New York 9 February 1782
Manuscript
1cm × 22·8cm
Ref: PRO 30/55/35
Public Record Office, London

Although Burgoyne remained in England he was still technically a prisoner, and a valuable bargaining commodity for the Americans. As late as 1782, before the final peace was settled, they were negotiating for his exchange. Prisoner exchanges worked on a points system, with a tariff worked out according to rank: colonels were worth a hundred, majors twenty-eight, captains sixteen, lieutenants six and ensigns four. A rank and file soldier was worth one, while a lieutenant-general, like Burgoyne, rated 1044. As long as the sum tallied the exchanges could be made.

In this exchange the two commissary generals from the British and American armies had balanced the books; Burgoyne would be officially handed over to the British, if thirty-two officers, Brigadier-General Moultrie, Colonel Pinkney and 443 privates were relinquished in turn. The British would still then be owed three privates, but as Burgoyne was in London when these arrangements were being made, they were only a formality to discharge the debts of war.

THE PHILADELPHIA STORY

The plan for Sir William Howe to attack Pennsylvania, and thereby the focal point of Rebel activity, Philadelphia, was approved in the spring of 1777, a few days before Burgoyne's scheme for Saratoga was despatched to Carleton. The summer of that year saw both commanders busy with preparations for a major campaign.

In mid-July, 14,000 of Howe's men embarked into hot, crowded transport ships off Staten Island and waited. A week later, on 16 July, news arrived of Burgoyne's success at Ticonderoga, and with easy mind Howe ordered his ships to sail. They set out on the 23rd.

The delays placed Rebel commander Washington in a quandary, whether to deploy his 8000-strong army in defence of Philadelphia or to send them, should Howe be headed north to support Burgoyne, to the Hudson. The British fleet completely vanished for another month, which did not improve matters for the Americans.

Nor for the British, as after six weeks on their transports the men were sick and exhausted, the horses emaciated or dead. Howe had elected to sail round into the Chesapeake to avoid Delaware, apparently Rebel-infested. The agonising trip had cost him dear in terms of the fitness of his army, and he was no nearer Philadelphia than when he started.

On 25 August the army landed at Head of Elk and marched off to Philadelphia. On 11 September the Rebels made a final stand, at Brandywine Creek, to prevent the British invading their city. Howe chose a frontal attack, supported by a wide flanking action which, because the Americans had failed to reconnoitre properly, threw the enemy into confusion. As at New York, Howe failed to follow up his victory and most of Washington's men escaped the following night, but the day was his. On 26 September, Cornwallis led the British army into Philadelphia.

That winter was a time of relatively gracious living for both officers and men. Greeted warmly by Philadelphia Loyalists, they were involved in a social whirl, while the Rebel army squatted twenty miles away at Valley Forge. Howe was not prepared to undertake a winter campaign.

The entry of the French into the war caused a re-appraisal of policy back in London. It was decided that the army should be concentrated in the key maritime city, New York, and that garrisons in the West Indies, where French attacks were certain, should be strengthened. Howe was recalled, and Sir Henry Clinton, commander-in-chief until 1781, was sent to Philadelphia to mastermind its evacuation.

In a brilliant operation he organised the long column of troops, baggage, artillery and stores out of the city, ninety miles across New Jersey and into New York without loss, despite harassment by the Rebels. By early July 1778, Philadelphia was back in Rebel hands and the northern half of the war was over.

400
Sir Henry Clinton, 1738 ?–95
John Smart
1777. Miniature, watercolour on ivory
3·7 cm in diameter
National Army Museum, Chelsea, London

Henry Clinton reached Boston, with Howe and Burgoyne, in May 1775, and quickly distinguished himself at Bunker Hill, earning the local rank of lieutenant-general. The next year he fought alongside Howe at New York, for which his promotion was extended to the whole army, and he was knighted. When Howe left New York to capture Philadelphia, Clinton was left in charge.

Sir Henry was an able commander who was not sent supporting officers of sufficient imagination or calibre. After the evacuation of Pennsylvania, he was forced into a campaign of attrition based on New York, except when he led the attack on Charleston, South Carolina, in 1780, which has been described as 'the one solid British triumph of the war'. But he then returned to base in New York and left the winning of the Southern Campaign to Cornwallis, his second-in-command.

Clinton never trusted Cornwallis; Cornwallis thought Clinton failed to give him necessary support. Wherever the blame lay, Clinton resigned after Yorktown and returned to England, where he was made the scapegoat for the British defeat.

401
Letter from the King to Lord North
13 March 1778, manuscript
23·4 cm × 18·5 cm
Her Majesty the Queen

The French signed a treaty of friendship and commerce with the Rebels on 6 February 1778. When news of the alliance reached Britain, policy regarding America had to change.

In this letter George III writes of the need to strengthen and consolidate against the eventuality of a French attack. 'It is a joke to think of keeping Pennsylvania,' he comments.

402
Three-part map showing the operations of the British army from southern Long Island to the Elk River, 12 August 1776–late 1779
Manuscript, coloured, untitled and unsigned
Map 1. N.E. New Jersey, Staten Island, Long Island
   34·9 cm × 68·5 cm
Map 2. Delaware, Pennsylvania and Central New Jersey
   57 cm × 105·3 cm
Map 3. Pennsylvania, Delaware, Maryland and New Jersey
   38·1 cm × 50·1 cm
The Duke of Northumberland, Alnwick

This three-sheet map provides an overall view of the British campaigns to the south-west of New York. The Battle of Long Island, the positions at Trenton, Brandywine, Germantown and Freehold (during the Philadelphia evacuation) are shown as if concentrated into one long season. The map illustrates well the repeated forays made by the British into the area – which they finally conquered only to abandon.

403
Major Patrick Ferguson, 1744–80
Artist unknown

Wax bust of the period
17·8 cm high
Private collection

Patrick Ferguson, trained at the Royal Military Academy, Woolwich, heard of the marksmanship of Rebel riflemen and set about devising a rifle himself which could counter it. In June 1776 he conducted a series of experiments at Woolwich, before high-ranking officers, and proved beyond doubt the advantages of his breech-loading rifle.

Ordered back to America to join his regiment, Ferguson was allowed to form for himself a company of riflemen consisting of volunteers from other regiments. They excelled at Brandywine, but Ferguson was badly wounded and Howe, said to have been insulted because the corps was raised without his knowledge, disbanded it, returning Ferguson's men to their units.

For the next two years Ferguson led raids with small bodies of troops in the Jerseys and the south and fought under Tarleton. In 1779 he was appointed to the 71st Highlanders and was commissioned to rally Loyalist armed support in the south. While doing this he was trapped, the only British officer with over a thousand loyal Americans, on top of King's Mountain in North Carolina, and was killed.

404
Ferguson rifle
c. 1776. Made by D. Egg of London
Overall length, 47½ in (120·5 cm); barrel length, 43 in (109·2 cm)
Private collection

Ferguson's demonstration of his new ·560 calibre rifle in 1776 was designed to show how the disadvantages inherent in the smooth-bore Brown Bess musket (standing up to load, for example) could be overcome. The new breech-loading system meant that the gun could be loaded while the soldier was kneeling or lying down, thus exposing himself less to danger.

The rifle was quick to load and fire (Ferguson managed four shots a minute continuously for five minutes at a target 200 yards away). One turn of the complex ten-thread screw was enough to reveal the open breech. The rifle was also less vulnerable in bad weather than the Brown Bess.

Ferguson patented his seven-groove rifle in Deember 1776. This example has the word 'FERGUS' stamped behind the breech; further on is the Ferguson crest, and then the words 'D. Egg 15 London'. Egg was Gunmaker to the Board of Ordnance; he had the main contract for the manufacture of the Ferguson rifles. The '15' indicates that the rifle was intended for use by Ferguson's Corps. This may have been Ferguson's own rifle, or one used in his trial at Woolwich.

Despite its success at the first demonstration, the King, when he saw the gun fired at Windsor, was not so impressed. (It was fired by men not accustomed to it.) It was never generally adopted as an army weapon, and its popularity died with Ferguson.

405
Ferguson's double-barrelled pistol
c. 1776. Made by Wogdon of London
Overall length, 33 cm; barrel length, 20·3 cm;
bayonet length, 8·9 cm
Private collection

First-class evidence suggests that this pistol, one of a pair, was carried by Ferguson on campaigns: they accept the same size ammunition as that fired from his own rifle. The bayonet was a folding, hinged sword-bayonet, which was opened by hand and locked in position. It did not spring open. Of their kind, the pair are very rare.

Each pistol was made also to take a carbine stock, and could be used this way by mounted officers. A silver escutcheon is inscribed with the word 'Pitfour', the name of Ferguson's family estate.

406
Letter from Patrick Ferguson describing how he could have killed Washington
Three sheets written by a clerk, signed 'PF' and dated 31 Jan 1778
Each 32 cm × 20 cm
Edinburgh University Library

Before the Battle of Brandywine, while Howe and Knyphausen were drawing up their troops, Ferguson, with twenty of his rifle corps, took up position on the edge of a wood. A Rebel in dark green or blue with a cocked hat, rode to within 100 yards of Ferguson's position. Ferguson despatched three of his best marksmen to shoot him but then recalled his men – to shoot the Rebel in the back would have been dishonourable.

As the officer rode back, Ferguson stood up and called to him; he looked, but calmly rode away.

Ferguson describes how easily he could have 'lodged half a dozen of balls' in him, but 'it was not pleasant to fire at the back of an unoffending individual who was accquiting himself very coolly of his duty'. Next day he discovered from a doctor who was treating the wounded of both sides that the man in his sights was General Washington.

During the battle Ferguson was seriously wounded in the right hand. His letter, dictated to a clerk, was initialled with his left.

Extract from Patrick Ferguson's letter
We had not l(a)yn long when a Rebell Officer remarkable by a Huzzar Dress passed towards our army within 100 yards of my right flank, not perceiving us – he was followed by another dressed in Dark Green or blue mounted on a very good bay horse with a remarkable large high cocked hat. I ordered three good shots to steal near them and fire at them but the idea disgusted me and I recalled them. The Huzzar in returning made a circuit but the other passed within 100 yards of us upon which I advanced from the wood towards him, upon my calling he stopd but after looking at me proceeded. I again drew his attention, and made signs to him to stop levelling my piece at him, but he slowly continued his way. As I was within that distance at which in the quickest firing I have seldom missed a sheet of paper and could have lodged a half a dozen of balls in or about him before he was out of my reach I had only to determine but it was not pleasant to fire at the back of an unoffending individual who was accquiting himself very coolly of his duty so I let him alone. The day after I had just been telling this story to some wounded officers who lay in the same room with me when one of our surgeons who had been dressing the wounded Rebell Officers came in and told us that they had been informing him that Gen.[1] Washington was all the morning with the Light Troops generally in their front and only attended by a French Officer in a huzzar Dress he himself mounted and dressed as above described, the oddness of their dress had puzzled me and made me take notice of it – I am not sorry that I did not know all the time who it was.

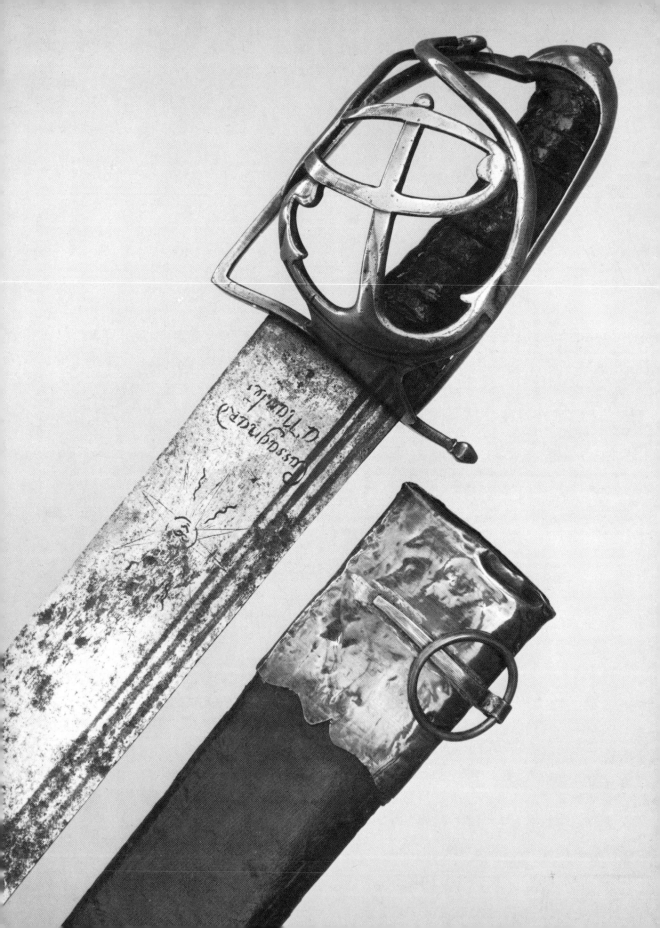

Enter The French

FRANCE MADE A CRUCIAL CONTRIBUTION to the success of the American Revolution. Yet her entry into what was a domestic issue between Great Britain and the Colonists was a protracted affair, and the French decision to intervene was not taken without considerable misgivings. It was only the victory of the Colonists at Saratoga on 7 October 1777 which forced the French Government to make up its mind. Before then, it had been content to play an indirect role in the conflict. The Rebels needed powder (their supply had failed in January 1776) and also wanted to check British naval supremacy because it made possible the unrestricted movement of troops along the Atlantic seaboard. As she was England's natural enemy, France seemed a natural ally for the Colonists.

As early as November 1774, American agents in London had approached the French chargé d'affaires with a request for assistance. The French were cautious; they sent unofficial observers to America to obtain information and to encourage the Rebels, and to England to assess the strength of the Government's determination to put down the rebellion. These were only passive moves, but it was inevitable that France would have to decide sooner or later whether to take advantage of developments in America to restore the position she had lost to Britain in the Seven Years War and to regain her military glory. The arguments for intervention seemed overwhelming: the American involvement was a drain on Britain's resources, and Britain stood to lose all the strategic advantages offered by the possession of the colonies. In the light of these powerful arguments, why did France hesitate?

In France, the first consideration was the weak financial position of the Government. In the course of the debate in the Royal Council on secret aid for the American Rebels in the spring of 1776, Turgot, the Controller-General of the Finances, reminded Louis XVI that expenditure already exceeded revenue by twenty million *livres*. Secondly, both the army and the navy were in the throes of reform: the navy after the ravages of an incompetent minister, and the army in order to put it on an equal footing with the forces of Austria and Prussia. Thirdly, opinion within the Government was divided on the question of giving active support to the Colonists, and this division partly reflected the rivalries among ministers.

Turgot and the leading minister, the aged Comte de Maurepas, were against involvement. After all, they argued, there was always a danger that the resistance of the Rebels would collapse or that they might come to terms with Britain. In the debate in the Royal Council these two ministers were opposed by Vergennes (Foreign Affairs), St Germain (War), and possibly Sartines (Marine). Vergennes always argued that France was in some danger from the growing strength of British forces in America; should they succeed in putting down the rebellion, these British forces might take advantage of their position to attack French possessions in the West Indies. With the removal of Turgot in May 1776, Maurepas gave way over secret aid but was nevertheless able to delay military intervention for more than a year. His main support probably came from the King himself. The young Louis XVI had great reservations about whether a colonial power like France could justify giving aid to the rebellious subjects of another and whether it was right for him to encourage rebellion against the legitimate authority of a brother monarch. The British ambassador paid tribute to him when he wrote that the King 'is averse to war and averse to it from motives that do him honour'. Although the King overcame his scruples in the matter of giving secret aid, those scruples continued to stand in the way of any deeper involvement.

The victory at Saratoga in October 1777 took the French Government by surprise. 'We no longer have any time to lose,' wrote Vergennes, who was afraid that France might miss the opportunity of consolidating the success of the Colonists. Yet if Saratoga was the moment of decision for the French, that moment could not have come at a worse time for them. Powerful external factors were against intervention. First, there was an imminent danger that France might repeat the error of 1756 by becoming involved in a war on two fronts: on the Continent as well as in America. Since 1774 the question of the Bavarian succession had brought Prussia and Austria, France's ally, close to war. There was now a risk that the Austrians might ask for French military assistance under the treaties of 1756–7.

Secondly, any effective French intervention required the participation of Spain. The alliance with Spain was regarded as the cornerstone of French moves on the colonial scene, for the combined navies of the two Bourbon monarchies could outnumber that of Britain. But Spain refused to help. She was already engaged in a war with Portugal. Moreover, as the ruler of his own large colonial empire, King Charles III had even less sympathy than had his nephew, Louis XVI, for movements towards colonial independence; besides, he was afraid that if they obtained their independence, the Americans would eventually encroach on Spanish territory in Louisiana and elsewhere.

It was clear that if they wished to take advantage of the victory, the French had to act alone. Maurepas had already given way, and the decision now rested with the King. After a last refusal from Spain, Louis XVI succumbed and dictated to Vergennes the terms of a formal treaty of friendship and commerce with the 'United States of North America'. It was signed on 6 February 1778, and its implicit recognition led to an immediate breach of diplomatic relations and to a state of war between Great Britain and France. 'The final decision was taken by the King,' wrote Vergennes. 'He did not take it under the influence of his ministers.' In March the French refused an Austrian request for military assistance in case of war in Germany and continued their negotiations to bring the Spaniards into the war. Meanwhile, French naval forces successfully harried the British off Ushant in June.

The British mishandled their own negotiations with Spain, and in April 1779 Charles III signed a treaty with France. The French paid a heavy price for the treaty. Spain insisted that the area of naval operations should be limited to Europe and should include a direct attack on England. The attack by the combined fleets (sixty-six ships in all) on the Isle of Wight failed in August. Spain again resorted to negotiations to obtain Gibraltar by peaceful means, but the British had by then obtained successes and were not disposed to take the negotiations seriously. They dragged on until March 1781 and effectively paralysed some of the military operations of the French, who now found themselves committed to campaigns against the British for the recovery of Gibraltar and Minorca.

In July 1780 a French division under the command of the Comte de Rochambeau had at last been sent over to America under the protection of a fleet. It arrived at Newport and stayed there for the winter, and its presence deprived the British forces in New York of their freedom of action. In the spring of 1781 Rochambeau crossed Connecticut to meet Washington's Continentals on the Hudson. From Newport they moved with speed down through New Jersey and Pennsylvania to Delaware and Virginia. At Yorktown, after a resistance of thirteen days, Cornwallis surrendered. When the news was brought to the dying Maurepas, he quoted a line from Racine's *Mithridate*: 'Mes derniers regards ont vu fuir les Romains'.

The old French monarchy, then, had recovered some of its earlier military and naval glory, and American independence was a fact. That monarchy, however, was unable to survive the hopeless disarray of its finances which the war engendered, nor the spread of revolutionary ideas.

J. M. J. ROGISTER

407
Marquis de Lafayette, 1757–1834
Charles Willson Peale

1781. A replica painted by Peale after his life portrait
Oil on canvas
58·7 cm × 46 cm
Independence National Historical Park,
Philadelphia, Pennsylvania

Lafayette's father was killed at the Battle of Minden in 1759, fighting against the British. A sense of revenge may well have been one of the motives which led the young Frenchman to America.

Whatever ideas of revolution and glory invaded Lafayette's mind, the aristocrat was one of a group of adventurers who landed in South Carolina on 13 June 1777. Six weeks later Lafayette was in Philadelphia. There some of his compatriots were disappointed with their reception; few were given instantly the high ranks they expected. Lafayette, on the other hand, offered to serve at his own expense, and he was rewarded with an appointment as major-general.

It was Lafayette's meeting with Washington that was crucial to his career. A strong relationship, almost like that between father and son, grew between them. The Marquis was still only nineteen. After the French general's blooding at Brandywine, where he was wounded, Washington began to increase the size of Lafayette's commands. He shared American hardships at Valley Forge, fought in New Jersey and in the Southern Campaign, where he showed great skill in hounding Cornwallis and avoiding attempts by the British general to 'trap the boy'.

There is a distinction to be made between French officers such as the Marquis, who volunteered to fight for the Rebels while France sat on the sidelines, and those who commanded the French regular forces in America later in the war. Both types were represented when Rochambeau and Washington moved south in 1781 for the Yorktown siege, when Lafayette was given his highest command, over the light division, for the final action. His dash, bravery, breeding and enthusiasm for the cause had made him a popular hero.

408
The prow of Marie-Antoinette's barge
Paris, 1777. Painted wood
171 cm × 105 cm
Musée de la Marine, Paris

Though a rough wood carving, the mermaid figurehead of the Queen's barge speaks in some way for the

414

COUNT D·H
French General of the Land Forces

409

HAMBEAU
Reviewing the French Troops 25 Nov 1780

elegance of Versailles. While Louis XVI discussed the Revolution with his ministers, Marie-Antoinette entertained in her pretty barge as it floated serenely on the canals of Versailles.

409
Silas Deane, 1737–89
Charles Willson Peale

1776. Miniature watercolour on ivory
3·9 cm × 3·1 cm
Connecticut Historical Society, Hartford

Instigator, with others, of the Ethan Allen capture of Fort Ticonderoga, Silas Deane, lawyer and business-man, was one of Connecticut's delegates to the first two Continental Congresses. In 1776 Deane was appointed as the first American diplomat to serve abroad, and he arrived in Paris with two missions. The first was to act as a kind of commercial attaché guiding necessary supplies back to America; the second, authorised by the Secret Committee of Congress, was to purchase uniforms and arms. As he had been invited also to recruit suitable foreign officers, it was a Deane letter that introduced Lafayette to Philadelphia.

On the arms-running side, Silas Deane had a hand in setting up Hortalez et Cie, a legitimate-looking company which in fact smuggled guns to the Rebels. Its leading French operator was Beaumarchais, the Parisian playwright.

Through all his dealings Deane worked closely with an old friend, the American-born Edward Bancroft, passing to him all sorts of information of a highly confidential nature. Bancroft was a double agent.

410
Two promissory notes to Louis XVI's Treasury signed by Benjamin Franklin
Paper, mounted on paper
Each 24 cm × 18 cm
American Philosophical Society,
Philadelphia, Pennsylvania

As American Minister Plenipotentiary to the French Government, Franklin negotiated many loans for Congress. These two notes, signed during the height of the war, provided the Rebels with cash for food, arms and gunpowder.

430

411
Letter from John Jay, President of the Continental Congress, to Franklin on payment for smuggled arms
18 June 1779. Paper
30·4 cm × 19 cm
H. E. Monsieur Jacques de Beaumarchais, French Ambassador to the Court of St James, London

A typical example of the letters which Congress was sending to Paris to enable its agents to pay Beaumarchais for his gun-running.

This letter in part reads: 'Sensible of Mr. Beaumarchais efforts to serve these United States and of the Seasonable Supplies he has from time to time furnished, Congress are earnestly disposed to make him this payment. They would gladly have done it in produce; but the State of our finances and the hazardous navigation render it impracticable . . .'

412
Five cheques from Congress to Beaumarchais, payment for guns
Paper
Each 12·7 cm × 26·6 cm
H. E. Monsieur Jacques de Beaumarchais, French Ambassador to the Court of St James, London

These exhibits are clear evidence of the gun-running which Caron de Beaumarchais, the French playwright, operated on behalf of the American rebels.

Beaumarchais, author of *The Barber of Seville* and *The Marriage of Figaro*, operated under cover of an honest-sounding commercial house, Hortalez et Cie. With a million livres from the French Government, a million from Spain, and a third million from French private sources, in the summer of 1776 Beaumarchais was in business.

By 1777, the dramatist had twelve ships working out of Le Havre, Bordeaux, Marseilles and Nantes. One historian reckons that nine-tenths of the military equipment and supplies that made the Rebel victory at Saratoga possible had come from France or foreign merchants.

Beaumarchais never directly received the cash for these cheques.

413
Letter from Franklin on the need for secrecy over a French treaty of alliance
Passy, 24 March 1778
22·7 cm × 18·3 cm
Maryland Historical Society, Baltimore

'Dr. Franklin presents his compliments to Mr. W. Lee and informs him that the Treaty of Alliance is ordered by the Court of France to be kept secret until they think fit to publish it.' (The Treaty had been signed on 6 February.) The letter was addressed to the Hon. William Lee, joint commercial agent for Congress in Paris.

414
'Count de Rochambeau French General of the Land Forces in America Reviewing the French Troops'
25 Nov 1780. Engraving, published by T. Colley, Strand, London
20·9 cm × 33 cm
Ref: BM 5706
Trustees of the British Museum, London

A burlesque of Rochambeau's army. The General himself stands on the right with an officer's spear and an exaggeratedly long pigtail. His troops, distinguished by a wide range of noses, carry knapsacks resembling large muffs.

415
'That for Lewis, Dem-me Whos afraid of Frogs'
1 September 1780. Hand-coloured engraving; published by E. Hedges, 92 Royal Exchange, London
19 cm × 25·4 cm
Ref: BM Add. 994
Trustees of the British Museum, London

With rumours of French invasions, and French ships now and then in the Channel, the satirist strikes a most patriotic note. The local militia is not afraid of Louis XVI (Lewis) and is able to frighten away the be-laced invader by slapping his own buttocks – a very rude 18th-century gesture.

416
'Coiffure à l'Independence ou le Triomphe de la Liberté'
17 June 1778. Coloured engraving
29 cm × 20·5 cm
Le Musée de la Coopération Franco-Américaine, Château de Blérancourt, Aisne

This is said to be a satirical illustration of a Parisian coiffure inspired by a famous French victory at sea earlier that year.

417
Lieutenant-General Jean Baptiste Donatien de Vimeur, Comte de Rochambeau

The Comte de Rochambeau (1725–1807) commanded the French army in America after France entered the war in March 1778. Rochambeau had enjoyed a distinguished military career before playing a leading role in the Revolution. For that, the general sailed from Brest with 5500 men and arrived in Newport, Rhode Island, on 10 July 1780.

Rochambeau first conferred with Washington in Hartford, Connecticut, where it was agreed that France should provide more troops before a combined attack on New York. The reply from Versailles denied Rochambeau further reinforcements but bore the news that the fleet of Admiral de Grasse was headed for the West Indies and could be called on for help over a limited period on the American coast. The fleet would bring with it a number of troops from the French West Indies also on temporary loan.

The two generals met again, this time at Wethersfield, Connecticut, in May 1781. They agreed that, with the promised support of a French fleet giving them naval supremacy for a time, the British army of Cornwallis in the south should be their target. Yorktown was the result (see item 551).

This is a photograph of the Charles Willson Peale portrait at the Independence National Historical Park, Philadelphia.

THE FORCE OF FRANCE

The Brunon Collection is one of the most distinguished military collections in the world. Its holdings in the equipment of the 18th-century French army are unique. The collection is the child of the Brunon family of Salon-de-Provence, near Marseilles, and it is housed in the Château de l'Empéri overlooking that town. Its fame has grown through more than thirty international exhibitions from Tokyo to Montreal. This is the first time it has been to Britain. While the military collection itself now falls under the wing of the Musée de l'Armée in Paris, the library still belongs to the family. This is their introduction to the French section of '1776':

'Thanks to the diplomacy of Franklin and Jefferson, to the impulse of Lafayette, and faced with a worsening Anglo-American conflict, Louis XVI signed a treaty of alliance with the American nation in 1778.

'Frenchmen fought on sea and on land for seven years, from 1776 to 1783, either alongside the Americans, or in the West Indies to defend her own colonies from the English.

'The French navy made much progress during this period, and Louis XVI possessed the first great French fleet with leaders such as Suffren, Bougainville, Guichen, d'Estaing, de Grasse, La Motte-Piquet and La Pérouse. Every year, several squadrons sailed for America and the West Indies, or returned from there, well tested.

'As for the army, about fifty infantry regiments took part in the operations, more often sending some companies from each. All together their numbers totalled about twenty thousand men. The majority came from France, but the West Indian garrisons contributed in a large way. Some regiments were seconded to act as "naval troops" on board ship. The most illustrious corps fought of course with Rochambeau.

'All the objects presented here are original, and, with few exceptions, belonged to units who fought in the American Revolution.'

418
Uniform of a French marshal of camp (brigadier-general), according to the Royal Order of 1775
Life-size figure
Musée de l'Empéri, Salon-de-Provence, Bouches du Rhône

Uniforms worn by Lieutenant-Generals the Comte de Rochambeau and the Baron de Vioménil, also at Yorktown, were similar to this one, but with double braid on the sleeves and pockets, indicating their rank. This one is of the design prescribed by the Royal Order of 1775 (see next item), and belonged to Brigadier-General Nault de Champagny. It is the only uniform of a general officer of the Old Monarchy known to exist in France.

The embroidery is in gold thread. The sword has a handle of chased silver decorated with war motifs. The figure bears the Decoration of Commander of the Order of St John of Jerusalem (Malta), and of a Knight of Saint-Louis.

419
'King's regulations concerning the Uniform of General Officers and others in his Armies and his Garrisons. 2 September, 1775.'
Printed booklet of sixteen pages and five colour plates
Bibliothèque Raoul et Jean Brunon, Salon-de-Provence, Bouches du Rhône

This is the first order ever to set out the rules for the uniforms of general officers. These engravings illustrate the braiding and buttons for the different ranks.

420
Flagstaff finial of the Louis XV and Louis XVI periods

Gilt bronze; the finial decorated with a pierced
fleur-de-lys
16 cm high
Musée de l'Empéri, Salon-de-Provence, Bouches du Rhône

421
Decoration of Knight of the Royal and Military Order of Saint-Louis

Musée de l'Empéri, Salon-de-Provence, Bouches du Rhône

This order was instituted by Louis XIV in April
1693. The Ribbon and Grand Cross of the Order was
awarded to Rochambeau in 1771. The obverse includes the effigy of Saint-Louis surrounded by the
words 'LUD. MAGNUS. INST. 1693.' On the reverse there is a sword with the motto 'BELLICAE
VIRTUTIS PRAEMIUM'.

422
Officer's epaulettes

Musée de l'Empéri, Salon-de-Provence, Bouches du Rhône

The epaulette, distinguishing mark of rank, was
instituted by the French Minister Choiseul in 1762.
The epaulette of the field officer had a large twisted
fringe; the subaltern's was smaller. The colour of the
metal (silver or gold) depended on the corps.

423
Officer's holster pistol

Louis XVI period. Silver mounting, polished
steel lock
40 cm long
Musée de l'Empéri, Salon-de-Provence, Bouches du Rhône

The lock-plate bears the inscription 'Louis Lamotte –
Arquebusier de plusiers régiments à Saint-Etienne'.

424
Officer's pocket pistol

Louis XVI period
20 cm long
Musée de l'Empéri, Salon-de-Provence, Bouches du Rhône

The cap is shaped like a bird's head. The lock bears
the words 'Fouré et Angénieux à Saint-Etienne'.

407

410

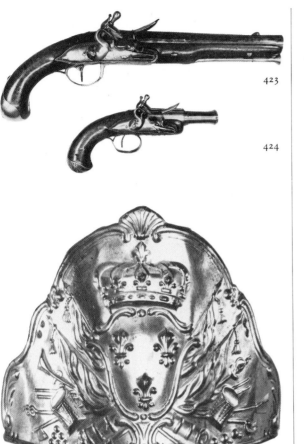

423

424

428

438 (detail)

425
'Royal Order for the payment etc of Troops for a special expedition. 20 March 1780'
Bibliothèque Raoul et Jean Brunon, Salon-de-Provence, Bouches du Rhône

The order is non-specific in order to disguise its purpose. It concerned the army soon to set sail for America under Rochambeau. The printed booklet contains ten pages giving details of salaries. In the French infantry, a colonel was to receive 13,200 livres a year, a captain 3000 livres, a soldier 171 livres. Details of the food ration to be given to a soldier each day: 24 ounces of bread (720 g), 8 ounces of beef (240 g), and 1 ounce of rice (30 g). 'His Majesty intends that only men fit and able to endure long sea voyages shall embark.'

426
Accounts for the Port of Lorient
Musée de l'Empéri, Salon-de-Provence, Bouches du Rhône

The manuscript gives details of amounts handed over to the Port of Lorient 'for the service of the American Colonies' from 1 November 1780, to 31 October 1782.

427
A soldier of the Régiment de Hainaut-Infanterie, company of Grenadiers
Life-size figure
Musée de l'Empéri, Salon-de-Provence, Bouches du Rhône

The Brunon mannequin is dressed with hat, coat, arms and equipment of the period. (Only the waistcoat is modern.)

The French infantry was dressed entirely in white. Each regiment had distinguishing colours – here crimson facings. The grenadiers wore woollen epaulettes and carried a sabre.

A battalion of 500 men of the Hainaut regiment embarked with d'Estaing's fleet for the West Indies in 1777. It was involved in the naval battle there against the British squadrons under Admiral Byron, distinguished itself at the fall of Grenada, and took part in the siege of Savannah in 1779 where the British drove off the combined American and French forces.

428
Grenadier officer's cap front plate
Gilded copper, the Arms of France surrounded by trophies
20 cm high
Musée de l'Empéri, Salon-de-Provence, Bouches du Rhône

429
Cartridge-pouch badge of an officer of the
Port-au-Prince Regiment
Musée de l'Empéri, Salon-de-Provence, Bouches du Rhône

The badge bears the Arms of France on an anchor surmounted by a banderole with the inscription 'Reg^t du Portauprince'. Frequently involved in the engagements of the West Indies, this regiment provided one detachment for the siege of Savannah in 1779.

430
Gorget of an officer of the
Régiment de Berry-Infanterie
Musée de l'Empéri, Salon-de-Provence, Bouches du Rhône

It is typical, with its fleur-de-lys and other ornament, of those worn by French officers in America.

431
Rank and file epaulettes
Musée de l'Empéri, Salon-de-Provence, Bouches du Rhône

These epaulettes of wool were used to distinguish the élite companies of light infantry and grenadiers.

432
Pair of soldier's shoes
Louis XVI. Only known example
Musée de l'Empéri, Salon-de-Provence, Bouches du Rhône

433
Infantry officer's sword
Model of 1767. Sword-belt in white buffalo hide with stitched and embossed decoration. Fittings in gilded copper. Blue steel blade with gilt motifs
120 cm long overall
Musée de l'Empéri, Salon-de-Provence, Bouches du Rhône

434
Junior officer's sword
Model *c.* 1770. Iron guard and ebony handle. On the blade is inscribed 'De la manufacture de la marque de l'Extra-Fin à Solingen – Gilbert Marchand fourbisseur Place Sainte-Croix à Angers'
95 cm long
Musée de l'Empéri, Salon-de-Provence, Bouches du Rhône

435
Sabre-briquet of a grenadier
Model 1767–70. On the blade: a grenade, the monogram of the King, 'L' and 'Grenadier'. Brass guard
Musée de l'Empéri, Salon-de-Provence, Bouches du Rhône

The blades of French side-arms were manufactured at Klingenthal and Solingen. The guards and furnishings were entrusted to a great number of workshops around Paris and in the provinces.

436
Infantry musket
Model of 1766. Weight 3·8 kg, calibre 17·5 mm, with a range of 200 m
Musée de l'Empéri, Salon-de-Provence, Bouches du Rhône

This musket was the model chiefly used by French troops in the American Revolution. Those that were earlier made for the Rebels were manufactured officially for the 'Compagnie des Indes'. This gun carries the manufacturing mark of 'Maubeuge'. The principal French gunmakers were to be found at Saint-Etienne, Maubeuge, Tulle and Charleville.

437
Infantry musket
Model of 1777
Musée de l'Empéri, Salon-de-Provence, Bouches du Rhône

Some French units were issued with a newly-developed musket towards the end of the Revolution. It shows only minor alterations compared with its predecessor. It was also made at Maubeuge.

438
Infantry officer's musket
Model of 1770
Musée de l'Empéri, Salon-de-Provence, Bouches du Rhône

The Royal Orders of 1754 and 1759 prescribed the bearing of a rifle by officers. This weapon is lighter than that of a soldier and more refinement has gone into its manufacture.

439
Light infantry officer's cartridge pouch
White buffalo hide, stitched and embossed with grenades, fleur de lys, and the monogram of the King, 'L'
Musée de l'Empéri, Salon-de-Provence, Bouches du Rhône

440
Cartridge-pouch badge of the
Boulonnais Regiment
Metal, decorated with the Arms of France surrounded with flags, and with the inscription, 'Boulonnois'
Musée de l'Empéri, Salon-de-Provence, Bouches du Rhône

The regiment left Brest in March 1781, and arrived in Boston with a convoy of eight ships escorted by *Le*

Sagittaire under Bourgainville. The 600 men of the convoy were intended as replacements. The Boulonnais relieved troops from the Saintonge regiment.

441
Soldier of the Régiment de Royal-Auvergne Gâtinais-Infanterie
Nikolaus Hoffmann

Undated. Coloured engraving
Bibliothèque Raoul et Jean Brunon, Salon-de-Provence, Bouches du Rhône

This regiment arrived from the West Indies with the de Grasse squadron in 1781 to take part in the siege of Gloucester, the British position on the other side of the York River from Yorktown. After the surrender the French regiment received the personal congratulations of Washington.

The involved name of this regiment, split like many others, arises out of the fact that in order to expand the French army rapidly, some regiments were divided in two, one half then given a new name, and both halves raised to full strength.

442
'Engraved plates showing the positions in which soldiers should be placed in accordance with the Royal Order on Infantry Exercise 1 January 1766'
Engraving made from drawings by Gravelot on handling the musket for firing
80cm × 31cm
Bibliothèque Raoul et Jean Brunon, Salon-de-Provence, Bouches du Rhône

443
Drum of the Régiment de Languedoc-Infanterie
Painted wood; blue background strewn with large yellow fleurs-de-lys, and on the front, the Arms of France with flags and cannon
Musée de l'Empéri, Salon-de-Provence, Bouches du Rhône

The first detachment of the regiment left Brest at the end of 1778 for the West Indies. A second detachment arrived in Boston with the Boulonnais in June 1781, as replacements (see item 440).

444
Parade tools: pick and shovel
Musée de l'Empéri, Salon-de-Provence, Bouches du Rhône

These are symbolic parade tools of carpenter-soldiers, dated towards the end of the 18th century.

445
'Orders which the King has issued for the provisional regulation of the exercise of his infantry troops. 30 May 1775'
Book of 145 pages, accompanied by twenty-six folding plates
Bibliothèque Raoul et Jean Brunon, Salon-de-Provence, Bouches du Rhône

446
Collection of orders of 1779, bound in leather, concerning the new regulations on distinguishing colours for the infantry
Bibliothèque Raoul et Jean Brunon, Salon-de-Provence, Bouches du Rhône

The book contains the crimson facings of the Régiment de Hainaut.

447
'Uniforms of the French infantry according to the regulations signed by the King on 25 April 1767.'
Paris. A series of 101 coloured engravings by Lattré, 'engraver-in-ordinary to Monseigneur le Dauphin, rue Saint-Jacques...'
Bibliothèque Raoul et Jean Brunon, Salon-de-Provence, Bouches du Rhône

448
Hussar officer's sabre
Louis XVI period. Guard and fittings in gilt chased bronze. Pommel and fittings of the scabbard adorned with trophies. Blue steel blade decorated with gilt motifs: 'Vivat hussard', and 'Ier Rgt d'Hussards'. Sword-knot in silver thread. Sword belt in red morocco embroidered with a course of rings of silver thread. Buckle with a lion's head
Musée de l'Empéri, Salon-de-Provence, Bouches du Rhône

449
Hussar's sabre
Period of Louis XVI. Guard and trimmings in brass. Engraving on blade: 'Vivat hussard', the Arms of France and 'Vive Le Roy'
Musée de l'Empéri, Salon-de-Provence, Bouches du Rhône

450
Cavalry musket
Model of 1763–6; adapted with the addition of a bayonet for the Corps of Mounted Constabulary
Musée de l'Empéri, Salon-de-Provence, Bouches du Rhône

451
Cavalry pistol
Model of 1763–6. This is one of a second series of
manufacture dated 1776. Made in Saint-Etienne
Musée de l'Empéri, Salon-de-Provence, Bouches du Rhône

452
Cavalry pistol
Model of 1777, manufactured in Saint-Etienne
Musée de l'Empéri, Salon-de-Provence, Bouches du Rhône

This model was adopted later by the United States
as a regulation weapon.

453
Mounted constabulary pistol
Model of 1770. Manufactured at Maubeuge
Musée de l'Empéri, Salon-de-Provence, Bouches du Rhône

454
Hussar of the Régiment de Lauzun
Lieutenant Barbier

c. 1789. Watercolour
40 cm × 30 cm
*Bibliothèque Raoul et Jean Brunon, Salon-de-Provence,
Bouches du Rhône*

Two hundred and eighty hussars in all formed the
only cavalry unit of the French forces in America.
They belonged to the Volontaires Etrangers de
Lauzun of the army of Rochambeau. They took part
in the battles of the York river and won fame at the
siege of Gloucester against Tarleton as well as at Yorktown. After Rochambeau's departure, they served
under the direct orders of Washington until 1783.

455
Hussar bridle
Late 18th century. Hungarian-type fitting, lead
ornaments
Musée de l'Empéri, Salon-de-Provence, Bouches du Rhône

[However great the impact of the French army on the
American Revolution, it was the French navy which
set Britain the greatest problems. The combined fleets
of France and Spain could outnumber the British, and
this fact alone induced hesitation in Admiralty decisions when clear-cut action was required. However
many ships were needed in American waters, invasion
threats in the Channel prompted great caution in the
allocation of existing squadrons.]

442

454

456
Naval sabre
c. 1760–80. Guard formed by an 'L' (monogram of Louis XVI) and an anchor interlocked. Blade with engraved decoration of a sun, a moon, and a signature: 'Cassagnard à Nantes'
Musée de l'Empéri, Salon-de-Provence, Bouches du Rhône

457
Sabre of the Navy and of the French marines
Model of 1772. Guard in moulded copper
Musée de l'Empéri, Salon-de-Provence, Bouches du Rhône

458
Naval pistol
Model of 1779, with belt hook
35cm long
Musée de l'Empéri, Salon-de-Provence, Bouches du Rhône

459
Naval blunderbuss
c. 1780, with earlier lock of 1777
Musée de l'Empéri, Salon-de-Provence, Bouches du Rhône

The pivoting fork of a blunderbuss enabled it to be rested on the bulwark of a ship. The gun had a short range but it could fire a volley of missiles.

460
Fragments of ship ornaments
18th century. Gilded wood, from the Arsenal of Toulon
Musée de la Marine, Paris

461
Model of machine for drilling cannon
1779. Wood, steel and brass
49cm high
Musée de la Marine, Paris

462
Pivoted mortar in bronze
18th century. Wooden cap
39cm high
Musée de la Marine, Paris

463
Small compass
1778. The work of J. Charles Chesse at La Rochelle
Musée de la Marine, Paris

464
Astronomical aid to navigation
1772. Wood and brass
8·5cm in diameter
Musée de la Marine, Paris

465
Magnet of Admiral Comte d'Estaing
Brass and iron
Musée de la Marine, Paris

This loadstone, belonging to the French admiral who fought three actions with the British, was used by him to remagnetise compasses on board his ships.

466
Shipyard on the Thames
John Cleveley

1762. Oil on canvas. Signed lower left corner: 'I: Cleveley. 1762.'
55·3cm × 95·1cm
Glasgow Museums and Art Galleries

Cleveley's view of the Thames below London takes in a shipyard on the far bank, with a man-of-war on the stocks and the dockside to the left loaded with timber.

To construct a ship the size of the *Royal George*, one of Britain's largest, required 5739½ cartloads of oak, elm and fir. Each cartload carried the amount of timber cut from a full-grown oak.

By the end of 1777 the Royal Navy had forty-two ships in commission at home, thirty-five of them manned for sea. In one year the navy had converted twenty Channel guardships into a fighting force more than twice that size.

467
The Dockyard at Deptford
Richard Paton

1775. Oil on canvas
101·6cm × 147·3cm
Her Majesty the Queen

With the dockyard on the right, the view embraces a Royal yacht firing a salute, a barge with the Royal Standard near it, St Alfege Church in the middle distance, and, on the bend of the river, the Greenwich Hospital reaching down to the banks of the Thames as it does today. The site of the '1776' Exhibition, where the Royal palace and manor grounds once stretched, lies behind the Hospital.

Waging War at Sea

THE WAR AT SEA was neither a phase nor an aspect of the American Revolution but the fundamental fact on which the operations, even the land campaigns, were based. A sea battle, more than any other single action, gave the United States their independence. 'It was the Battle of the Chesapeake Bay,' wrote my predecessor, Sir Geoffrey Callender, 'which decided the final issue of the war, crowned the work of Washington and reduced to ashes our grandiose ambition to keep North America under the Crown.'

A fleet is both ships and men, each needing tending. Supplies (naval stores), pitch and tar, hemp and canvas, mast and spar timber to maintain the wooden sailing ships' hulls, masts, yards and rigging were even more vital than the powder and shot for the guns. The men needed food, such as it was, and drink, including large quantities of alcohol, and the outbreak of hostilities found the British navy, victorious in the recent wars with France, in a sadly run-down state, with none of the essentials in ready or plentiful supply. The near fatal disease of maladministration sapped what supplies of money and stores there were. Dockyard officers, contractors, Admiralty and Navy Board officials, workmen, clerks, even Their Lordships, were infected with it. But France, who in the last war had lost her America through a similar disease, had taken the warning and did not let her ships and seamen languish.

Of course, the British found the power to make good some of the defects, to keep the fleet at sea, manned, victualled and stored. Supreme effort in adversity has more than once in British history saved, if not the day, at least the war. The man of the moment was Sir Charles Middleton, better known by his title of Lord Barham, who was from 1778 the Comptroller of the Navy in charge of supplies and the shipbuilding programme, and later to become Admiral and First Lord. He stirred up the sluggish and defective administration so that commanders-in-chief might be able to rely on what ships they had, and the Commissioners at home should bring their dockyards into effective production.

At sea there were famous names, well known already, destined to become more renowned. Richard Kempenfelt, seaman and scholar, devised a much-needed signal system based on pairs of numbered flags and what he had absorbed of the pioneer work of the Frenchman, de Villehuet. This system was adopted in 1778 by the commander-in-chief on the North American station, Lord Howe, who also

facing page: item 470
(detail)

urgently felt that same lack of communication. In 1782 the two admirals were able to introduce an improved and enlarged version of the signal book in the Channel fleet, but Kempenfelt was lost almost at once in the tragic sinking of the *Royal George*.

Admiral Lord Howe, patrician, leader, tactician, disciple of Hawke in the previous war, was also an innovator. He had sought a way in which admirals could communicate with their fleet to free them from the dead hand of the printed Fighting Instructions, which, after a hundred years, had begun to cramp initiative. He introduced a signal book of his own for his North American squadron in 1776. He also acquired the doubtful distinction of being the first Admiral to be attacked by a submarine, for his flagship, H.M.S. *Eagle*, was the target of American inventive genius in the shape of David Bushnell's underwater weapon of 1776.

Sir George Brydges Rodney, senior to Howe and already a rear-admiral by the end of the last war in 1763, was not universally popular but had a reputation as a fighter and a man of energy. The Hon. Augustus Keppel, also rear-admiral, another of Hawke's dashing captains, Sir Samuel Hood, who was Commissioner of Portsmouth Dockyard in 1778 and became an able second to Rodney, and the Hon. Samuel Barrington, who was in command in the West Indies in the same year, were all men of mark.

In addition to the obvious task of supporting the army, convoying its supplies and covering its positions near the coast, it was often the navy's task to move military forces by sea, since land communications were poor and ran through hostile country. There were never enough ships, and on top of this was the need to blockade and control that vast eastern coastline, to try to stop colonial shipping. The task was almost impossible. After a time practically all the army's supplies had to come in ships from Europe, and the Americans, who were in part a maritime people with an extensive fishery and coasting trade, proved themselves adept at privateering warfare, where small, heavily armed and manned merchant vessels cruised on the lookout for the enemy's merchantmen and transports. The privateers did not operate only on the western side of the Atlantic. They demonstrated the beginnings of true sea power and were encountered as fierce marauders around the British coasts. It is appropriate that the resourceful and troublesome John Paul Jones is sometimes called the father of the United States Navy.

The intervention of France added to the scale of operations and made the sea conflict one of oceanic warfare and the strategy of fleets. Powerful squadrons appearing off a coast could profoundly influence events on land, and American operations were near the seat of Britain's most valuable West Indies trade. Maintaining prosperity at home and appeasing the vocal merchants' lobby were both essential and, with the entry of Spain in 1779 and Holland the following year, the campaigns for the sugar islands were waged with vigour in the appropriate season, the hurricane exercising its influence from time to time. Garrisons surrendered and islands changed hands, but in the meantime the convoys of laden merchantmen continued under the protection of the fleets of both sides.

Against the combined naval force of its enemies, the British navy in this war was latterly a numerically inferior force and its strategy was therefore a defensive one. The Fleet in Being, the concentration of fighting ships in a state of preparedness, prevented invasion of the homeland, relieved besieged outposts, like Gibraltar, and covered the arrival and departure of the vital deep-sea merchant ships. Again and again events turned on the passage of merchant vessels from all parts in convoy through the dangerous coastal areas where enemy squadrons could be expected and where privateers operated.

The chief naval adversary, supporter and champion of the aspiring Colonists, was France, whose commanders afloat, d'Estaing, for example, and de Grasse, were men of great calibre. Barrington outwitted the former and secured the fortified island of St Lucia as a valuable haven for the Royal Navy right on the doorstep of France's main base at Martinique. From there Sir George Rodney was to be able to operate, and eventually to crush de Grasse off the little islands in the Antilles called Les Saintes. The glorious 12 April 1782 was celebrated in song and verse, in china, silver and pretty objects for fashionable people to wear.

Unhappily, Thomas Graves, the British admiral commanding the squadron sent to relieve the pressure on General Cornwallis's position in Virginia in 1781, had neither the determination to make the most of his opportunities, and they were good, nor the means of making his orders, conveyed by flag signal, unmistakeable. To captains schooled in the old-established tactics of the Line of Battle, it was unthinkable to interpret a meaning. Never, it has been said, was adherence to the letter of the law, in this case the Admiralty's printed Instructions, more fatal than off the Chesapeake in 1781. The surrender at Yorktown followed three weeks after, and there were no celebrations or commemoration of that event on the British side.

BASIL GREENHILL

468
Captain Squire, Royal Marines, *c*.1760–*c*.1796
J. S. Copley

c. 1780. Oil on canvas
76 cm × 64 cm
Sigmund Samuel Canadiana Collection
Royal Ontario Museum, Toronto

This portrait of a marine in the uniform of the period
is rare. The subject is Captain Edward Squire, who
was appointed a second lieutenant with a Chatham
company in 1778, a first lieutenant in 1780 in a Portsmouth company, and promoted to captain on 1 May
1795. He died in the West Indies in about 1796.

Many army regiments were drafted to various
British fleets to play the part of marines, but the
marines themselves saw action in America at Lexington, Bunker Hill and in the Southern Campaign. And
because of the nature of the Caribbean, the marines
were heavily involved in the many battles of the West
Indies.

469
Admiral James Gambier, 1723–89
J. S. Copley

Signed and dated in the lower right corner:
'J. S. Copley 1773 Boston'. Oil on canvas
127 cm × 101·6 cm
Miss Amelia Peabody, Boston, Massachusetts

From 1770 to 1773, Gambier served as commander-
in-chief on the North American station. He was
typical of those long-serving naval officers more distinguished for their steadfastness than for their
panache in battle. From July 1773 onwards Gambier
filled posts back in England for an Admiralty that
never seemed to trust him with high commands in
battle areas. Promoted to rear-admiral in January
1778, Gambier was sent to New York as second-in-
command to Lord Howe. There, much to his disgust,
he was made Port Admiral of New York.

Admiral Gambier's complaint, in the winter of
1777–8, that the army demanded protection for
almost every move it made, however insignificant,
exemplified the conflicting duties of the Royal Navy
in the American Revolution. It was asked to blockade
the American coastline against foreign supplies
reaching the Rebels; to support and transport the
army in its campaigns; and, after 1778, to be in a
constant state of readiness against the appearance of
French and Spanish fleets. In May 1776 there were
fifty-nine British ships on the American station, with

485 (detail)

468

a fair percentage of those always in harbour for repairs. This force had to control more than 1500 miles of hostile shoreline.

Copley's portrait shows a New England farming scene in the lower left corner with a typical Dutch type of barn.

470
The engagement between the 'Quebec' and the 'Surveillante'
After Rossel

Copy of 1789. Oil on canvas
115 cm × 163 cm
Musée de la Marine, Paris

Much marine painting concerns itself with battle scenes of an almost impersonal nature. This French canvas, however, carries the full impact of the war at sea.

The Royal Navy frigate, the *Quebec* (32 guns), encountered the French frigate, *La Surveillante* (32 guns), off Ushant, close to Brittany, on 4 October 1779. What followed was one of the most violent engagements of the war. The two ships, commanded by Captain George Farmer and the Baron du Couëdic de Kergoualer, were at one moment locked together, pouring broadsides into each other.

After two-and-a-half hours both ships were totally dismasted, but in the case of the *Quebec*, her sails fell across the gunports, blocking the view of the English gunners. Eventually the sails caught alight, the fire spread through the frigate, and the *Surveillante* just managed to free herself before the *Quebec* blew up. Those English seamen who were saved by the *Surveillante* then had to struggle alongside their captors to get what was left of the French frigate back to Brest. Captain Farmer was killed in the action. Du Couëdic died of his wounds three months later.

This picture was copied from an original by the Marquis de Rossel, a French naval captain with great expertise as a marine painter.

471
The London press-gang
This photo-mural shows a detail from a satire on the London press-gangs, 'The Liberty of the Subject', by James Gillray. It is a well-aimed attack on the naval system of recruitment, with all its horrors of family separation.

This method of recruitment was forced on the navy by the fact that the fleet was never kept up to strength in peacetime, and, faced with sudden

486

emergencies, there were never enough volunteers forthcoming. Whatever the life of a soldier, life at sea was even harsher. At a time of naval mobilisation, the steps to be taken included the issuing of warrants empowering officers to take those who 'used the sea'. The pressing of able-bodied landsmen was not the usual practice.

A typical press-gang is represented by Lieutenant Reddish who established a rendezvous (or a 'Rondy') at the Red Lion at Godalming on the Portsmouth road in 1782. He was assisted by a midshipman aged forty-two, who had never been to sea, and a gang of eight men, mostly agricultural labourers. He raised only 155 men in three years at a cost of £1618.

In 1779, 1019 officers and men were employed on shore with the impressment service. They raised 21,367 men at a cost of £106,591. 5s. 1d.

This engraving of 1779, by Gillray, is reproduced by permission of the Trustees of the British Museum, where the original is to be found.

472
Man-of-war flying before the wind

Seldom in a marine picture does one see an entire crew working in a peacetime setting. This rare picture, a detail from a crayon drawing by the French artist, Ozanne, shows something of the frightening conditions under which most seamen would have worked. The original picture, found in the Musée de la Marine in Paris, is called 'A ship flying before the wind', and it shows a vessel with all its yards manned in an attempt to lower and secure almost all the sails before damage occurs. Ozanne has captured with extraordinary sensitivity the power of the elements which both animated and endangered ships at sea.

473
Ship's equipment salvaged from the sunken 'Royal George'
Three blocks, four sheaves, deep sea line block, lead numbers
National Maritime Museum, Greenwich, London

The *Royal George* (100 guns), built in 1756, was one of the great ships of the Revolution. She had been Hawke's flagship in the victory of Quiberon Bay in the Seven Years War in 1759, and she had taken part in Rodney's action during a relief of Gibraltar in 1780.

In dramatic circumstances (through a fault of her structure), the *Royal George* sank suddenly at anchor at Spithead in August 1782, with the loss of 900 lives including that of Rear-Admiral Kempenfelt. These

recovered objects give some small idea of the equipment of the ships of the time.

474
James Jameson's brass speaking trumpet
47 cm long
Scottish United Services Museum, Edinburgh

This aid to issuing orders on board, and from ship to ship, belonged to the seaman who was Nelson's sailing master from 1777 to 1786.

475
Brass model of a carronade
1779
19.7 cm long
Scottish United Services Museum, Edinburgh

Early in 1779, Scottish artillery officer General Melville invented a new form of cannon. Known first as the 'smasher', it soon took its name from its place of manufacture – the Carron Iron Works at Falkirk, Scotland.

The carronade could discharge a much heavier ball from a barrel which was shorter than usual although it was fired by a lighter charge. Its gunners relied on the weight of the ball, rather than on its impetus, to do the damage. The angle of the barrel was governed by a screw rather than the old wedge of the earlier cannon. The new gun suited the British style of close-in fighting. By 1781 there were said to be 604 carronades in service.

476
Sea service flintlock pistol
Model 1760–96. Steel, brass and wood
48.3 cm long
Scottish United Services Museum, Edinburgh

477
Royal Navy pistol
c. 1770. Inscribed on lock: 'Tower'. With belt hook
Musée de l'Empéri, Salon-de-Provence, Bouches du Rhône

478
Five boarding pikes
Washington Navy Yard Museum, Washington, D.C.

These were used to repel boarders or to attack the seamen of ships alongside.

479
One boarding pike
Late 18th century. Wood and steel
238.8 cm long
Scottish United Services Museum, Edinburgh

480
One boarding pike
National Maritime Museum, Greenwich, London

481
Two navy cutlasses
Iron and bone
Blade lengths: 74·9 cm and 71·7 cm
Guthman Collection, Westport, Connecticut

482
A naval cutlass
Mr Francis A. Lord, Columbia, South Carolina

483
Blue and white Staffordshire bowl
7·6 cm high, 19 cm diameter
Private collection

This patriotic naval souvenir aimed at lending Olympian stature to 18th-century top-ranking naval personnel:

> May all British
> ADMIRALS
> have the Eye of a
> HAWKE
> the Heart of a
> WOLFE
> and the Spirit of a
> RODNEY

484
Captain Sir Richard Pearson
Charles Grignion

1780. Oil on canvas
91·5 cm × 71·1 cm
National Maritime Museum, Greenwich, London

Captain Richard Pearson, in command of the *Serapis* on the afternoon of 23 September 1779, was escorting forty-one ships of a Baltic convoy towards the Yorkshire coast. The ships were carrying supplies and timber for the Royal Navy. The *Serapis*, rated at 44 guns but actually carrying fifty, was accompanied by the *Countess of Scarborough* (22 guns), and had the responsibility of seeing the convoy safely through.

Towards three o'clock, Pearson saw to the south, near Flamborough Head, the outlines of a ship heading towards him. The vessel was flying the British flag, but it was in fact the Rebel frigate, the *Bonhomme Richard*, commanded by John Paul Jones. Because of

adverse winds, the American frigate did not close with the *Serapis* until well after six in the evening, when the *Bonhomme Richard* struck the Union flag, raised one with red, white and blue stripes, and the battle began.

For three-and-a-half hours the two ships manoeuvred, shooting each other almost to a standstill, until, with the *Bonhomme Richard* sinking under him, John Paul Jones boarded the *Serapis* and forced Pearson to strike his flag.

A day later the *Bonhomme Richard* sank. Pearson and the remains of his crew were later released. Jones, now on the *Serapis*, sailed to the Texel, off the Dutch coast, where he was received by Europe as a hero.

Richard Pearson was also received as a hero. He was court-martialled, acquitted, and later knighted; for despite his own loss, he had saved the Baltic convoy. John Paul Jones's reaction was characteristically sardonic: 'Should I have the good fortune to fall in with him again,' he said, 'I'll make a lord of him.'

485
'Bonhomme Richard' and H.M.S. 'Serapis'
Thomas Mitchell

Signed lower right, 'Mitchell 1780'. Oil on canvas
53·3 cm × 71·1 cm
United States Naval Academy Museum,
Annapolis, Maryland

Mitchell exhibited a painting of this naval battle at the Free Society of Artists in 1780 and at the Royal Academy in 1781.

John Paul Jones, when he first encountered the *Serapis*, was accompanied by a small squadron of American and French vessels – the *Pallas*, *Vengeance* and *Alliance*. The first two played little part in the main action, but at one point the *Alliance* turned up and began firing in the general direction of the battle, only to blast John Paul Jones.

The *Serapis* is seen in this picture sandwiched between the *Bonhomme Richard* and the *Alliance*. In the distance, beneath the moon, lies Flamborough Head.

486
Bust of John Paul Jones, 1747–92
Jean Antoine Houdon

Marked under the subject's right shoulder,
'houdon 1780'. Plaster
71·1 cm high; 30·5 cm deep; 55·9 cm wide
United States Naval Academy Museum,
Annapolis, Maryland

A bust of Jones was commissioned from Houdon in Paris in 1780. Subsequently the sculptor and his studio were responsible for one marble copy and several plaster copies in the 18th century. Many plaster and bronze copies have been made since, but none of them shows the delicacy of line, as this one does, of the earlier busts.

John Paul Jones was born the son of a gardener in Kirkbean, Kirkcudbrightshire, in July 1747. He first went to sea from Whitehaven, and settled in America on a deceased brother's property in 1773. His real name was John Paul and at this time he added the 'Jones'. With the outbreak of hostilities he offered himself to the American Continental navy for a commission to serve at sea.

His first adventures in British waters were with the *Ranger* from which he took prizes in the Irish Sea. He then landed at Whitehaven, and stole the silver from the Countess of Selkirk while the Earl was away in London. After his success with the *Bonhomme Richard*, John Paul Jones's career was a sad one. He had unparalleled style as a sea captain, but lacked the personality to harness his gifts to greater commands. He served with the Russian navy, that period too a failure, before he died in Paris in 1792.

487
Miniature of John Paul Jones
Constance de Lowendal Turpin de Crissé

1780. Watercolour on ivory
Oval; 6·3 cm × 5·6 cm
National Portrait Gallery, Smithsonian Institution, Washington, D.C.

488
Quadrant and box container of John Paul Jones
Quadrant: brass, reflecting mirror, and two sunglasses; marked 'Simon Graham'
29·8 cm × 30·5 cm
Wooden case: 34·3 cm × 30·5 cm × 7·3 cm deep
United States Naval Academy Museum, Annapolis, Maryland

The interior of the case is painted with two scenes. The first shows John Paul Jones striking a sailor as the man attempts to pull down the flag of the *Bonhomme Richard*. The second shows a man with top hat and telescope pointing to a ship at sea (presumably one of Jones's).

The quadrant is said to have come from the estate of John Paul Jones to his aunt in Scotland, and to have been given to her nephew, Simon Graham.

489
Musket taken from the 'Serapis' by John Paul Jones and given to Benjamin Franklin
1762, made by Edge. Decorative brass mounts
Overall length, 51¾ inches (131·4 cm);
barrel length, 36½ inches (92·6 cm)
Georgia Historical Society, Savannah

COUNTING THE CANNON
Naval ships were divided into six rates according to the number of guns they carried. First rates, with 100 guns or more (like the *Royal George*), and second rates, with between 90 and 98 guns, were fairly rare but most powerful, with their three decks of cannon. They were often used as the flagships of senior officers.

The standard ship of the Revolution period was the third rate, with between 64 and 84 guns, constructed for the most part as a two-decker – the workhorse of the fleet. All three rates were considered powerful enough to be in the forefront of battle; they were known as 'ships of the line'.

The frigate was the favourite command of the junior officer. She was fast, worked as escort, scout or messenger carrier (like the *Serapis*), and armed with between 28 and 40 cannon. The Revolution was the scene of very few set-piece battles (Rhode Island, the Chesapeake, the Saints, Gibraltar, etc.), but the one-to-one engagement between opposing frigates was a fairly regular event.

Once the Admiralty machine had lumbered into motion, the build-up of Royal Navy ships in the Revolution was impressive. At its outbreak Britain had 340 ships in service and had mustered 15,062 men. By 1783, under the pressure of what had become a world war, the figures had grown to 617 ships carrying 107,446 seamen.

In a classic battle, with opposing forces sailing past each other, line astern, the British, with a fleet of, say, thirty ships of the line and Europe's fastest gunners, poured out broadsides from 1000 guns at a time.

490
Model of H.M.S. 'Lion'
Contemporary model on launching skids, flying pre-launching flags
121·9 cm long; 61 cm high; 30·5 cm across beam
Dorset County Museums, Dorchester

The *Lion* itself was built in 1777, a two-decker of 64 guns. Five years later she was commanded by Captain W. Fooks in the Delaware, where she scored a notable victory later in the war over a French opponent.

The model is seen flying the usual pre-launching flags, normally five in number – the Union flag at the bow, the Admiralty flag, the Royal Standard, a second Union flag, and, at the stern, the Red or White ensign according to squadron.

After being launched in this state a ship would be towed by rowing boats to a fitting-out berth where masts would be placed in position and the ship rigged, and guns and supplies would be taken on board for her first trip to sea.

491
Sword surrendered by French captain to commander of H.M.S. 'Lion'
With bird-head hilt finial and decorated guard
81·3cm long
Dorset County Museums, Dorchester

This sword belonged to the Comte de la Touche, commander of *L'Aigle*, who surrendered it to Captain Fooks after the battle on the Delaware on 15 September 1782.

492
Model of 'Hercules' or 'Thunderer' class
Contemporary model
175 cm long; 148 cm high; 79 cm wide
National Maritime Museum, Greenwich, London

This model has been specially rigged for the exhibition. The hull and masts etc. are of the period, and if the model is of the *Hercules* (these classes resemble each other closely), she was a third rate with 74 guns. The *Hercules* herself saw action at the Battle of the Saints, close to a French group of small islands called Les Saintes in the Caribbean, in April 1782.

493
Model of H.M.S. 'Romulus' (?)
Probably *c.* 1799
213·4cm high; 243·8 cm long; 76·2 cm wide
Montagu Ventures Limited and the National Trust at Buckler's Hard Maritime Museum, Beaulieu, Hampshire

The model, normally seen at Buckler's Hard on loan from the National Trust, was reputed to be a replica of H.M.S. *Romulus*, 44 guns, launched at Buckler's Hard by Henry Adams in 1777. An investigation of the lines and dimensions made at the museum proves the ship to be at least a frigate of the late 18th century. It is a fine representation of the role the Hampshire New Forest region played during the Revolution: thirty-two men-of-war were built in the Southampton area during the period.

494
Model of the American Continental frigate 'Confederacy'
Model built 1971–2
119·4cm high; 167·6cm long; 68·6cm wide
Division of Naval History, Smithsonian Institution, Washington, D.C.

Twenty-one frigates were purchased or built for the Continental navy between 1775 and 1783. Five of them were sold at the end of the war; the rest were captured or destroyed by the British.

The original of this model was built at Norwich, Connecticut, in 1778 and captured by H.M.S. *Orpheus* and H.M.S. *Roebuck* off the Delaware Capes, taken into the Royal Navy and renamed the *Confederate*.

This model was constructed by Robert V. Bruckshaw of Norwalk, Ohio.

495
Continental Congress broadside permitting American privateering
3 April 1776. Printed notice with name of John Hancock, President of Congress
35·5 cm × 23·5cm
Ref: PRO HCA 32/4/75/14
Public Record Office, London

On 23 March 1776, Congress passed a privateering resolution which was then published as a broadside. The key part of the resolution included the words: 'the inhabitants of these colonies be permitted to fit out armed vessels to cruise on the enemies of these united colonies'.

In the first two years of the Revolution it is reckoned that the Rebels put 136 privateers to sea. By 1781 there were 449 in action. Privateers and Continental navy ships took prisoner about 16,000 British seamen. The House of Lords was told in February 1778 that American privateers had captured or destroyed 733 British prizes, with cargoes valued at over £2 million.

496
British frigate with four captured American merchantmen
Francis Holman

Signed and dated: 'F. Holman 1778'. Oil on canvas
101·6cm × 165·1cm
National Maritime Museum, Greenwich, London

The taking of prizes by both regular naval ships and privateers was not confined to the Rebels. The scene in the Holman picture shows the British ship, centre, with a figure, most likely the captain, standing in the middle of the deck. With the British vessel are four American prizes each flying the Union flag over the Rebel striped flag. They are anchored, or anchoring, off a strip of unidentified American coastline.

497
Admiral Peter Rainier, *c.* 1741–1808
Mather Brown

c. 1783–7. Oil on canvas
76·2 cm × 63·5 cm
Museum of Fine Arts, Boston, Massachusetts

Rainier was born in Sandwich, Kent, and entered the Royal Navy in 1756. He was promoted to the rank of lieutenant in 1768 but was not involved in sea service until he was appointed to the *Maidstone* in 1774 in the West Indies. In May 1777, he was promoted to the command of the sloop *Ostrich*, and in her, on 8 July 1778, in a hard-fought action during which he was severely wounded, he captured a large Rebel privateer.

Rainier was promoted to the rank of captain in 1778, and his portrait must have been painted either late in 1778, or between the years of 1783 and 1787 when he was in England. He wound up a distinguished career in the East Indies, where at one time he was commander-in-chief.

498
Commodore Abraham Whipple, 1733–1819
Edward Savage

1786. Oil on canvas. Signed on pillar, top centre: 'Painted in Charleston (South Carolina), May 9, 1786, E. Savage pinx 1786'
198·1 cm × 134·6 cm
United States Naval Academy Museum, Annapolis, Maryland

Abraham Whipple, born in Providence, Rhode Island, had little formal education and soon chose a seafaring career. He commanded the privateer *Game Cock* towards the end of the Seven Years War and in a six-month cruise captured twenty-three French ships. In 1772, with fifty men, he burned the British schooner *Gaspée*, which had run aground while on patrol against American smugglers.

In 1775, when the Rhode Island General Assembly agreed to set up the first ships of its own navy, the colony turned to Whipple to command the miniature fleet. Later, in Philadelphia, his ship the *Katy* was taken into the Continental navy and he was appointed a captain. Almost always in some sort of action, in

496

497

1779 he was entrusted with the defence of Charleston in South Carolina, where he used most of the cannon on his small squadron to arm the city. When Clinton captured Charleston in May 1780, Whipple was taken prisoner. Paroled later, he was sent to Chester in Pennsylvania, where he spent the rest of the war.

It was Rhode Island's own lead in forming a tiny navy and the colony's resolutions to Congress which brought about the birth of the first Continental navy. In a sense Rhode Island and Commodore Whipple were the founders of a great tradition.

499
The British occupy Rhode Island
Robert Cleveley

1777. Watercolour
55.9 cm × 83.8 cm
National Maritime Museum, Greenwich, London

As the final phases of the New York campaign were drawing to a close with the retreat of Washington south through the Jerseys and his crossing of the Delaware into Pennsylvania, the British army was striking north to another success. Clinton, with 6000 men, occupied Rhode Island with no opposition on 6 December 1776.

The Royal Navy needed this deep, easily defended harbour for the fleet. The rivers of New York, likely to ice over, were not the best winter anchorage for Admiral Howe's ships.

In Cleveley's watercolour British ships are lying close inshore for a bombardment to cover the boats rowing in from the transports with men and supplies.

500
'Destaing Shewing how he Cut the Englishmens heads off'
24 February 1780. Engraving, 'Pub by E Hedges Royal Exchange' and 'Pub by T. Colby Portsmouth Street Clare Market'
25.4 cm × 20.3 cm
Ref: BM Add. 479
Trustees of the British Museum, London

'There me had him,' cries the 18th-century Englishman's idea of a French admiral: pigtail like a bullwhip, lace frills at the wrist and chest. The Comte d'Estaing's career in the American Revolution was not very distinguished. The engraving refers to those victories he enjoyed in 1779 in the West Indies, where his forces captured St Vincent and Grenada.

There me had him.

DESTAING
— *Shewing how he Cut the Englishmens heads off*

501
Bust of the Comte d'Estaing, 1729–94
Huguenin

Early 19th century. Marble
81 cm high; 61 cm wide
Musée de la Marine, Paris

Charles Hector Théodat, the Comte d'Estaing, was born in the Auvergne. He was first commissioned in the French army, and subsequently captured in India during the Seven Years War, when he was imprisoned in Portsmouth before being released.

This experience no doubt strengthened his bitterness towards the English, a feeling in no way eased by the attitude of Admiral Boscawen, commander-in-chief in India. If he ever caught d'Estaing, he said, he would 'chain him up on the quarter-deck and treat him like a baboon'.

D'Estaing, confusingly, was appointed a lieutenant-general in the French navy in 1763, but then became a vice-admiral in 1777. On 13 April 1778, he sailed from Toulon and after a very slow crossing of eighty-seven days his fleet arrived off the Delaware.

Contemporary Frenchmen held d'Estaing's strategic expertise in fairly low regard, a view shared by the Rebels with whom he fought. He failed to bring Admiral Lord Howe to battle off New York in July 1778; he was outmanoeuvred by Howe at Rhode Island before a storm broke up the impending battle in August of that same year. And despite his victories in the West Indies in the middle of 1779, at the siege of Savannah, his forces were driven back in a fierce action in which the British saved the city and d'Estaing himself was severely wounded.

He was executed during the French Revolution.

502
Nine-pounder cannon recovered from H.M.S. 'Cerberus' sunk at Rhode Island
236 cm long
State of Rhode Island and the University of Rhode Island

On 5 August 1778, as a prelude to the full Rebel attack on Rhode Island, the French admiral, Suffren, sailed through the East Passage into Rhode Island harbour. With French ships now outside in the Atlantic and others cutting off retreat further into the harbour, the small British squadron of ships trapped there was faced with three choices: (a) to surrender, adding more ships to the French navy; (b) to fight, with the knowledge that the French ships of the line would blast the British out of the water; (c) to scuttle. They chose the third.

That day the 32-gun frigates *Cerberus, Juno, Orpheus* and *Lark*, the 16-gun *Kingfisher* and the *Pigot* galley were all run aground and burnt by their captains. Other British ships scuttled to bar the entrance to Newport harbour itself.

Three years ago a team from the University of Rhode Island, under Professor Joel Cohen and Mr A. Davies, began searching for the wrecks. With the help of a ship's log, the divers were able to locate the *Cerberus*. The sea-bed, it was reported, was covered with cannon and artefacts from these 18th-century British frigates.

It seemed most appropriate that Anglo-American co-operation should be celebrated in this exhibition (after all, such co-operation was the ultimate outcome of this war) by bringing back to Britain one of the *Cerberus*'s cannon and a selection of everyday objects to show something of life on board a British vessel during the American Revolution.

Joint action was agreed. Mr Davies and his divers brought two cannon up from the floor of the harbour. The American minesweeper *Direct* took them from Newport to Halifax, Nova Scotia, where H.M.S. *Minerva* accepted them and sailed them from Halifax to Portsmouth. There they were conserved in the laboratories of Portsmouth Museums by a method unique to Britain.

The first cannon is on display here and will stay in the National Maritime Museum on permanent loan from the State of Rhode Island. The second has gone back to the State to be exhibited there. After 200 years, the story of that day in August 1778 grows more vivid.

503
Boston, Capital of the United States
Pierre Ozanne

Boston, 1778. Pen and ink. Inscriptions read: 'Campagne du Vice-Amiral Cte d'Estaing en Amérique, Commandant une Escadre de 12 vaisseaux et de 4 frégattes, sortie de Toulon le 13 Avril 1778 No XII', and 'Boston capitale des Etats-Unis de l'Amérique Septentrionale Vue de la Rade nommée Kings Road'
29·5 cm × 61 cm
Metropolitan Museum of Art, New York

Boston, recovered from its battle scars of three years earlier, is shown here in a peaceful scene dominated by a small American vessel firing a salute as it enters the harbour.

Calling Boston the 'capital' is an error of a French officer, Pierre Ozanne, official artist and engineer of d'Estaing's fleet. The Count used Boston only once, in 1778, after the Rhode Island storm had damaged his ships and they needed repairs.

504
D'Estaing's squadron entering the harbour at Newport, Rhode Island
Pierre Ozanne

Newport, 1778. Pen and ink. Inscription reads: 'L'Escadre francoise entrant dans Newport sous le feu des Batteries en forcant le passage le 8 Aoust 1778. Jour que les Américains passerent sur l'Isle de Rode Island par le chemin d'howland's Ferry.'
24·1 cm × 40 cm
Ref: LC-USZ62-900
Library of Congress, Washington, D.C.

This pen and ink sketch is one of the Ozanne series (see item 503) which recorded the Comte d'Estaing's participation in the naval warfare of the American Revolution. It shows his fleet forcing the Middle Passage into Narragansett Bay, the main anchorage.

Beyond the island on the right lies the site where, surprised by the unexpected approach of the French, British frigates had been fired and scuttled three days earlier. Newport itself, which was occupied by the British, lies to the extreme right.

505
'Lord Howe and the Compte d'Estaing off Rhode Island, August 9th, 1778'
R. Wilkins

Undated. Oil on canvas
52 cm × 92·7 cm
The Earl Howe, Amersham, Buckinghamshire

As Rebel forces, supported by the French fleet of d'Estaing and the infantry he had on board, were about to launch an attack on Newport, Rhode Island, Admiral Lord Howe arrived from New York. Fearing to be trapped inside the harbour, the French admiral sailed out to do battle. He had the advantages of numbers and the weather, but with skilful manoeuvres, drawing the French further south, Howe was slowly sailing into a position where he would have the weather gauge. (It gave a fleet a following wind and therefore more control over its actions.)

A large storm prevented a full-scale battle, but several minor engagements resulted in advantages for the British. Howe returned to New York; d'Estaing called off his part in the Rhode Island attack, which finally collapsed.

506
Ship model in section showing stabling in horse transports
Contemporary model. Wood, canvas, metal
56 cm long; 128 cm high; 67 cm wide
National Maritime Museum, Greenwich, London

Horses in the Revolution were needed by the British Army for cavalry, officer duty, scouting and for hauling transport. In the hostile areas of the Colonies, the Rebels were able, with guerrilla tactics, to deny the British access to local supplies of food and horses.

A need arose, growing with the years, for more and more horses to be shipped across the Atlantic. As the model shows, transports converted to this purpose were furnished with stables, with hay above and water below, and the horses were supported with broad slings to prevent damage to them on rough sea voyages.

[Other naval material, sextants, compasses, telescopes etc., has been provided by the National Maritime Museum.]

506

The Struggle moves South

UNTIL 1778 THE SOUTHERN COLONIES were virtually ignored by the British Government. Apart from an expedition to Charleston in 1776 under Clinton and Admiral Sir Peter Parker, which ended in fiasco, the war effort had been limited to the northern theatre. It was generally believed that the south was predominantly Loyalist, a support that could be called upon when needed, and indeed Georgia's Tory population was second in size only to New York.

The French involvement, and the promise of the opening up of a new area of operations in the West Indies, altered the situation radically. Strategically, the south changed from a relatively untroublesome backwater to a key base from which to control the war in the Caribbean. East Florida was already securely British; to expand that hold north into Georgia and South Carolina was the next step.

In the last days of 1778 Lieutenant-Colonel Archibald Campbell, with two battalions of the 71st Highlanders, landed in the Savannah swamps and captured the city. Within a short while he had advanced inland into Georgia and became 'the first officer . . . to take a stripe and star from the rebel flag of Congress'.

The following autumn a combined American-French force laid siege to Savannah, but was severely beaten when it tried to storm the city. The French under d'Estaing retreated to lick their wounds in the West Indies; the Americans suffered a great loss of morale; the British, the Rebel defeat having rallied strong Loyalist support, prepared for the next attack.

It came in the spring of 1780 when Sir Henry Clinton, in one of the most efficient military operations of the whole war, captured Charleston from Rebel General Benjamin Lincoln. At the cost of 250 British casualties he took 6000 prisoners, with their arms, three enemy frigates and 400 guns. The humiliation of 1776, when Charleston had eluded him, was avenged.

The day Charleston surrendered, 12 May 1780, was a watershed for Britain in the south. The army now occupied the key ports, thus securing for the navy control of the New York–Caribbean seaways. The next step was to push inland over the swampy coastal plain and establish forts and outposts along the fall-line, where the land began to rise to the foothills of the Appalachians over an arc of some 350 miles. Clinton himself withdrew to New York leaving Cornwallis, his second-in-command, with 4000 troops to bring the south to submission. This meant rallying Loyalist support to help patrol the vast region of 15,000 square miles; Major

acing page: item 528

Patrick Ferguson, now of the 71st, was one of the leading activists.

The terrain in the south was unlike anything the British army had yet encountered, and at last the light cavalry could be used to full effect. Fine sand roads and woods clear of undergrowth meant that dashing horsemen like Banastre Tarleton and George Hanger, at the head of their cavalry troops, could move around the country winning lightning victories and drumming up support. They quickly earned a name for brutality, and Rebel leaders of the same ilk, men like Francis Marion, the 'Swampfox', and Thomas Sumter, the 'Carolina Gamecock', soon emerged to counter them. The story of the Southern Campaign is largely one of bloody skirmishes and swooping cavalry raids.

But Cornwallis had an overall plan. He believed, contrary to Clinton, that to secure South Carolina it was essential to move steadily north, through North Carolina into Virginia, stamping out Rebel resistance and thus minimising the chances of rekindling anti-British feeling to the south. Germain, 3000 miles away, agreed that Virginia was the key to holding the southern colonies. This triangle of opinion, formed by Germain, Clinton and Cornwallis, probably did more to hinder co-operation and undermine the chances of British success than any other factor.

The Rebels, meanwhile, realised that it would take a greater leader than Benjamin Lincoln to oust the British, and Horatio Gates was sent to repeat his Saratoga victory. Militia support would flock to his side from the Carolina backwoods, Congress hoped, as it had done from the Hudson Highlands. Gates promptly conceded a major victory to Cornwallis at Camden, losing all but 700 of his 4000-strong army, and returned north as fast as he could.

It was a setback for the Rebels, but it was to be their last. The appearance of Continental regulars, in place of local militia, did much to stir up support, while cooling down many lukewarm Loyalists. In September 1780, having moved from outpost to outpost to protect Cornwallis's rear as he pushed north, Patrick Ferguson was killed while defending King's Mountain with 1000 of the Loyalists he had been working so hard to raise. Cornwallis, his rear exposed yet again, drew back for the winter.

The new Rebel general sent to deal with Cornwallis and his 4000-strong army was Nathanael Greene. Greene seized the initiative without delay, seeing that, too weak to fight face to face, he had to attack the British lines of communication and divide their strength. This he did. Cornwallis sent Tarleton off in one direction, to be crushingly beaten by Daniel Morgan at Cowpens, and set out himself to cut off Greene.

The American backed away, drawing Cornwallis's depleted force into the position he wanted, and on 15 March 1781 the two armies met. In a masterly action, Cornwallis, with 1900 tired, hungry men, defeated 4400 Rebels at the Battle of Guilford Court House, but it was a Pyrrhic victory. His force was spent and, as Greene's army slipped round behind to occupy the territory Cornwallis had left vacant in South Carolina, the British commander had no choice, with over 500 casualities, but to advance north and join up with the British army in Virginia.

On 20 May 1781 Cornwallis linked up with Arnold and the British at Richmond,

Virginia. General Phillips, the senior commander, had died the previous day. Failing to do battle with the small enemy unit in the area under Lafayette, Cornwallis camped at Williamsburg and awaited orders. After some disagreement and indecision it was agreed that he should fortify Yorktown on the end of the Peninsula at the mouth of the York river, which could protect the anchorage for a future offensive up the Chesapeake. August saw Cornwallis's troops digging the defences in sweltering heat. They might as well have been digging their graves, for on the last day of the month the French fleet appeared off the Capes, cutting the army off from all support by sea.

In May, Washington and Rochambeau had been undecided about what to do. By August, with the promise of additional French support arriving with de Grasse, Washington set out for Virginia. His army, 7000 Americans and French, covered 200 miles in fifteen days, and by mid-September, when de Grasse arrived in the Chesapeake, the American fortunes were flying high.

On 29 September, with no support from Clinton, Cornwallis withdrew his 6000 troops inside the Yorktown fortifications. The enemy, now 16,000 strong, was closing in. (It is estimated that the British force numbered over 8500, but many of these men were unfit or not part of the actual fighting force.) On 9 October the enemy siegeworks broke ground and the bombardment began. Cornwallis's men fell rapidly, from fever if not from wounds, and by the 16th the number fit to fight had been reduced to half. With all hope gone, Cornwallis decided to end the agony. On 18 October 1781, the British army laid down its arms before the combined forces of the United States and France, and marched out of Yorktown to the popular tune, 'The World Turned Upside-Down'.

PATRICIA CONNOR

507
A Plan of the Siege and Surrender of Charleston
Captain Charles Blaskowitz

1780. Coloured manuscript
Full title: 'A Plan of the Siege and Surrender of
Charlestown South Carolina to His Majesty's Fleet
and Army. Commanded by their Excellencies Sir
Henry Clinton Knight of the Bath, General and
Commander-in-Chief, And Mariot Arbuthnot, Esq.
Vice Admiral of the White, and Commander-in-
Chief of His Majesty's Ships and Vessels in North
America &c &c &c May 12th. 1780 Surveyed during
& after the Siege by Charles Blaskowitz Cap.
Guides & Pioneers.'
67·2 cm × 73·6 cm
Ref: PRO MPH 666
Public Record Office, London

Clinton set sail from New York on 26 December
1779. He had an appalling voyage south which lasted
thirty-eight days. Most of the artillery and horses
were lost; several transports were swept away into the
Atlantic by currents (one even reached Cornwall
eleven weeks later).

He put into Savannah on 1 February to regroup
and replace lost equipment, and on 10 February set
out for Charleston, where he waited for naval support. Arbuthnot's ships at last crossed the bar in
Charleston harbour, and on the night of 28–29
March, Clinton's men crossed the Ashley River in
boats with muffled oars. Two days later they broke
ground 800 yards from the town defences. Charleston,
on the tip of a peninsula, was cut off by land and sea.

Clinton's army worked closer and closer to the
Rebel-held town in intense heat and under constant
fire. Eventually the Rebels gave in, and after a six-
week siege surrendered, with heavy losses, on 12 May.

Charles Blaskowitz was one of the outstanding
mapmakers of the Revolution. Trained under Samuel
Holland, Surveyor-General of the Northern District,
he joined the Guides and Pioneers, as did his master,
at the outbreak of war, and remained in this Loyalist
regiment, travelling with it to Halifax in 1784. He
also produced a sketch of the American floating
battery at Boston (see item 289).

508
American Light Cavalry and Dragoons
1775. Ink and watercolour drawing
In two strips, each 19 cm × 43·7 cm
Anne S. K. Brown Military Collection,
Providence, Rhode Island

The Continental army contained four regiments of
cavalry, all light dragoons, which were raised early in
the war. Washington was aware of the potential of
mounted troops, but through lack of horses, saddles
and money there were probably never more than
1000 raised. Like the British cavalry, they were used
mostly in the south.

509
The 17th Light Dragoons Charging
c. 1779. Ink drawing
11·1 cm × 27·9 cm
Anne S. K. Brown Military Collection,
Providence, Rhode Island

Only two light cavalry regiments of the British army
travelled to America. The ground was considered too
rough for the manoeuvres to which they were best
suited. The 16th Light Dragoons served the first two
years, then were posted home, although some of their
effective men and horses were drafted into the 17th
Light Dragoons. This regiment was present in small
numbers at Bunker Hill, and in force during the New
York and Pennsylvania campaigns. One troop was
attached to Tarleton's legion in the Southern Campaign, and interned at Yorktown.

The dragoons were armed with swords, a pair of
pistols with 9-inch barrels and a flintlock carbine.
This weapon had a 29-inch barrel and was carried
either in a bucket just in front of the rider's leg, or
slung over his shoulder on a belt. The gun was
attached to the belt by a swivel, and could be picked
up from its loaded, muzzle-down position and fired
in one movement. The use of the three types of
cavalry weapon can be seen in the drawing.

510
British saddle holster for pistol
c. 1770. Leather
Mr Francis A. Lord, Columbia, South Carolina

511
Brass stirrup
c. 1750
Mr Francis A. Lord, Columbia, South Carolina

512
Cavalry bit
Late 18th century. Steel
Scottish United Services Museum, Edinburgh

The list of 'horse furniture and accoutrements' that
was required by a light dragoon was long and expen-

ive. However, most of it was provided, unlike the uniform, which he himself had to buy. A saddle would have cost the Treasury £1 1s, holsters 5s. 8d., tinned stirrups 3s. 6d., and a tinned bit 3s. Officers' accoutrements were probably more costly, being made of brass and steel.

513
Lieutenant-Colonel Banastre Tarleton

Engraved by J. R. Smith from the portrait by Sir Joshua Reynolds (see item 1)

London, 1782. Hand-coloured mezzotint
52·4 cm × 39·6 cm
Anne S. K. Brown Military Collection, Providence, Rhode Island

Tarleton arrived in America as a volunteer in 1776 and joined the 16th Light Dragoons. When they returned home in 1778 he stayed as Lieutenant-Colonel, Commandant of the British Legion, a provincial unit of mounted troops. Although Tarleton had served well in the war until 1780, it was only when he began to command light cavalry operations in the south that his talents as a leader came to the fore.

At the head of his Legion and of a troop of the 17th Light Dragoons he became the scourge of the Carolinas, inflicting defeat on Rebel leaders such as Gates, Sumter and Marion, severely damaging their forces. Only when he encountered Daniel Morgan, 'the Old Wagoner', at Cowpens did he meet his equal and get thoroughly beaten. In two weeks he was back in action, raiding and skirmishing, ending up in Virginia, across the river from Yorktown at Gloucester. He was interned with the rest of the army, but paroled home.

Tarleton was much disliked by many senior British officers who thought the young daredevil lacked 'military maturity'. He was feared by the Rebels, to whom he showed little mercy, but he was respected by fellow cavalry officers like Hanger and Simcoe, and his men never performed in battle under other commanders as successfully as they did for him.

514
Major George Hanger, later 4th Lord Coleraine

Thomas Beach

1782–3. Oil on canvas. Signed: 'T. Beach p.'
76·2 cm × 63·5 cm
Her Majesty the Queen

Hanger arrived in America in 1776 with a purchased commission in the Hessian jägers, and served with them in New York and Pennsylvania. In 1780 he was named commander of a detachment and sent to Charleston, where he distinguished himself by reconnoitring the defences, and advising Clinton on the plan of attack.

Hanger's reward was an appointment to aide-de-camp, and a position as second-in-command to Ferguson, responsible for rallying Loyalists. This was too dull for Hanger, who then organised a command under his friend Tarleton in the Legion. Though tarred with the same brush as Tarleton, Hanger was not a successful cavalry leader.

The two men remained close friends back in England, and became part of the Prince of Wales's set of boisterous gadabouts. Beach painted Hanger in the uniform, green coat and feathered helmet of Tarleton's Legion, in which he was a major. It is almost identical to the uniform worn by Tarleton himself in the portrait by Reynolds (see item 1). Some authorities believe that the British Legion wore white when actually campaigning in the south.

515
Helmet of the 17th Light Dragoons

1775–83. Black leather, front-plate and mounts in black metal with silver ornamentation. Skull and crossbones motif on front. Red horse-hair plume, red silk pleated turban around back
Musée de l'Empéri, Salon-de-Provence, Bouches du Rhône

The distinctive light dragoon helmet gave protection from sabre slashes during fast-moving cavalry action. The 17th Light Dragoons wore this headgear in America; their troop in the south, however, on attachment to Tarleton, wore white sheepskin turbans on the back of the helmet in place of the usual regimental red.

516
Light cavalry trooper's sword

c. 1780. Steel
National Army Museum, Chelsea, London

517
Light cavalry sabre, with basket hilt

c. 1780
Scottish Infantry Depot Museum, Penicuik, Midlothian

The sword, issued to both officers and other ranks in cavalry regiments, was the most important weapon to the horseman, equivalent to the infantryman's bayonet. The trend at the time of the Revolution was, as with all military equipment, towards lightness. Accordingly, the swords were getting shorter, and the hilts, though vital to the protection of the hand, less cumbersome. A contemporary description tells us that the swords were 'either crooked or straight according to the regulations of the Regiment'.

518
Major-General Sir Alexander Leslie, 1731–94
Thomas Gainsborough

c. 1783. Oil on canvas
76·2 cm × 63·5 cm
Luffness Limited, St Peter Port, Guernsey

Leslie was commander of the 64th Foot while it was garrisoned in Boston before the outbreak of the Revolution, and several times was involved in situations which promised to erupt into violent demonstrations. Leslie established a reputation for tactful handling, and was military adviser to Gage.

At New York he commanded a brigade, and played a prominent part in the actions. His most important mission of the war came in 1780 when, now major-general, he embarked for the south with a command of 2500 men. His orders were to land at Portsmouth, Virginia, destroy Rebel stores and link up with Cornwallis, who was moving north. But when Leslie arrived he found orders from Cornwallis to sail straight on to Charleston, and support him in South Carolina.

These orders were much regretted by Germain, who saw Leslie's Chesapeake expedition as vital to the southern strategy. Cornwallis, however, was relying on Leslie's force (1500 men marched to join Cornwallis) to push on into North Carolina. Leslie commanded the British right flank at Guilford Court House.

As Cornwallis headed north with his depleted force in spring 1781, Leslie returned to Charleston, and then to New York, where he conferred with Clinton during the Yorktown crisis. With Cornwallis interned he was sent by Clinton to command the southern operations from Charleston, but there was nothing to do except hold British garrisons for as long as possible. On 11 July 1782, Leslie organised the evacuation of Savannah, and in December the army withdrew under his command from Charleston. The Southern Campaign was over.

508

514 (detail)

509

519
British Orderly Book kept by brigade under the command of Major-General Leslie
28 August 1780–20 March 1781, manuscript, 365 pp
20 cm × 11 cm
North Carolina State Archives, Raleigh

This orderly book, which belonged to one of the units under General Leslie, the Brigade of Guards commanded by Colonel Charles O'Hara, details the events from 28 August 1780, when Leslie was preparing in New York for his expedition to the Chesapeake, to 20 March 1781, five days after the unit had fought in the battle of Guilford Court House. Though wounded twice, O'Hara led his men of the 2nd Battalion in the final thrust which drove Greene from the battlefield.

520
Captain Jacob Shubrick
1st South Carolina Regiment
Henry Benbridge

c. 1778. Oil on canvas
77·5 cm × 63·5 cm
Society of the Cincinnati, Washington, D.C.

The 1st and 2nd South Carolina regiments were raised in June 1775 for service within the State, but were soon taken into Continental service. They were present at the British attempt to take Charleston in 1776, and contributed significantly to its failure by defending Fort Moultrie on Sullivan's Island at the entrance to Charleston harbour.

Shubrick, who joined the regiment at its raising, gained promotion just before the Sullivan Island fiasco. He died at the end of 1777. The picture may have been painted posthumously. In 1779 his fellow officers, dressed in identical distinctive uniforms of dark blue coat with red lapels and hat with silver crescent, fought bravely alongside the French in the attack on Savannah. In 1780 they defended Charleston to the last and made up the bulk of Clinton's prisoners when he captured their city.

515

521
Flintlock rifle
American, *c.* 1775. Made in Pennsylvania
Bright steel lock, curly maple stock with brass and silver decorated mounts, silver escutcheon plate engraved with 'JT'. Cheek rest inlaid with a thirteen-point silver star inscribed 'UNITED: STATES: WE ARE ONE'. Bright steel barrel rifled with seven grooves

Overall length: 59¾ inches; barrel length: 43¾ inches; calibre: 0·47 inches
Her Majesty the Queen

This rifle originally belonged to Colonel John Thomas of the American Riflemen. Thomas, whose initials appear on the escutcheon plate, was killed in North Carolina in action against the British Legion. His rifle was brought back to England and presented to the Royal family by Colonel George Hanger in the first years of the 1800s.

With its patriotic American star, this fine rifle was repaired by D. Egg in 1803 when some of the original American parts were replaced.

522
Lord Francis Rawdon, 1754–1826
After Gainsborough

Crayon drawing
62·1 cm × 41·2 cm
Worcester Art Museum, Massachusetts

Lord Rawdon, despite his youth, was one of the outstanding British officers to serve in the war, particularly in the south. He arrived in America as a lieutenant in the 5th Foot and survived Bunker Hill with two bullets through his hat. He fought at New York with the 63rd, and by 1778 had risen to the rank of lieutenant-colonel and adjutant-general (when he resigned that post in 1779, the ill-starred André took over). Also in 1778, while in Philadelphia, he raised a provincial regiment, the Volunteers of Ireland, which later became the 2nd American and then the 105th Foot on the regular British army establishment, one of the only two Loyalist units to be so honoured.

In 1780 Rawdon, with his Volunteers, went to support Clinton's siege of Charleston, and was then placed under Cornwallis by Clinton (who did not like Rawdon). At Camden his leadership did much to facilitate Cornwallis's rout of Gates, and so, when the commander made his offensive push into North Carolina, Rawdon was left with 8000 men to hold South Carolina and Georgia. He began well, stopping Greene with a daring attack at Hobkirk's Hill, but realising that his resources were too dissipated he ordered the evacuation of some outposts.

In the summer of 1781, his orders to evacuate not having arrived in time to prevent a siege, he marched to the inland fort of Ninety-Six, which was surrounded by Greene and his army. With 2000 men, under a blazing sun, Rawdon covered 200 miles in a forced march to save the garrison, which had been bottled up for twenty-eight days. In a brilliant tactical

operation he saved his men and evacuated the fort, but it was the end of his career in America. Fifty of his troops had died of sunstroke, and Rawdon himself, debilitated by the heat, had to return to England. He was still only twenty-six. Captured by a French privateer en route, he spent a year as a prisoner in Brest before being paroled home.

Gainsborough's portrait of Rawdon, now in São Paulo, Brazil, from which this drawing was taken, was painted *c.* 1783.

523
Brown Bess musket, Short Land pattern
After 1768. Walnut stock, lock engraved 'TOWER' with crowned 'GR', breech stamped with ordnance mark and private proof. Barrel inscribed '71 REG'
57·75 inches overall length; 42 inches barrel length
Colonial Williamsburg Foundation,
Williamsburg, Virginia

This musket is said to have belonged to a member of the 71st Foot, shown by the engraving '71 REG' on the barrel. The 71st were raised in Scotland for the Revolution, and called Fraser's Highlanders. They were disbanded in 1783, having served at New York and Brandywine. When Lieutenant-Colonel Archibald Campbell took Savannah, two battalions of the 71st were prominent in his force, and when Cornwallis surrendered at Yorktown part of the regiment was interned. Patrick Ferguson, killed at King's Mountain, was a major in the 71st, although the regiment was not with him at the disaster.

524
The Siege of Savannah
The siege of Savannah, which began in late September 1779, ended on 8 October after two weeks, when Admiral d'Estaing, commander of the French forces, ordered the combined French and American troops to attack the defences. Fighting was at its fiercest around the Spring Hill redoubt, where wave after wave of Rebels were repulsed by the British. The onslaught failed badly and over 1000 French and American troops were killed or captured, while the British lost as few as 100.

In this wash drawing, Pierre Ozanne was looking at the defences of Savannah, which enclosed it on the land side, from the camps behind the zigzag siege trenches. The French camp is to the right, the American on the left. The Spring Hill redoubt, where d'Estaing led his attack and Pulaski was killed, can be seen in the concentration of activity at the left, where smoke is rising from the defences. Masts of ships anchored on the Savannah river can be seen beyond the town.

The original drawing is in the Library of Congress, Washington, D.C.

525
British cross-belt plate, with Royal cipher and crown
Brass
Mr Francis A. Lord, Columbia, South Carolina

526
Three steel bayonets
One button of the 52nd Foot
Musket balls and grapeshot
Georgia Historical Society, Savannah

These relics of the battle for Savannah were picked up from the ground at the Spring Hill redoubt, where fighting was fiercest. The 52nd Foot fought in the early part of the war, but returned to England in 1778. Members of the regiment who were fit were drafted to other units; this button was lost by a soldier on attachment to a regiment at Savannah.

527
Plume said to have been taken from Sergeant Jasper's shako
Red and white feathers
38 cm high
Mrs Margaret E. Wood, Stinchcombe, Gloucestershire

As the Rebels attacked the Spring Hill redoubt for the third time, Sergeant William Jasper of the 2nd South Carolina Infantry tried to plant the regiment's flag on top of it. In two previous attempts fellow soldiers had died, and Sergeant Jasper was also killed. The plume from his helmet and the flag he had been attempting to raise were taken from his body by British soldiers to mark their victory.

528
Powder Horn with wampum sash
Engraved: '1770 by D.B.'
Metropolitan Museum of Art, New York

This powder horn is engraved with a plan of Charles Town (Charleston), South Carolina, showing the strategic points of defence: 1 The Battery, 2 East Fort, 3 Old Barracks, 4 New Barracks.

529
Cast button marked '2' for 2nd South Carolina Infantry
University of South Carolina, Columbia

Colonel William Moultrie and his 2nd South Carolina Infantry regiment were in Charleston during Clinton's siege, and at the city's fall Moultrie became a prisoner for two years.

530
Map of the Battle of Camden
1780. Coloured manuscript map
Full title: 'Sketch of the disposition and commencement of the Action near Camden in South Carolina 16th August 1780. As discribed in the Letters of the Right Honb^le Earl Cornwallis to the Secretary of State: and the Rebel Gates to Congress. Most respectfully inscribed to the Right Honb^le Earl Percy, by his Lordships most Humble Servant Ed. Barron.'
Oval, 20 cm × 25 cm
The Duke of Northumberland, Alnwick

When Horatio Gates arrived to command the Continental army he marched straight to Camden to attack the main British inland supply base. Cornwallis hastened from Charleston, 150 miles away, and confronted Gates on 16 August 1780. The experience of the British outweighed the raw Rebel militia and the exhausted Continentals, and Gates was put to flight. His army of 4000 was completely destroyed – either killed, captured or scattered – while British losses were 324.

531
British short sword from Hobkirk's Hill
Steel
Ross E. Beard Jr Collection, Camden Historical Commission, South Carolina

A second battle took place at Camden, on Hobkirk's Hill, on 25 April 1781. Rawdon, who was based there after Guilford Court House while Cornwallis moved north, was able to use his knowledge of the terrain to outmanoeuvre Greene when he attacked. Rawdon had fought there six months earlier.

Rawdon won a tactical victory, but Greene managed to evacuate his artillery and supplies, so with losses equal on both sides Rawdon was forced to withdraw towards Charleston. The sword is a relic of the battle.

532
Sketch map of the Battle of Guilford
1781. Rough manuscript
40 cm × 31.9 cm
Ref: Faden Collection 53
Library of Congress, Washington, D.C.

Greene and Cornwallis skirted each other for a while at the beginning of 1781, until Greene took up position at Guilford Court House, North Carolina, and waited for Cornwallis to be drawn into the attack. The British were outnumbered, with only 1900 men against the Americans' 4400. Cornwallis in fact believed the odds were even greater than that, but was sure that his veterans could overcome. After a twelve-mile approach march, on empty stomachs, the British army went straight into the attack at dawn on 15 March. In three lines the British forces advanced obstinately until, with enormous losses, they emerged victorious.

Many of the finest officers were killed or wounded that day, and with his small force reduced by over 500 men, Cornwallis could not fully celebrate or follow up his victory. From Guilford he moved on towards Yorktown.

533
British map of the siege of Yorktown
Lieutenant John Hills, of the 23rd Foot

1781. Coloured manuscript
Full title: Plan of Yorktown and Gloucester in Virginia Shewing the Works constructed for the Defence of the Posts by the R^t Honble Lieu^t General Earl Cornwallis with the Attacks of the Combined Army of French and Rebels under the Command of the Generals Count de Rochambaud and Washington which Capitulated October 1781
91 cm × 59 cm
Ref: Faden Collection 91
Library of Congress, Washington, D.C.

The first enemy siege works were built on 1 October. On 6 October they broke ground and began a first parallel around the southern perimeter of Yorktown, and on the 9th the first artillery bombardment began.

Two British outposts near the York River, redoubts 9 and 10, were the next positions to fall, on 14 October, and two days later the French batteries in the newly-dug second parallel opened up only 350 yards from the British lines. On the night of the 16th–17th, Cornwallis tried to ferry his able-bodied men across the river, hoping he could fight his way out through Gloucester, on the opposite bank, which was also besieged, but a storm ended this venture. On 17 October, when the enemy heavy artillery opened up, Cornwallis started overtures for surrender.

534
German colours of the Ansbach-Bayreuth Regiment, surrendered to the Americans at Yorktown
Oil on canvas
92·6 cm × 111·7 cm
West Point Museum, United States Military Academy, West Point, New York

Two Ansbach-Bayreuth infantry regiments, 1285 men in all, served at the battle for New York in 1777, in Philadelphia in 1777–8, and were based in the New York region until 1781 when they went to Virginia. They were interned at Yorktown and held in America until exchanged in 1783.

The field of this colour is white damask; on the obverse is a crown, garlands and the initials CCFSA, the initials of the ruling Prince of Ansbach-Bayreuth and MZB, for 'Margrave zu Bayreuth'. On the reverse is a red eagle with a ribbon and the motto 'Pro Principe et Patria'.

535
The Siege of Yorktown
The model of the siege of Yorktown shows the disposition of the British forces within the confines of the town, and the combined American and French armies occupying the territory encircling the perimeter of Cornwallis's defences.

Yorktown was situated on a thirty-five foot bluff overlooking the York River, across from Gloucester Point half a mile away over the water, and also under siege. The British defences were laid down with an average 300 yards only between the perimeter and the river. Inside, Cornwallis had about 6000 men. Outside, the French and Rebel armies numbered about 16,000.

Siege works in the form of approach trenches were laid down to the east of the town so that the French and American artillery could work closer to the British defences. Dysentry and constant enemy bombardment daily reduced the number of defenders until on 17 October 1781, after eighteen days of siege, Cornwallis surrendered with only 3273 rank and file left fit for duty.

536
The Storming of Redoubt no. 10
The eastern defences of the British line, as the diorama shows, were secured to the York River bank by redoubt no. 10. Before the French and the Rebels could complete their approach works, this redoubt and one other had to be taken. On the night of

14 October, the French attacked one redoubt; the Americans under Alexander Hamilton took on redoubt no. 10. The small fortress was assaulted in a bayonet charge with swift success. It cost the Americans only nine dead and twenty-five wounded.

537
Charles, Earl Cornwallis, 1738–1805
Thomas Gainsborough

1783. Oil on canvas
75 cm × 63 cm
National Portrait Gallery, London

Cornwallis was a Whig, and before the Revolution broke out he resolutely disagreed with the Government's policies which exacerbated the American crisis. However, liked by George III, his sympathies were not held against him and he earned high command and respect. Even after the disaster at Yorktown, he was not blamed. Clinton bore the brunt of that.

Cornwallis served three tours of duty in America. The first time he took reinforcements for Lord Howe to Halifax, and then served at New York and Brandywine and led the victorious British army into Philadelphia in the autumn of 1777. After a visit home, he returned a year later to act as second-in-command to Clinton, with whom he violently disagreed regarding policy. Resigning, he travelled home again, but on the death of his dearly loved wife, he agreed to go back to America. This time it was for the Southern Campaign, where despite a far-sighted strategy he lacked support, and headed into defeat.

538
Letter: Cornwallis to Washington
York, Virginia, 17 October 1781
30·4 cm × 19 cm
Ref: PRO 30/11/74
Public Record Office, London

In this short letter (a copy kept by the clerk) Cornwallis requests a twenty-four hour cessation of hostilities 'that two Officers may be appointed by each side to meet at Mr Moore's house to settle terms for the surrender of the Posts of York & Gloucester'. In signing off, he describes himself as honoured to be Washington's 'most obedient and most humble Servant'.

539
Autograph letter from Washington to Cornwallis
Undated (17 October 1781)

20·3 cm × 19 cm
Ref: PRO 30/11/74
Public Record Office, London

Washington returns the honour. 'Suspension of Hostilities during two Hours from the Delivery of this Letter will be granted –'.

540
The Articles of Capitulation
'Done in the Trenches before York
October 19th 1781' (in Washington's hand)
Three-page manuscript, signed:
'Cornwallis and Tho? Symonds for Britain,
G. Washington for the United States, le Cte de Rochambeau et le Cte de Barras (en mon nom et celui du cte de Grasse) for France'
43·1 cm × 38·1 cm
Ref: PRO 30/11/74
Public Record Office, London

The surrender terms were worked out at the Moore House during a long, heated session between two British officers, Dundas and Ross, representing Cornwallis, and Noailles and John Laurens for the Rebels. By the morning of 20 October the document was ready for signing. Soon after midday the names of Cornwallis, Captain Thomas Symonds (the senior British naval officer present), Washington, Rochambeau and Barras had been added.

The terms were honourable. Following a precedent set by the British when Lincoln surrendered Charleston, the troops had to march out with colours cased, playing a British or German march, the traditional honour of playing a tune of the victor being denied. Apart from this the British were satisfied. After the ceremony of laying down of arms and colours the British army marched off to captivity in, according to witnesses, an untidy ill-disciplined fashion, to the tune *The World Turned Upside Down*.

541
Letter from Cornwallis to Sir Henry Clinton
'York Town, Virginia. 20th Oct: 1781' (Clerk's copy)
30·4 cm × 19 cm
Ref: PRO 30/11/74
Public Record Office, London

After the surrender Cornwallis wrote to his commanding officer in New York: 'I have the mortification to inform your Excellency that I have been forced to give up the Posts of York and Gloucester, and to surrender the Troops under my command, by Capitulation on the 19th instant, as prisoners of War to the combined Forces of America & France.'

Cornwallis had handed over to the enemy 8081 prisoners, 214 artillery pieces, 7320 small arms and twenty-four transport ships. He had 600 casualties. American losses amounted to 125; those of the French were higher, but nothing like those of Cornwallis.

542
Parole of Lieutenant Eyre Coote of the 37th Foot after his internment at Yorktown
30 April 1782. Signed by the Assistant Commandant of Prisoners
33·3 cm × 21·1 cm, folded
National Army Museum, Chelsea, London

Coote had served throughout the Revolution. As ensign in the 37th he carried the Colours at the Battle of Brooklyn aged only fourteen. He served at New York, in Pennsylvania and at the siege of Charleston. After the defeat at Yorktown, the parole gave Coote freedom of movement on condition that he did not attempt to escape.

543
Colonel John Laurens, 1754–82
Charles Willson Peale

1780. Miniature, oil paint on ivory
Oval; 3·6 cm × 2·8 cm
Gibbes Art Gallery, Charleston, South Carolina

Laurens served in the Revolution as confidential secretary to Washington. After the fall of Charleston, Laurens' gallantry in the Southern Campaign having achieved special notice, he was sent to France as a special envoy to Louis XVI to request further supplies.

The support Laurens elicited helped the Americans considerably at Yorktown, and the young southerner was back in Virginia, fighting, to see the victory. With Noailles, he arranged the surrender terms, which must have given some satisfaction as his father, Henry Laurens, was at that time a British prisoner in the Tower of London.

The father, however, who became a Peace Commissioner in Paris on his release, did not see his son again, for John was killed in a small, futile skirmish just before the British evacuated South Carolina.

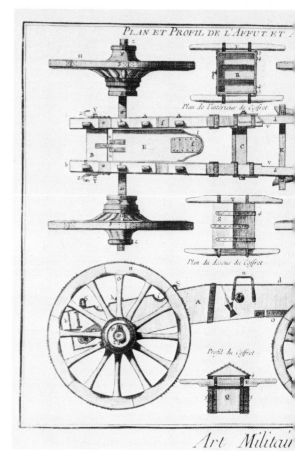

550

547 (detail)

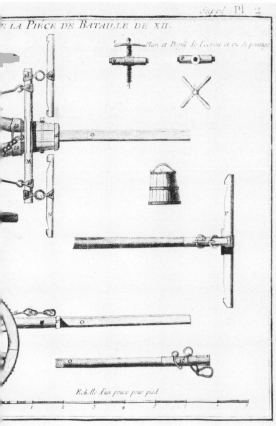

544

Washington and his Generals at Yorktown

James Peale

c. 1781. Oil on canvas
51·4 cm × 74·8 cm
Colonial Williamsburg Foundation,
Williamsburg, Virginia

Washington is seen, after the British capitulation, on the shore of the York river at the western end of Yorktown. British ships are sunk in the water and horses lie dead on the beach.

The identity of the generals standing on the beach has never been established with any certainty. However, the latest ideas name them as (in the front row from the left) Lafayette, Washington, Rochambeau and Tench Tilghman, who was military secretary and aide-de-camp to Washington and in that capacity carried the news of Yorktown to Congress. Behind them could be the Chevalier de Chastellux, a French major-general under Rochambeau, on the left, and Benjamin Lincoln.

545

Lieutenant and Captain Francis Dundas,
1st Foot Guards

Daniel Gardner

Gouache and pastel
83·8 cm × 53·3 cm
Private collection

A battalion of guards was sent to America in March 1776 composed of companies taken from the 1st Foot Guards, the Coldstream Guards and the 3rd Foot Guards. It took part in all the major campaigns: New York, Pennsylvania and the south, featuring well at Brandywine and Guilford Court House.

Dundas was a typical young officer of this unit. When the Brigade of Guards, under O'Hara, surrendered at Yorktown, Dundas was taken prisoner. He was one of many young officers who had fought for the King against Rebel colonists and been defeated by the allied might of France and the new United States of America.

546

Orders issued by de Grasse for the
disembarkation of the French
troops at Yorktown

22 August 1781. Printed on the flagship's presses
Full title: 'Ordre concernant les Troupes de

Débarquement. A Bord de la Ville de Paris, le 22 du mois d'aoust 1781'
21·5 cm × 17 cm
Le Musée de la Coopération Franco-Américaine, Château de Blérancourt, Aisne

François Joseph Paul, Comte de Grasse, arrived in the West Indies in July 1781 with orders to support Rochambeau and Washington as he thought best. He had served sporadically during the war against Britain, at Ushant off Brittany, under d'Estaing at Savannah and in minor engagements in the West Indies. The new mission of this immensely tall, handsome admiral was of a completely different order.

On 13 August he sailed north with 3000 men, money and thirty-four ships, and arrived off the Chesapeake Capes a day after Hood who, when he arrived from the West Indies and found no de Grasse, had sailed on for New York.

On 2 September de Grasse landed his troops. The orders instructing the commanding officers how to conduct this operation had been printed while the flagship, the *Ville de Paris*, was under way. The order sheet stipulates how the equipment must be in perfect condition, how each man must carry his equipment, no one taking any excess, how the victuals must be divided for transport, that each soldier must have thirty cartridges and that the units must carry extra arms for some volunteers from France expected any day.

Hood and Graves returned with haste from New York hoping to cut off a French supply fleet under Barras on its way from New England. Instead, they were engaged by de Grasse at the indecisive Battle of the Capes. After an initial barrage lasting two-and-a-half hours, on 5 September, the two fleets remained in contact for two days, drifting south, with no action. On 9 September the French fleet broke away; de Grasse returned to the Chesapeake and found that his compatriot Barras had slipped his supply fleet in while the British were otherwise occupied.

Graves departed, with his badly damaged fleet, to return to New York on 14 September, leaving the Chesapeake in the hands of de Grasse. Cornwallis's days were numbered.

547
The Thomas Nelson house
The Thomas Nelson house, the finest in Yorktown, was badly damaged by American bombardment during the siege. On 10 October Thomas Nelson, Governor of Virginia and commander of the Virginia militia, was invited by Lafayette to attend one of the batteries to give advice on where best to train the guns. Nelson indicated his own house, standing near the cliffs over the York River and well behind the British defence lines. Because, he explained, it was the finest house standing, Cornwallis would surely be inside, using it as headquarters.

Fifteen years after the battle, architect and water-colour artist Benjamin Latrobe found the house still badly damaged and the British trenches and banks still intact. Even today, the house has a cannon ball lodged in its bricks as a memento of 10 October 1781.

Latrobe's sketch, part of a journal, is in the State Archives of Virginia, Richmond.

548
Rampart siege carbine
Steel lock
Ross E. Beard Jr Collection, Camden Historical Commission, South Carolina

Carbines were short-barrel muskets used for short-range fire. A wall carbine like this was too heavy to be fired as a shoulder weapon. It would have been rested on the rampart or in a hole in the fortress wall. Many had a swivel fork on the forestock to help support them. Guns like this would have been used during the Yorktown siege to support the cannon fire.

549
Quarter-size model of an eight-pound Gribeauval field cannon
French. 18th century
Eight-pound cannon ball
Musée de l'Empéri, Salon-de-Provence, Bouches du Rhône

In 1765 the French army adopted an artillery system perfected by Jean-Baptiste Vaquette Gribeauval, which standardised the sizes of cannon, their uses and the shot they took. Gribeauval also stripped the gun of embellishment which made the cannon cumbersome, liable to explode because of the different barrel thicknesses, and wasteful of precious metal. The carriages were also lightened and made more mobile. Gribeauval's standardised system was so popular that it remained in use until the 1830s.

This model, complete with carriage and accoutrements, was made at the time Gribeauval was working. Guns like these, with their 1300-yard range, contributed greatly to the French success at Yorktown. Thirteen gunners manned the weapon, and it was drawn by a four- or six-horse team.

550
French artillery equipment, and its use
Three engravings, entitled 'Art Militaire. Nouvelle Artillerie'
Each plate 25 cm × 40 cm
Bibliothèque Raoul et Jean Brunon, Salon-de-Provence, Bouches du Rhône

The three engravings show: field guns; the construction and equipment of a twelve-pounder gun carriage; and the manoeuvre positions of the thirteen-man team operating a Gribeauval cannon.

551
Lieutenant-General Rochambeau's map of his army's march from New England to Yorktown and back, 1781–2
Coloured manuscript
44 cm × 164 cm
Ref: Rochambeau Collection 65
Library of Congress, Washington, D.C.

Rochambeau and Washington met in Wethersfield, Connecticut, in May 1781 and formulated a plan to draw British pressure away from Greene in the south and Lafayette in Virginia. They were to stage a strategic diversion to draw the British in defence of New York. News reached them of Cornwallis's arrival in Virginia, and the scheme had to be implemented as soon as possible.

The French infantry left their Newport camp and marched via Providence to join Washington's army at Peekskill, New York, at the end of June. A month later, after several raiding operations, Washington and Rochambeau were camped near Dobb's Ferry on the Hudson above New York, awaiting news from de Grasse.

When his promise of support reached Washington on 14 August, the commander abandoned plans for New York and set out south, leaving a token force to hold the Hudson. By 25 August the American and French forces had crossed that river at King's Ferry. On 3 and 4 September the French marched into Philadelphia. Only then did Clinton in New York realise he had been duped into thinking the allied forces were encircling him. It was Cornwallis they were after.

The troops waited a while at Head of Elk for transport, but it was limited, so after the artillery and heavy equipment had been loaded for water transit they marched on towards Baltimore and Annapolis. Here they met transport ships and were carried down to the Yorktown Peninsula, where they arrived on 26 September 1781. After the battle, Rochambeau's troops stayed in Virginia, and did not start their march back to Newport until 23 June 1782.

Each camp occupied by Rochambeau's men on their way both to and from Virginia was plotted on this map, one of a set of campaign maps used by the French commander.

552
Gunner of the French Royal Artillery
Nikolaus Hoffmann

French. Coloured engraving
40 cm × 28 cm
Bibliothèque Raoul et Jean Brunon, Salon-de-Provence, Bouches du Rhône

A battalion of the Régiment d'Auxonne and two companies of the Régiment de Metz served in America under the command of artillery officer Chevalier d'Aboville. The French artillery was conspicuous at both the siege of Savannah and at Yorktown, where nine batteries were under French command.

553
Short French artillery sword
1771. Hilt in moulded copper representing the head of an eagle
80 cm long
Musée de l'Empéri, Salon-de-Provence, Bouches du Rhône

554
Portrait of an officer in the French Royal Artillery
Miniature
Oval; 10 cm × 8 cm
Musée de l'Empéri, Salon-de-Provence, Bouches du Rhône

An Explosion of Battlefronts

FROM THE MOMENT FRANCE AND SPAIN entered the war as allies of the Colonies, the British Government was like a man facing a perforated dyke. Even if the man used both hands to stem the flood, somewhere something was leaking. With a large part of the Royal Navy committed to the American station, Britain was confronted by an old enemy who could choose to fight where she pleased. The Cabinet's problem was to anticipate where the enemy might appear: in India, the Mediterranean, off the American coast, in the West Indies, or in that old battleground, the thought of which sent shivers through the most sanguine politician – the Channel. To these considerations, uncontrollable factors such as the wind added hazards that made nonsense of inspired decisions.

Nervous dispositions in the Government dared not let too great a part of the Navy serve on foreign stations for fear that their plans would open the south coast of England to invasion. One example will suffice to illustrate their dread. In the summer of 1779, with the threat of the combined French and Spanish fleets appearing in the Channel, Admiral Sir Charles Hardy was given the task of guarding the Channel entrance. Hardy, patrolling west of the Scillies, was kept there by weather conditions while, to the general horror, an armada of sixty-three French and Spanish ships slipped up from the Bay of Biscay and were to be seen sailing off Plymouth Sound, where for several days various authorities considered blowing up the Plymouth dockyard and taking other decisions of similar consequence. A change of wind brought Hardy up the Channel, where he was commander, into Spithead to revictual. While this was in progress, and the militia of southern England dreamed of a ghastly glory, the Combined Fleet, under orders from the Continent, sailed home.

Decisions to cover eventualities of this nature were not taken in isolation; their collapsing domino effect could influence events at least two years ahead. The defence of Minorca and Gibraltar was always bound up with planning for the Channel. The series of reliefs of Gibraltar were nearly always combined with other projects: supplies to go on to Minorca, or sailing west to the Caribbean.

It was public feeling that kept Gibraltar in the forefront of the British mind. Since its capture in 1704, many politicians had considered trading it for peace with Spain. No such considerations bothered national sentiment about the West Indies. These were prize objects to be cherished for economic reasons alone. In

facing page: item 560
(detail)

one year the British West Indian islands would send 300 or so merchant ships into London. West Indian imports in 1776 were valued at £4¼ million, mostly from sugar and rum.

Controlling the Caribbean strategically was like operating on a giant chess-board, where once again the disposition of the islands and the vagaries of the weather imposed on long-term planning. Though at one time the American Rebels had hoped that Canada, the Irish and the West Indies would join them in their cause, the Caribbean planters were dependent on European markets for the sale of their produce, and on London for their loans: ties not to be broken suddenly.

For most of the year, the trade winds across the Caribbean blew from south-east to north-west, which is why the curve of small islands bending eastwards and south from Puerto Rico to the South American coast was divided into the Leeward Isles and the Windward Isles. Possession of them belonged almost equally to France and Britain. A thousand miles away to the west, south of Cuba, lay Jamaica, one of the most valuable of islands. Its position put it at great risk for the British: the trade wind would blow a ship there from Barbados in a week, and it would take an unconscionable time to tack back against the wind. For this reason France and Britain played with the outer islands as if they were pawns: king and check-mate were 1000 miles downwind in Jamaica.

From 1778 Britain's anti-Rebel moves were more or less divided between the American colonies and the West Indies. Hood, Rodney and others outwitted and out-sailed the French; and in turn were defeated by them. The French admirals, de Grasse and d'Estaing, enjoyed at moments their victories over the British, when reinforcements from Brest gave them the edge in the number of ships of the line. Add to this temporary superiority in numbers the fact that the hurricane season in the Caribbean, from August to November, tended to ensure that Europe's Carib-bean fleets sailed north to safety on the American coast, and there developed a situation in which Britain lost short-term control of the high seas, and Yorktown was isolated long enough for it to fall.

There thus remained to be played in the Caribbean the grand finale, cast from the massed players of France and Britain. The French fleet under de Grasse had but to link up with the fleet of Spain, and the massed ships would sail downwind to take Jamaica. Rodney caught de Grasse near a collection of small islands be-tween Dominica and Guadeloupe called the Isles des Saintes. At the end of the battle the French had lost four ships and de Grasse's own flagship, the *Ville de Paris*. The admiral himself was taken prisoner.

Further ahead was the treaty of peace between all the combatant powers and Britain's recognition of American independence. But as one American historian said in 1974, 'It is not surprising that America won its independence. What sur-prises me is the fact that with half the world on its side, it took so long.'

KENNETH PEARSON

555
Model of twenty-four pounder with special carriage, invented at Gibraltar

1782. Wood and brass
50·8 cm long; 43·2 cm high; 35·6 cm wide
Royal Artillery Institution, Woolwich, London

This contemporary model demonstrates a brilliant invention conceived during the Siege of Gibraltar (1779–83).

Attacks by Spanish fire-ships revealed that the regular cannon of the Rock garrison could not be depressed enough to bear down on their targets. Lieutenant George F. Koehler of the Hanoverian Artillery, who was aide-de-camp and assistant engineer to the Governor, suggested the use of this depression carriage.

Of the first thirty test rounds fired on 15 February 1782, twenty-eight of them landed by the St Carlos battery – as one witness said, 'to the delight of all the British who witnessed this interesting event'. The gun was loaded in the horizontal position. The powder charge was rammed in first, then a wet wad of paper or cotton rags, then the red-hot shot, and finally a second wet wad. The cannon was depressed to the right angle, and fired as soon as possible.

556
Keys to the Spanish powder magazine captured at Gibraltar

14·5 cm long, 5·5 cm wide; 13·3 cm long, 5·5 cm wide
National Army Museum, Chelsea, London

The keys were taken during the siege when the British forces made a sortie to spike Spanish guns.

557
The Spanish floating batteries

c. 1782. Watercolour on paper. From a Spanish intelligence report. Inscribed: 'Vaisseau de 64 canons transformé en batterie flotante insubmersible et incombustible'
35 cm × 40·5 cm
National Army Museum, Chelsea, London

On 13 September 1782 a Franco-Spanish force of warships and floating batteries, with 40,000 men and 200 guns, anchored 1000 yards off the Rock of Gibraltar, and with 200 more guns on the Isthmus between the Rock and the Spanish mainland, they opened fire.

The British, returning the fire, concentrated on the floating batteries. These had been specially constructed with heavy timbers and lined with thick walls of sand to absorb punishment. Towards night the batteries began to look as if they were in trouble. Fires broke out everywhere and spread; the British red-hot shot had worked.

Through the night one battery after another burst into flames. On the morning of 14 September, the last of them blew up. British gunboats rescued and captured more than 350 prisoners. The red-hot shot was never needed again. The supply relief which arrived soon after ensured the security of the Rock.

558
Gibraltar on the morning after the great Franco-Spanish attack
Thomas Davies

1783. Watercolour over pencil, black ink margins, on paper. Inscribed in lower margin: 'A View of Gibraltar with the situation of the Spanish Flotantes on the Morning of 14 September 1782 taken from the North Pavillion'. And inscribed lower right: 'T. Davies fecit 1783.'
38·9 cm × 59·2 cm
Sigmund Samuel Canadiana Collection
Royal Ontario Museum, Toronto

After the great attack was repulsed the Rock of Gibraltar was secure. Small groups of British officers on the left of the picture watch the burning Spanish floating batteries.

559
'Oh! Lord, Howe – they Run or Jack English Clearing the Gangway before Gibraltar'

London, 2 November 1782. Hand-coloured engraving, 'Pub: by T: Colley'
14·3 cm × 22·9 cm
Ref: BM 6037
Trustees of the British Museum, London

Gibraltar was relieved three times during its siege. The third and final relief arrived just a month after the great combined Franco-Spanish attack on the Rock had been thrown back. Admiral Lord Howe was threatened by the Spanish admiral, Cordoba, with a joint fleet of forty-nine ships of the line. Howe was heading south with only thirty-four, but all were copper-bottomed and therefore fast sailers. Taking advantage of a storm, Howe outmanoeuvred the enemy and arrived to anchor off the Rock on 16 October 1782.

This satire shows an English sailor loaded with provisions for Gibraltar as he fires a blunderbuss at a Frenchman running off, and a Spaniard falling.

560
Governor Eliott and staff
George Carter

Oil sketch on millboard
41·9 cm × 55·9 cm
National Portrait Gallery, London

Another view of the morning after the attack. On the left, soldiers cheer as the Spanish floating batteries explode. In the lower centre there stands one of the many furnaces used to heat the British shot. It was the red-hot cannon balls from these which eventually set fire to the batteries. A British naval sortie that night finished off the enemy. To the right stands the Governor of Gibraltar, George Augustus Eliott, surrounded by his staff.

Eliott (1717–90) enjoyed a very distinguished military career. He was trained as an engineer at Woolwich. He took great pride in his troops and looked after them well in the field while he himself lived a spartan existence. He was second-in-command at the capture of Havana in 1762, and with his share of the prize money bought Heathfield in Sussex. Gibraltar needed a strong man to make its defences secure, and Eliott was chosen for the job. At the end of the war he returned to England and was well rewarded, being raised to the peerage as Lord Heathfield.

561
Major General de la Motte
J. S. Copley

1787. Oil on canvas
53·3 cm × 43·2 cm
Fogg Art Museum, Harvard University, Cambridge, Massachusetts

562
Colonel Dachenhausen
J. S. Copley

1787. Oil on canvas
53·3 cm × 43·2 cm
Fogg Art Museum, Harvard University, Cambridge, Massachusetts

By the end of the Revolution Copley was gaining a great deal of fame and earning a lot of money from his historical paintings. Wishing to celebrate the siege of Gibraltar, the Corporation of London commissioned Copley to paint 'The Repulse of the Floating Batteries at Gibraltar'. Copley laid out a canvas twenty-five feet by twenty and worked six years on the painting.

In 1787, the Corporation sent the artist to Germany so that he could paint the portraits of four Hanoverian officers who had taken part in the defence of the Rock. These oil sketches are two of those portraits.

563
Francis Augustus Eliott and a Spanish officer
Benjamin West

1783. Oil on canvas
99·1 cm × 124·5 cm
Lloyds Bank Limited, Cox and King's Branch, London

Francis Eliott was the son of the Governor of Gibraltar. He was colonel, successively, of the 25th Light Dragoons, the 20th Light Dragoons, and the First or King's Dragoon Guards. Though none of these served in Gibraltar, young Eliott was seconded to the garrison there to be with his father. He probably had his portrait painted with the Spanish officer to celebrate a meeting after the peace was signed. It is amusing to note that the two men have exchanged hats.

564
Rear-Admiral Sir Samuel Hood, 1724–1818
Sir Joshua Reynolds

c. 1783. Oil on canvas
127·2 cm × 130 cm
City of Manchester Art Galleries

When Samuel Hood entered the Royal Navy he served some of his first years as a midshipman with Rodney (see item 566); it was the beginning of a sometimes difficult but fruitful relationship. Fame came to Hood in his fifties. In September 1780, he was promoted to rear-admiral and sent to the West Indies, where he proceeded to handle his squadron with the finesse needed in the complicated chess-like naval game of moves and counter-moves.

In the summer of 1781, Hood was sent north with fourteen ships to support Admiral Graves on the North American coast; Hood was to play a subordinate role in the Battle of the Chesapeake, when the British were outmanoeuvred and Cornwallis thereby isolated in Yorktown. Back in the Caribbean, Hood's seamanship showed itself again in brushes with the French admiral, de Grasse, at the island of St Kitts.

But all these incidents were leading to the final confrontation: the Battle of the Saints (see item 566). There, with Hood at the top of his form in his flagship, the *Barfleur* (98 guns), the admiral finished the day engaged with de Grasse's own flagship, the *Ville de Paris* (110 guns). At 6.29 p.m. (noted in Hood's own journal) on 12 April 1782, the French admiral surrendered to him. It was Hood's greatest moment.

565
Midshipman Joseph Yorke, 1768–1818
George Romney

c. 1782. Oil on canvas. Inscriptions, on top wooden block under naval trophy: 'Joseph Sydney Yorke Aetatis 13 April 12, 1782'. On bottom block: 'ROMNEY'.
91·4 cm × 71·1 cm
Private collection

Yorke joined the Navy in 1780, aged twelve. In March 1781, as a midshipman, he was moved to the *Duke* (98 guns), under the command of Sir Charles Douglas. In December that same year, both captain and midshipman transferred to the *Formidable*, Rodney's flagship in the West Indies. The young boy was in the thick of the fighting throughout the Battle of the Saints.

Later in his career Yorke was knighted and made an admiral. He was drowned when his yacht overturned on its way from Southampton to Portsmouth.

566
Admiral Sir George Rodney, 1719–92
Studio of Reynolds

c. 1790. Oil on canvas
238·7 cm × 146 cm
National Maritime Museum, Greenwich, London

George Bridges Rodney knew the West Indies well. He was first sent there in 1761 as commander-in-chief of the Leeward Islands, where during the Seven Years War he took Martinique, St Lucia, Grenada and St Vincent from the French. In the peace that followed, Rodney was Governor of Greenwich Hospital.

In 1779, Admiral Rodney was offered the Leeward Islands again and was ordered to relieve Gibraltar on the way. In January 1780, nearing Gibraltar, his fleet intercepted a Spanish squadron of nine ships. Two of them were blown up in the action that followed, and seven were captured later. The Rock was relieved for the first time, and Rodney continued to the West Indies with four ships of the line.

During the next two years, with occasional breaks in England because of ill-health, Rodney played the continuous chess game among the islands. One

moment he had the advantage in numbers of ships; the next the French held the superior power.

At the beginning of 1781, soon after Holland came into the war, Rodney captured the Dutch West Indian island of St Eustatius, a previously neutral back door into the West Indies for the merchant-smugglers of the world. Rodney, always impecunious, spent the next three months auctioning their goods and sharing the proceeds.

In January 1782 Rodney returned from one of his visits to England with reinforcements for the Caribbean. Meanwhile, de Grasse, back from his crucial intervention off Yorktown, had retaken St Kitts and captured Nevis and Monserrat. British fortunes were at a low ebb. But de Grasse had an even more ambitious plan in mind: he was to link up with a Spanish fleet at San Domingo and sail on to capture Jamaica.

On 7 April, as the French admiral marshalled his forces between the islands of Dominica and Guadeloupe – close to a group called Les Saintes – his fleet consisted of thirty-three ships of the line, two more of 50 guns each, and a convoy of troops and supplies. Rodney had thirty-six ships of the line under his command. From 9 to 11 April, as the two fleets moved north-westwards, accidents began to whittle away the strength of de Grasse. Two ships collided, others were detached to escort one back; suddenly, when Rodney's fleet threatened the limping ships, de Grasse made the mistake of turning to help . . . and battle was about to be joined.

On 12 April, as Rodney's line ran parallel to that of de Grasse, Rodney's flagship, the *Formidable*, eighteenth in the column, turned with a shift in the wind and sliced through the enemy line, firing broadsides on both sides. Others did the same. The French column was cut up into more vulnerable pieces, and eventual victory lay with the British. The Battle of the Saints was won.

At the end of the day, de Grasse was a prisoner and five enemy ships were in Rodney's hands; two more struck to Hood a week later. The combined forces abandoned their objectives in Jamaica. Hood much criticised Rodney's failure to follow the French for the absolute kill, but it did not matter. Rodney was Britain's hero.

The original of this portrait was exhibited at the Royal Academy in 1789 and is in St James's Palace. This one appears to be the portrait sold in auction in 1821 to the King, having previously belonged to Reynolds's niece.

567
The Ville de Paris, flagship of Admiral de Grasse
Fauconnier

1771. Watercolour on paper. Inscription reads:
'Le vaisseau . . . La Ville de Paris l'encée au port de
Rochefort le 29 janvier 1764. Le nouveau vaisseau a
été donné au Roy par la Ville de Paris de la deuxième
Prevoté de Messire le Camus De Pontecaré de Viarme,
Conseillier d'Etat Provost Des Marchands.'
96 cm × 126 cm
Musée de Carnavalet, Paris

This ship was a gift of the people of Paris to the King.
It became the flagship of Admiral de Grasse.

568
Ship's lantern from the Ville de Paris
55·8 cm high; 27·9 cm diameter
National Maritime Museum, Greenwich, London

This lantern is traditionally held to have been taken
from de Grasse's flagship at its surrender at the Battle
of the Saints.

569
'Count de Grasse delivering his
Sword to the Gallant Admiral Rodney'
T. Colley (?)

'Pub. by P. Mitchell May 27th 1782 as the Act directs
North Audley St'
27·6 cm × 41 cm
Ref: BM 5991
Trustees of the British Museum, London

News of the victory at the Battle of the Saints reached
London on 18 May 1782. This satire may be crudely
executed, but was published with some speed.

The engraving shows an imaginary view of
Rodney's quarter-deck. De Grasse, with the bag-wig
and top boots loved by English satirists, surrenders
his sword to Admiral Rodney. Sailors cheer and
drink a toast. The deck is littered with cannon balls.

In fact, de Grasse surrendered to Admiral Hood's
flagship, and was taken on board Rodney's flagship,
the *Formidable*, two days later.

570
Miniature of Lieutenant-Colonel
Robert Prescott
John Bogle

1776. Signed with initials and dated
Oval; 3·4 cm × 2·8 cm
National Portrait Gallery, London

564

558

71

Prescott was heavily involved in the American Revolution, fighting with the 28th Foot on Long Island, at Fort Washington, Brandywine and Philadelphia. In 1778 he was appointed the first brigadier under General James Grant to fight the French in the West Indies, his first expedition being against St Lucia. He was promoted to the rank of major-general before the end of hostilities, and most of his subsequent career was spent in the West Indies.

571
Captain Horatio Nelson, 1758–1805
Francis Rigaud

1780. Oil on canvas. Inscribed (later): 'Capt Horatio Nelson 1781'
127 cm × 101·6 cm
National Maritime Museum, Greenwich, London

Eighteen years before his first famous victory at the Nile, Horatio Nelson was in action during the American Revolution. Now at war with Spain, ally of the American colonies, Caribbean-based officers decided to attack Fort Juan in Nicaragua, part of the Spanish Main. In April 1780 a force of 500 regulars and 1000 blacks and settlers, depleted en route by sickness, set out to attack a fort situated on the San Juan river. In a week of cannonading, the guns were laid either by the chief engineer or by the young Nelson.

Captain Nelson is seen here in the full dress uniform of a captain (of over three years). In the background is Fort Juan. The picture was begun in 1777, when Nelson was a lieutenant, and finished in 1786.

572
French attack on St Lucia is thrown back
Pierre Ozanne

1778. Watercolour on paper. Inscription: 'Vue de l'attaque de L'Isle de Ste Lucie le 15 et le 17 X^bre 1778.'
25 cm × 42 cm
Ref: LC-USZ62-7702
Library of Congress, Washington, D.C.

Two more watercolours from the series painted by Ozanne, engineer and artist, who travelled from France in the fleet of the Comte d'Estaing. In this one he records the attack on St Lucia by d'Estaing's forces in December 1778, just after the British had captured it.

Forced from the first two landing targets by heavy cannonades, d'Estaing switched his 9000 troops to a landing five miles north of the British. Five thousand

Frenchmen then attacked three British battalions on a hilly peninsula (right of centre). Three times they were thrown back. And from what Piers Mackesy calls 'this Bunker Hill of the Caribbean', the French retreated with thirty per cent casualties.

573
The French capture Grenada
Pierre Ozanne

1779. Watercolour on paper. Inscription: 'Vue du fort et Ville de S^t· George dans L'isle de la Granade et du Morne de l'hopital emporté d'assaut par les troupes francoises aux ordres de vice-amiral d'Estaing. le 4 Juillet 1779'
25 cm × 42 cm
Ref: LC-USZ62-7697
Library of Congress, Washington, D.C.

By the middle of 1779 more reinforcements had arrived in the West Indies from France. The balance of power now rested with the enemy. On 2 July d'Estaing attacked Grenada. The British garrison numbered 159 regulars and 300 militia, and soon surrendered. The richest sugar island was lost.

NEW MAPS AT VERSAILLES
574
The American Signers for Peace
This photograph of an unfinished Benjamin West oil sketch shows the American signers of the preliminary articles of peace. From left to right, they are American diplomat John Jay, John Adams, Benjamin Franklin, Henry Laurens and William Temple Franklin, grandson of Benjamin. The articles, completed on 30 November 1782, were signed for Britain by Richard Oswald and Caleb Whitefoord.

The original picture is at the Henry Francis du Pont Winterthur Museum, Winterthur, Delaware.

575
The British Witness
Caleb Whitefoord, as he is seen in this photograph of a Gilbert Stuart portrait, had been a neighbour of Franklin in London. Because of their friendship, Lord Shelburne, first Secretary of State for Home and Colonial Affairs and by this time Britain's Prime Minister, had chosen Whitefoord to act as intermediary between the British Government and Franklin, who was then United States minister at Versailles. In Paris with Richard Oswald, Whitefoord served for a year as secretary to the peace commission.

The original portrait is at the Montclair Museum, New Jersey.

574

579

576
The Map of the Peace Treaty

'A Map of the British Colonies in North America with the Roads, Distances, Limits, and Extent of the settlements, Humbly inscribed to the Right Honourable the Earl of Halifax . . . By . . . Jnº Mitchell. Tho: Kitchin Sculp. London: Publish'd by the Author, 1755 (1775).' MS additions by Richard Oswald, c. 1782

197 cm × 140 cm. Scale: 1 : 2,000,000
Ref: K.118d.26 (K. Top. CXVIII 49.b)
Trustees of the British Library, London

The Red-Lined Map, as it is known, was brought to the negotiating table by Richard Oswald, and the boundary line and other annotations are in his own hand. The red line, defined as 'The Boundary as described by Mr. Oswald', marks the limits of the United States and her neighbours. This map appears to have been prepared as the copy for George III.

Richard Oswald (1705–84) spent many years in business in the American colonies and married into estates there and in the West Indies. During the Revolution, because of his friendship with Franklin, he was often consulted in Britain on American affairs. When Henry Laurens, one of the American peace signers, was earlier captured on the high seas and imprisoned in the Tower, Oswald went bail for him for £50,000. Though Oswald signed the preliminary articles of peace in November 1782, he was not there to sign the definitive treaty in September 1783. Britain had a new government and a new representative, David Hartley.

577
Preliminary articles of peace between Great Britain and America

30 November 1782
38·1 cm × 48·3 cm open
Ref: F.O.93/8/1
Public Record Office, London

The articles signed on 30 November 1782 immediately recognised the independence of the United States of America. According to protocol, Oswald signed first as the representative of the most venerable state. After that, the Americans signed in alphabetical order. This page of the treaty, signed, and witnessed by the secretaries of the two commissions, covered a separate article on the future of West Florida which was supposed to be secret, but which soon leaked out.

578
The definitive Treaty of Paris between Great Britain and the United States

3 September 1783
38·1 cm × 48·3 cm open
Ref: F.O.93/8/2
Public Record Office, London

The treaty was signed at the apartment of David Hartley at the Hotel d'York in Paris. Representing a crowned head, he signed first. His signature was followed by those of Adams, Franklin and Jay. The secret article of the preliminary treaty was missing.

579
David Hartley M.P., 1732–1813
George Romney

c. 1784. Oil on canvas
127 cm × 101·6 cm
Fidelity Union Trust Company as executors of the estate of the late Geraldine R. Dodge, Newark, New Jersey

David Hartley, politician and scientist, was an intimate friend and correspondent of Benjamin Franklin. Throughout the Revolution he stood firmly against the war with the Colonists. He represented Hull as a Member of Parliament from 1774–80 and 1782–4. The regard in which Hartley was held by the new Government ensured that he would be sent to Paris as Britain's plenipotentiary to sign the final treaty of peace with the United States.

The portrait shows a rolled document on the table on the left. Romney has incorrectly inscribed it: 'Definitive Treaty with the United States of America Sept 1780'.

580
Cabinet minute ordering evacuation of New York

30 March 1782
30·5 cm × 19·8 cm
Ref: RA 4583
Her Majesty the Queen

This Cabinet minute is in the handwriting of Lord Shelburne, then Secretary of State for Home and Colonial Affairs. It is addressed to the King and advises the evacuation of the garrison of New York to Halifax, and of Charlestown and Savannah. This delicate task was to be carried out by Sir Guy Carleton, former Governor of Quebec and commander-in-chief in Canada, and at this point to be commander-in-chief in North America. The evacuation was completed on 25 November 1783.

A Kind of Kinship

> By the rude bridge that arched the flood
> Their flag to April's breeze unfurled,
> Here once the embattled farmers stood
> And fired the shot heard round the world.

O F COURSE EMERSON GOT IT WRONG. In 1775 the first shots in anger were fired not at Concord, but eight miles away and six hours earlier at Lexington: and no one knows or will ever know who ordered or shouted 'Fire!'. But, thanks in part to poetry – which matters more than facts in the making of legends – Concord Bridge is where it all began. And of course there is another legend, of those who came without any choice over 3000 miles of ocean from the slums and the fields of the Old Country to die to farmers' bullets on alien soil.

> They came 3000 miles and died
> To keep the past upon its throne.

This was a clash of two competing calls of duty. And on both sides of the water there were Patriots and Loyalists, for it was the first of international ideological wars, a war for and in the minds of men.

There is today another bridge: London Bridge, moved bodily to Arizona in 1970 and carefully re-erected there, along with a specially constructed river, and imported old London buses. For running through the special Anglo-American relationship there has always been an American love-hate affair with a trad and untrendy Britain, an ancestral yearning perhaps for their missing past, in a nevernever land of porticos and lawns, tea-on-the-terrace above a fog-bound river, with the sound of a hansom cab just audible in the distance.

The aristocratic virtues of spirit, courtesy and style – what Hemingway called 'grace under pressure' – have been admired by generations of American writers, and they have found them exemplified in particular types of Englishmen, especially if they happened to be born on a ducal estate, played cricket with a straight bat, and with the church clock at ten-to-three.

But bitterness after 1783 was slow to fade. Lord Sheffield wanted to exclude the U.S. from the Navigation system and campaigned hard to do so. Britain, shaken by the war, became cool to the idea of colonies for a whole generation. It is true that in 1815, after the final defeat of Napoleon, the map of the world was dotted

facing page: item 591

with red ports of call and victualling bases aptly located 400 or 500 miles sailing distance from each other; but for at least two generations, colonies were now seen as millstones. The aftermath of Independence in 1783 was not an era of good feelings. And – sometimes at Canada's expense – there were waves of ill-will through much of the 19th century.

What brought the sense of a special relationship into being? It did not exist at the time of the first centennial of American independence in 1876, when the United States seemed brash and vulgar, and Britain was looking east rather than west. Within twelve months of that event, Queen Victoria was proclaimed Empress of India, and within a decade Britain was beginning to push the Empire deeper into East and West Africa. It looked to and beyond Suez, not just to the New World. The United States was moving west, and the railroads were snaking their way across the plains and over the high sierras. In the wake of them the continent was being unified by the telegraph and by the telephone, and in the forty years up to 1914, 40 million immigrants, overwhelmingly non-English, moved into the United States, with names like Lewis and Carnegie, Dubinsky, Knudsen and Frankfurter, Schurz, Pabst and Budweiser, Capone and Kennedy, Adamic, Toscanini, Stokowski, Mann and Einstein.

The special relationship is a 20th-century phenomenon. It started when, at the end of the 19th century, the American people began to invest abroad, to have a two-ocean navy and interests in China and the Pacific, in the Middle East and the Caribbean. 'Take up the white man's burden, send forth the best ye breed . . .': Kipling's advice was designed for American ears, and was written in Vermont.

Behind the facts of their direct and indirect empires was the awareness of George III's ties of language and blood as voiced now by politicians like Joseph Chamberlain and Cecil Rhodes, Theodore Roosevelt and Admiral Mahan, and by professors in both countries in a wave of 'Nordic' and 'Anglo-Saxon' nostalgia. Part of it became the fashionable 'history' of the period. The ducal marriages of the Edwardian age among Vanderbilts and Marlboroughs, Astors and Langhornes, made Mirador, Virginia, and Newport, Rhode Island, Ditchley, Blenheim and Cliveden, centres of Anglo-Americanism. The 8th and 9th Dukes of Manchester and the 8th and 9th Dukes of Marlborough married American brides, and the last of these got, as well as a bride, $2½ billion with which to rebuild – and maintain – Blenheim. When the cynic said, Good Americans – when they die – go to Paris, he could with more truth have said London. Both Churchill and Macmillan had American mothers, and Churchill could properly claim, in addressing Congress in December 1941, that if his father had been American and his mother English he might have reached Congress on his own.

By 1941 the waning authority of Britain and the waxing power of the u.s. had made war between them unthinkable. Not that they were necessarily permanent friends, simply that they now had permanent and complementary interests. These were apparent strategically as early as 1922, in the naval treaties of Washington where Britain and the United States were brought together as equal partners in the face of the threat of Japan. The United States had come into World War I late, and reluctantly, driven in less by Woodrow Wilson's Anglophilia than by the folly of the German U-boat attacks on American shipping. In 1919, the United States withdrew into a dangerous isolation, so complete that it permitted – because it had no power in Europe to avert – the rise of the dictators.

The high point of the relationship was in 1939–45, in the remarkable friendship of Franklin D. Roosevelt and Winston Churchill. In the years from September 1939, when Britain's war started, until April 1945, when President Roosevelt died, they exchanged over 1700 letters. This was roughly one per day, often long, always frank and comradely, occasionally snappily astringent. That correspondence began on F.D.R.'s initiative, by-passing the then Prime Minister, Neville Chamberlain, and it continued until his death. This was the exchange of two men with total trust and deep affection for each other – the special relationship at its supreme best, and in its finest hour. Oceans no longer divided those who spoke Shakespeare's or Milton's language, the language of liberty.

This friendship was buttressed thereafter by NATO, the joint and interdependent commitment of American and British troops to Europe for fifty years – the first occasion that Britain as well as the U.S. undertook permanently to station its forces in Europe in peacetime. As a consequence, in all the fifty-two minor or major outbreaks of war in the world since 1945, an uneasy truce has held in Europe. Ironically it was in the last months of his life that F.D.R., working from strength, tried to play the role of 'fixer' and pragmatist with Stalin; it was Churchill, working from the weakness of the drain of two world wars, who at Fulton, Missouri, in 1946, as before and after, spoke for firmness. It was in this speech that he not only spoke of an iron curtain across Europe but of 'a special relationship across the Atlantic'. On the Anglo-American accord rests the security and the stability of all western Europe, and of much of Asia.

The alliance now is rooted in things other than a common concern over security. In all their differences of political structure, each is an open and democratic society; each shares a faith in law, and in the binding character of a Constitution, whether written or unwritten; each shares those assumptions about freedom and order in government and society of which the British Magna Carta has become the symbol – and a copy of it goes as the British Government's Bicentennial gift to sit beside the Declaration of Independence; a host of easy educational exchanges cement the ties of political necessity.

Each country now, behind the largely artificial distinctions of sovereignty and independence, is but a complement of the other in a world grown one and interdependent. Benjamin Franklin, the wisest, shrewdest and most prescient of all Anglo-Americans, saw it all over 200 years ago:

There are suppos'd to be now upwards of one million English souls in North America . . . This million doubling, suppose but once in 25 years, will, in another century, be more than the people of England, and the greatest number of Englishmen will be on this side of the water.

ESMOND WRIGHT

[The end of the American Revolution saw not the birth of one nation but the creation of two. Forty-five thousand Colonists, loyal to George III, sailed or trekked north to Canada. In Ontario, in Nova Scotia and in New Brunswick, hundreds of families and companies of soldiers began, quite literally, to hack new homes out of the virgin wilderness.]

581
Halifax, Nova Scotia
Lieutenant-Colonel Edward Hicks

1781. Aquatint with watercolour on paper
35·1 cm × 52·1 cm
Public Archives of Canada, Ottawa

The view describes the north-west aspect of the Citadel of Halifax with soldiers and tents in the middle distance. Apart from the role Halifax was to play in Loyalist days after the Revolution, the town was an active military base throughout the war itself. Howe had retreated there from Boston, and the port was the first reception point on the North American coast for many regiments sailing from England.

Colonel Hicks was with his regiment, the 70th Foot, in America from 1778. In 1781 it was posted to Nova Scotia, where he executed his series of illustrations of Halifax.

582
A view of Montreal
James Peachey

Watercolour on paper. Inscription: 'Montreal – Surrendered, with all Canada, on the 8th Day of Sept! 1760, to His Majesty's Army Commanded by Lieu! General, now, Lord Amherst. Taken from the Top of the Mountain the 15th of Oct! 1784.' Signed bottom left: 'Ja.s Peachey 1785'
38·7 cm × 59 cm
Private collection

After the initial assaults of Rebel troops on Montreal and Quebec at the end of 1775 and the beginning of 1776, the two cities played the more passive roles of military bases. In 1784 they were attractive magnets to the incoming Loyalists.

583
View of Quebec
James Peachey

Watercolour on paper. Inscription: 'A View of Quebec taken from the Ferry House on the Opposite

584 (detail)

side of the River S! Laurence, Taken October the 3.ᵈ 1784'. Signed 'Ja.ˢ Peachey 1785'
Alternative title: 'Quebec in Canada. Taken by Major General Wolfe on the 18th of September 1759.'
38·7 cm × 59 cm
Private collection

The lower town of Quebec can be seen in the middle distance. To the left are the Heights of Abraham.

584
Loyalist encampment at Johnstown on the banks of the St Lawrence
James Peachey

Watercolour on paper. Inscription: 'Encampment of The Loyalists at Johnstown, on the Banks of the River S! Laurence in Canada, taken June 6th 1784'.
Signed lower left: 'James Peachey 1785'
31·7 cm × 49·8 cm
Private collection

An extremely rare view of Loyalists newly arrived in Canada. Tents and log huts were their first primitive homes. Survival depended on rural skills in the summer and on courage to live through the winter. It is June here; November and the snows are not so far away.

585
The King's Head Inn sign
c. 1794. Painted wood. One side reads: 'King's Head Inn 1794'. The other bears a portrait of George III with the inscription, 'George the IIIrd King of Great Britain'
77·3 cm × 62·2 cm
Joseph Brant Museum, Burlington, Ontario

An inn sign whose portrait would at this time be found in North America only in the Loyalist territories of Canada. The sign (possibly repainted since) was used for a hotel which served travellers passing along Lieutenant-Governor John Simcoe's new road from Newark (now Niagara-on-the-Lake) to London, Ontario.

586
Miniature of Sir Guy Carleton, 1724–1808
Artist unknown. 'From a picture by Mr. Wellengs 1783'
Oval brooch, circled stones
4·4 cm × 3·8 cm
The Earl and Countess of Malmesbury, Basingstoke, Hampshire

Guy Carleton was wounded at the capture of Quebec on 13 September 1759, where he commanded the corps of grenadiers. He distinguished himself further at the siege of Havana. In September 1766 Carleton was appointed Lieutenant-Governor of Quebec. He was instrumental in furthering the cause of the Quebec Act, in which Roman Catholics in Canada were given freedom of religion, and he was warmly welcomed by the religious community when he returned after leave of absence in England.

During the American Revolution, Sir Guy Carleton commanded the successful defence of Quebec against Montgomery and Benedict Arnold, attempted the first invasion against the Rebels down Lake Champlain, and ordered the defences of Canada generally. Back in England, in February 1782, he was ordered to replace Clinton in America and he supervised the eventual evacuation of the British forces from the United States. As Lord Dorchester, Guy Carleton returned to Canada once again as Governor of Quebec where he stayed until July, 1796.

Some authorities consider Carleton to have been the most able commander in America. However, the personal feud he had with Germain inhibited the realisation of his full potential as a field officer.

587
Miniature of General Thomas Carleton, 1735–1817
Sampson Towgood Roche

c. 1795. Watercolour on ivory
Oval; 5·9 cm × 4·6 cm
The Beaverbrook Art Gallery, Fredericton, New Brunswick (Gift of Lady Dorchester, 1963)

Thomas Carleton, younger brother of Sir Guy (see item 586), served on the Continent in the Seven Years War, was four years at Gibraltar, and in 1774 obtained permission to serve with the Russians against the Turks. In 1776, Carleton arrived in Canada and became quartermaster-general to the forces his brother commanded. On 16 August 1784 he was appointed the first governor of the newly-created province of New Brunswick, fast filling with emigré Loyalists.

588
Letter from American colonists to the inhabitants of Canada
1774
21 cm × 13·8 cm
McCord Museum, Montreal, Quebec

At the time of the Quebec Act, which among other things gave Roman Catholics in Canada freedom of religion, potentially rebel Americans were attempting to seduce Quebec into becoming the fourteenth state of an American nation. This letter invited the Province to send delegates to the Continental Congress in Philadelphia in May 1775.

The English merchant class of Canada disliked the Act as a whole, but it was enough to secure some sort of allegiance to the Crown from the French-speaking population. Certainly it was true that the French of Quebec had no love for the New England Protestants.

589
Powder horn with Canadian map
Horn, with Royal Coat of Arms and initials 'A M'. The map marks the following places, lakes and rivers: La Riviere Sint Lorance, Lisle Au Galot, Fort Ontario, Fort Bruinton, Lake Onyda, Canada Creek, MowHock Rivier, Lake Ontario, Niagara, Wood Creek and Fort Stanwix.
Private collection

590
Pocket sundial
Brass. Butterfield type. Inscribed on the face: 'Pre Le Maire, Paris' On the reverse: 'Maison De la Trinité 51.5' Les piche Bourouni 49'
Private collection

This miniature sundial was manufactured in Paris for use in Canada, a necessary aid to travel there in the 18th century. Various useful latitudes were included on the reverse. They read:

québec 46–45'	lac St. jean 49
Montréalle 45–15'	lac Mistassin 52.
Louis bourg 45–40'	Michipcoton 41.45'
fort St anne 52.15'	fort Louis 51.50'
Abnakis 46.50'	port Royalle 44.10'
les jrocois 45.	labaye 44.15'

591
John Adams, first American Minister to the Court of St James
After Copley

c. 1785. Oil on canvas
50·8 cm × 34·3 cm
Museum of Fine Arts, Boston, Massachusetts

John Adams had served America as part of the commission in Paris which negotiated the peace treaty with Britain. He now had a new task: to help repair the natural bonds between Americans and Britons which the Revolution had torn apart. He was to be the United States' first ambassador to London.

On 1 June 1785, Adams approached George III in the King's Closet at St James's Palace to present his credentials. Adams had been reluctant to take part in the usual ceremony apart from presenting his credentials silently and leaving, but other diplomats in London had persuaded him to make a speech. Both men, the 'Rebel' and the 'Tyrant', were nervous of each other.

John Adams's speech included this passage: 'Sir . . . The appointment of a Minister from the United States to your Majesty's Court will form an epoch in the history of England and of America. I think myself more fortunate than all my fellow citizens in having the distinguished honour to be the first to stand in your Majesty's royal presence in a diplomatic character, and shall esteem myself the happiest of men if I can be instrumental in recommending my country more and more to your Majesty's royal benevolence, and of restoring an entire esteem, confidence, and affection; or in better words, the old good nature and the old good humour between people who, though separated by an ocean, and under different governments, have the same language, a similar religion and kindred blood.'

The King, much moved by the American minister's remarks, replied and ended his speech thus: 'I wish you, sir, to believe, and that it may be understood in America, that I have done nothing in the late contest, but what I thought myself indispensably bound to do by the duty which I owed to my people. I will be very frank with you. I was the last to consent to the separation; but the separation having been made, and having become inevitable, I have always said, as I say now, that I would be the first to meet the friendship of the United States as an independent Power. The moment I see such sentiments and language as yours prevail, and a disposition to give to this country the preference, that moment I shall say, let the circumstances of language, religion and blood have their natural and full effect.'

[In the '1776' Exhibition the two extracts are spoken by Mr Elliot Richardson, and His Royal Highness the Prince of Wales].

THE EPILOGUE

From the Bridge at Concord, where the Revolution began, to today's bridges across the Atlantic, the Exhibition's epilogue illuminates those special ties which further celebrate the Anglo-American connection.

592
Silver plate from Thomas Jefferson's home at Monticello
1792. Silver
23·8 cm diameter
The Lady Reigate, London

This silver plate from Monticello, Jefferson's home in Virginia, was made by Miguel Picazo in Mexico City in 1792. It is hallmarked and carries the Cary Arms (a Jefferson family connection), and the initials of Thomas Jefferson Coolidge, who was a great-grandson of Thomas Jefferson.

593
Centenary dress, 1876
Cotton
New York State History Collections, Schenectady

One hundred years ago the United States celebrated the Centenary of its Independence with a massive World Trade Fair in Philadelphia. Among the largest pavilions there was the British contribution, a wonderland of new technology. Somewhere among the crowds of thousands was this dress designed to celebrate a nation taking stock of itself.

The design shows the American eagle with thirteen stars over its head. The inscribed strips bear the repeated words: '1776. 1876. IN GOD WE TRUST', and: 'U.S. OF A. WELCOME CENTENNIAL'.

594
The Reconciliation
This photo-montage is based on a detail from the 18th-century engraving called 'The Reconciliation between Britania and her daughter America'. Britannia is saying, 'Be a good Girl and give me a Buss [a kiss].' And America replies, 'Dear Mama say no more about it'. In the full engraving Spain and France are trying to pull America away from Britain. Holland sits on the sidelines.

The engraving, published about May 1782, is in the British Museum, London; ref: BM 5989.

595
Whitsuntide Holidays
The photo-mural shows details of an engraving entitled 'Whitsuntide Holidays'. The year is 1783. The American Revolution is over. British admirals and a few generals have recovered some feeling of national pride: 'Rodney for Ever', proclaims a sailor's flag.

The original is in the British Museum, London; ref: BM 6346.

Notes on the Artists

James Barry Born Cork, 1741; died London, 1806. His work at the Dublin Society of Artists attracted the interest of Edmund Burke, who brought Barry to London. Elected to Royal Academy in 1773. His large-scale murals for the Society of Arts in the Adelphi (1777–84) won him recognition as the most distinguished epic painter of the day. He was buried in St Paul's.

Pompeo Batoni Born Lucca, 1708; died Rome, 1787. Influential painter, curator of the Papal Collections. Worked for many foreign patrons, and specialised in portraits. Members of the British nobility had their pictures painted by Batoni while visiting Rome on a Grand Tour.

Francis Bauer Born Austria, 1758; died London, 1840. A specialist in flower paintings, Bauer worked in Europe until 1788. Settling in London in 1790, he was employed by Sir Joseph Banks to execute the official botanical drawings at Kew.

Thomas Beach 1738–1806; Dorset-born. Pupil of Reynolds who concentrated on small portraits and groups. Sir Horace Walpole wrote: 'Mr Beach is a painter whose portraits never require the horrid question of – "Pray, who is that, Sir?" . . . his rooms may be said to exhibit the form and figure of the times.'

Henry Benbridge 1743–1811/2. Born in Philadelphia. Sent to Italy by rich stepfather, and may have studied under Batoni. In London in 1769, but back in Philadelphia by 1770. He moved to Charleston to become the leading painter in South Carolina. Said to have been a British prisoner during Revolution. Buried in Christ Church, Philadelphia.

John Bogle c. 1746–1803. Studied at the Drawing School in Glasgow, and subsequently practised as a miniaturist in Edinburgh and London. He exhibited at the Royal Academy from 1772–94.

Richard Brompton 1734–88. Pupil of Benjamin Wilson in London. Also worked in Rome and Venice. Released from Fleet Prison (he was in for debt) around 1778, Brompton travelled to Russia under the protection of the Empress Catherine. He was then appointed Court painter at St Petersburg.

Mather Brown 1761–1831. Son of a clockmaker, he had lessons at the age of twelve from Gilbert Stuart in Boston. In 1777 on trip through New England selling miniatures and wine, he wrote: 'The Yankeys are going to Philadelphia; I believe I shall follow them.' Instead, he went to Paris and in 1781 became a pupil of Benjamin West in London. He exhibited at the Royal Academy and hunted with the King.

Henry W. Bunbury 1750–1811. Of genial nature and some private means, Bunbury began to caricature at school and college. Later, he was a friend of Garrick and Reynolds. He stayed away from political subjects, but his comic observations of life were widely engraved by Gillray and others. He 'sold prodigiously'.

Jean-Jacques Caffieri 1725–92. French sculptor of family of artists descended from 17th-century papal engineer. Best known today for his statues and portrait busts for the Comédie Française.

George Carter 1737–95. Born in Colchester, and mainly a subject painter. His picture of Governor Eliott and staff at Gibraltar was probably painted in 1784. An Eliott letter refers to the artist's visit to the Rock in August of that year, two years after the siege.

John Cleveley c. 1712–77. A marine painter. He worked in Deptford dockyards, and studied watercolour painting with Paul Sandby during his training as a naval draughtsman. He exhibited at the Society of Artists from 1764 and at the Royal Academy from 1770.

Robert Cleveley 1747–1809. A one-time sailor and shipwright at Deptford, son of John Cleveley, he exhibited marine subjects and naval actions at the Royal Academy between 1780 and 1803. He was appointed marine painter to the Prince of Wales, and subsequently died falling from a cliff at Dover.

John Singleton Copley 1738–1815. An American of English-Irish origins. A self-taught portrait and history painter. First showed at the Royal Academy in 1776, and elected a full member in 1779 (see also item 353).

Richard Cosway 1742–1821. Born in Tiverton, Devon, his early drawings attracted the attention of the Duke of Richmond, Cipriani and Bartholozzi. Cosway was a student at the Royal Academy Schools and elected an R.A. in 1771. He became well known as a miniature painter.

Nathaniel Dance 1735–1811. Painter of portraits and historical subjects. He spent many years in Italy and was much enamoured of fellow-artist Angelica Kauffmann. He was a founder-member of the Royal Academy. In 1790, he retired from painting and entered Parliament.

Thomas Davies *c.* 1737–1812. A graduate of the Royal Military Academy at Woolwich and contemporary of Paul Sandby. He worked in America during the Seven Years War, at the beginning of the American Revolution (see item 252), and later in Canada during a peacetime posting to Quebec. His 'primitive' landscapes have only recently begun to be acknowledged for their true worth.

Edward Dayes 1763–1804. Began as a miniaturist and mezzotint artist. Engravings of his topographical tinted drawings of London circulated widely. He was also an art critic.

Robert Dighton 1752(?)–1814. Portrait painter, etcher and caricaturist. He first exhibited at the Free Society of Artists in 1769 and then at the Royal Academy in 1775. Later in his life, it was discovered that he had been systematically adding to his own collection of prints and watercolours by removing numerous items from the British Museum.

Ralph Earl 1751–1801. Born in Massachusetts. By 1774 he was painting portraits in New Haven, Connecticut, from where he travelled to Lexington and Concord in 1775 (see item 29). By 1779 he was painting in England, where he studied under Benjamin West, was made a member of the Royal Academy, and painted the King. He returned to America in the late 1780s.

Thomas Gainsborough 1727–88. Painter of portraits and landscapes. He worked in Suffolk, Bath and London where he exhibited at the Society of Artists and the Royal Academy. He settled in London in 1774 and by 1781 was working for the King, the Queen and the Prince of Wales. A contemporary described him: 'A natural Gentleman, and with all his simplicity he had wit, too.' Reynolds once raised his glass to 'The greatest landscape painter of the day.'

Daniel Gardner 1750–1805. Born in Kendal, Westmorland, and influenced in early years by his neighbour George Romney, whom he followed to London in 1767–8. Gardner entered the R.A. Schools in 1770. After showing one picture in 1771, he never exhibited again, though he was very active, working in pastel, gouache and oil.

Henry Gilder Dates unknown. Gilder was a pupil of Thomas Sandby, elder brother of Paul. He exhibited watercolours at the Royal Academy four times in the 1770s.

John Graham 1754–1817. Born in Edinburgh, he was apprenticed to the city's leading coach-painter. He later lived in Leicester Square in London and exhibited at the Royal Academy from 1780 to 1797. He was, by contemporary accounts, an inspiring teacher.

Charles Grignion 1754–1804. Son of a Covent Garden watchmaker, he was winning art prizes by the age of fourteen.

He was one of the earliest students at the Royal Academy and a pupil of Cipriani. In 1776 he won the gold medal for the historical painting, 'The Judgment of Hercules'. He exhibited regularly and went to Rome in 1782.

Francis Holman Active 1767–90. Very little is known about Holman, one of the finest 18th-century marine painters. Born in Cornwall, he lived at Wapping and exhibited at the Royal Academy between 1774 and 1784.

Nathaniel Hone 1718–84. Born in Dublin, he was a self-taught portrait painter. He was a founder-member of the Royal Academy, but when the Academy refused a painting, taken to be a satirical attack on Reynolds, Hone held the first known one-man exhibition in St Martin's Lane, showing sixty-six paintings and an account of his dispute with the R.A. He ran a prosperous studio.

Jean-Antoine Houdon 1741–1828. After working in Rome, Houdon settled in Paris in 1769 and was elected to the Academy in 1777. Considered the finest sculptor of portrait-busts in Europe in his day, he sculpted Franklin in 1778. In 1785, Houdon travelled to America to execute a full-length statue of George Washington, which today stands in Richmond, Virginia.

John Johnston 1753–1818. Born in Boston, son of Thomas Johnston. He achieved some local success for his portrait painting.

Thomas Johnston *c.* 1708–67. Boston-born, he was a man of wide talents, engraving maps, currency, trade cards, music sheets, etc. His own card advertised that he was skilled in varnishing, japanning, gilding, drawing and painting. He was also an organ-builder.

Tilly Kettle 1735–86. Born in London, son of a coach-painter. Walpole says he went 'to India in 1770, where he soon gained £30,000 by drawing portraits of nabobs and black merchants'. He first exhibited at the R.A. in 1777. On a return visit to the Indies, he died at Aleppo.

Philippe Jacques de Loutherbourg 1740–1812. Born in Strasbourg. Studied in Paris under Canova, and was then Court painter to the King of France. Brought to London in 1771 to become Garrick's chief designer at Drury Lane. He was elected a member of the Royal Academy in 1780, where he had exhibited from 1772 onwards. Away from the theatre, he was popular for his hunting scenes, battles and seascapes.

William Marlow 1740–1813. Born in Southwark, he was later a pupil of Samuel Scott. Walpole records that Marlow went through Flanders and France to Italy in 1765 and returned a year later 'improved in his colouring'. His early work included many views of country seats. He specialised in views of London, and of the Thames by Richmond and Twickenham where he settled.

Jeremiah Meyer 1735–89. A miniaturist born of German parents. He was invited to membership of the Royal Academy in 1769. His miniatures were very highly prized.

James Miller   Active 1773–91. Son of a German draughtsman and engraver. Became a landscape painter in watercolours. Exhibited at the Royal Academy from 1773 to 1775.

Thomas Mitchell   Active 1735–90. A shipwright by profession who also practised as a painter of marine subjects. In 1774 he was an assistant shipbuilder at Deptford, later to become assistant surveyor of the navy. He exhibited at the R.A. from 1774 to 1789.

Jean-Laurent Mosnier   1744–1809. Born in Paris, died in St Petersburg. A member of the French Academy, he came to Britain at the outbreak of the French Revolution. A diarist saw him as: 'The ingenious M. Mosnier, often talking with Sir Joshua Reynolds.'

Richard Paton   1716(?)–91. Held a post in the Excise Office and managed to paint by 'his early habits'. He was a marine painter and began to exhibit at the Royal Academy in 1776. Walpole wrote that Paton '. . . had the honour of waiting on His Majesty at the Queens Palace with some of his pictures . . . H.M. was pleased to honour the artist with his approbation . . .'

James Peachey   Active in Canada, 1781–93. An officer in the British army, he was a surveyor attached to the office of Samuel Holland, Surveyor-General of Canada. Peachey was later appointed Deputy Surveyor-General. He prepared maps and plans of Lower Canada, and illustrated the Book of Common Prayer which Indian Chief Joseph Brant translated into Mohawk. He exhibited his Canadian views at the Royal Academy 1786–7.

Charles Willson Peale   1741–1827. In 1766 eleven gentlemen of Maryland subscribed seventy-four guineas and eight pounds to send Charles Willson Peale to study in London. There he worked with Benjamin West, returning to the Colonies in 1769. His fame grew as he painted the leaders of Maryland, and in 1776 he moved with his family to Philadelphia, where he was elected an officer of a regiment that fought at Princeton. He was also present at Valley Forge. Peale became the portrait painter of the Revolution.

James Peale   1749–1831. Younger brother of Charles. Worked much in the shadow of the elder artist. He fought with the Continental army, and then resigned over promotion in 1779. It is likely that he followed the army to Yorktown, where he sketched scenes which would appear in some of the Peale 'Washington' studies.

Robert Edge Pine   Born London, 1730, died Philadelphia, 1788. The son of a well-known engraver, Pine was first interested in painting the theatrical world. Always sympathetic to the American cause, he left for Philadelphia in 1784. There, before he died, he painted Washington and many other figures of the Revolution.

Matthew Pratt   1734–1804. Born in Philadelphia, the son of a goldsmith. He began as a sign-painter and later studied in London from 1764–8 under Benjamin West. Finally, a portrait painter and miniaturist, he assisted the Peales in the establishment of their natural history museum in Philadelphia.

Henry Raeburn   1756–1823. Apprenticed to a goldsmith, his skill as a miniaturist set him on his way to becoming Scotland's leading portrait painter of the period. After studying in Rome, he settled in Edinburgh. In 1822 he was knighted and became His Majesty's Limner for Scotland.

Allan Ramsay   1713–84. Born in Edinburgh, settled in London in 1738 after the first of his Continental tours. Lord Bute later introduced him to the Royal Family. He was appointed Painter in Ordinary to the Court and from then on painted very little but portraits and replicas of portraits of the Royal Family.

Christian Remick   1726–73. A mariner and then a ship's captain, he was also a self-taught painter. He turned professional in 1769 when he advertised 'Specimens of his Performances, particularly an accurate View of the Blockade of Boston . . .' He died in an almshouse.

Sir Joshua Reynolds   1723–92. Born in Plympton, Devon, the son of a clergyman-schoolmaster. He studied in London and Italy, was inspired to experiment with colour from his contact with Venetian painters, and back in London soon won a queue of sitters (125 in 1755). In 1768 he became the first President of the Royal Academy and a year later was knighted. In 1784 he succeeded Ramsay as Principal Painter to the King, but Reynolds had more friends among the Opposition and was therefore not greatly liked by George III. Nevertheless he enjoyed a wide circle of friends and was described by Dr Johnson as 'essentially a clubbable man'. When he died in 1792 he lay in state at the Royal Academy and was buried in St Paul's next to Christopher Wren.

Francis Rigaud   1742–1810. Born in Turin, he studied in Italy and arrived in London in 1771. A year later he became an Associate R.A., and apart from his portraits was notable for his frescoes, ceilings and altarpieces. He later became Chief Painter to the Queen of Sweden.

Sampson Towgood Roche   1759–1847. Born in Waterford, Ireland. He was a deaf mute who later worked in Dublin. In 1792 he moved to Bath for a period before returning home.

George Romney   1734–1802. Arrived in London in 1762 after apprenticeship to a cabinet-maker. Gained Society of Arts award (£25) for his 'Death of General Wolfe'. Travelled on the Continent, 1773–5, and then returned to London to settle in Cavendish Square where 'there was a constant influx of sitters'. His charges rose to 'full-length, 80 gns; half, 40; head, 20'. By 1783 he was regarded as Reynolds' rival. Lord Thurlow, who sat for him, said: 'Reynolds and Romney divide the town, I am of the Romney faction.'

Thomas Rowlandson   1756–1827. Son of a Spitalfields silk merchant. Entered the R.A. Schools at the age of fourteen and won the silver medal in 1777. His 'Vauxhall Gardens' (see item 71) is regarded by John Hayes, a Rowlandson authority, as 'unquestionably among the most consummate and beautiful watercolours he ever produced'. But by this time he was becoming increasingly interested in the world of caricature, which was finally to dominate his exuberant professional life.

Paul Sandby 1725–1809. Often referred to as 'the father of the English School of watercolour', he started his career as a military surveyor at the Tower of London. His style evolved with his direct observation of landscape. As Drawing Master at the Royal Military Academy at Woolwich, his influence spread through a generation of surveyors and engineer officers, the impact of which is seen in this exhibition. Sandby was a great favourite of the King, whose children he taught. He was a founder-member of the Royal Academy.

Claude Joseph Sauthier 1736–1802. Born in Strasbourg. Sauthier, trained architect and surveyor, arrived in the Carolinas in the mid-1760s. With the outbreak of the Revolution, the cartographer began to work with Lord Percy, returning to England as private secretary to the future Duke of Northumberland. Sauthier remained with Percy till 1790, mapping and surveying the estates.

Edward Savage 1761–1817. Born in Massachusetts, he became a portrait painter, miniaturist and engraver, studying under Benjamin West in London for a short time in the early 1790s. Washington's diary records: 'Dec. 21, 1789. Sat from ten to one o'clock for Mr. Savage, to draw my Portrait for the University of Cambridge, in the State of Massachusetts.' He worked in Boston, New York, London and Philadelphia.

Dominic Serres 1722–93. Born in Gascony, he ran away to sea to avoid being entered in the Church. As master of a trader, he was captured by a British frigate and brought to England *c.* 1758, and there he settled. He gained a reputation as a landscape and marine painter, was elected to the R.A. and appointed Marine Painter to George III.

John Smart 1741–1811. A prolific miniaturist, Smart was Vice-President of the Society of Artists in 1778. In the mid-1780s he travelled to India for a period. He exhibited at the Royal Academy in 1794.

Gilbert Stuart 1755–1828. Born in Rhode Island. Already painting on commission at the age of fourteen, Stuart first studied in Scotland and later under Benjamin West in London from 1775 onwards. In 1783 he opened his own studio in London, but to avoid debts worked in Ireland from 1787 to 1793. He returned to Philadelphia and Boston to become one of the most successful painters of George Washington.

John Trumbull 1756–1843. Born in Connecticut, and a graduate of Harvard. He first arrived in London in 1780 but was briefly arrested in reprisal for the hanging of Major André.

He returned in 1784 to work under West and at the R.A. He painted at home in the United States from 1787 onwards. His aim, to produce large historical canvases of the Revolution, was achieved in 1816 when he was commissioned to execute four scenes for the Capitol in Washington. These he completed in 1824. None of them has the life of his early oil sketches (see item 53).

Benjamin West 1738–1809. Born in Pennsylvania, he travelled to Italy in 1760, and then with the right introductions found patronage in London in 1763. He was soon closely associated with the Court, and gained attention with his innovation of dressing historical groups in contemporary clothes rather than classical costume. He was one of the original members of the Royal Academy and was appointed in 1772 as Historical Painter to the King. In 1792 he succeeded Reynolds as President of the Royal Academy.

Joseph Wright 1756–93. Born in Bordentown, New Jersey, Wright was raised in London in his youth when his mother settled in England after the death of his father. He studied under John Trumbull and Benjamin West. He was painting portraits in Paris in 1782 under the patronage of Franklin. Back in America, he worked in New York and Philadelphia where his additional skill as a die-sinker earned him appointment to the newly-established United States mint.

Joseph Wright of Derby 1734–97. The wide variety of subjects and sitters painted by Wright reflects the span of his interest in science and the industrial developments of his day. When Copley's 'Boy with squirrel' was exhibited in 1766, West wrote that 'Reynolds was greatly struck with the piece, and took it to be by Wright, a young man that has just made his appearance in the art, with a surprising degree of Meritt.' Wright's one-man exhibition of twenty-four works in 1785, held in Spring (Vauxhall) Gardens, centred on his epic 'The Destruction of the Floating Batteries at Gibraltar'.

Johann Zoffany Born Germany, 1733; died England, 1810. Son of an architect, studied in Italy, came to England in 1760 after an unhappy marriage, where he soon obtained commissions from the Royal Family through a recommendation by Lord Bute. A founder member of the Royal Academy, who also exhibited at the Society of Artists 1762–1800, Zoffany was renowned for his portraits, particularly those of actors. Left England for lengthy periods for financial reasons, but returned to settle in 1797.

List of Lenders

Her Majesty The Queen
Lady Acland
Major-General Sir Alan Shafto Adair
The Lady Teresa Agnew
American Antiquarian Society, Worcester, Massachusetts
American Philosophical Society, Philadelphia, Pennsylvania
Major F. E. G. Bagshawe
Barclays Bank Limited, London
His Excellency Monsieur Jacques de Beaumarchais, French
Ambassador, London
Beaverbrook Art Gallery, Fredericton, New Brunswick
Bennington Museum, Vermont
Berkshire Museum, Pittsfield, Massachusetts
Château de Blérancourt, Musée Nationale de la Coopération
Franco-Américaine, Aisne
Mrs L. G. Bladon
Library of the Boston Athenaeum, Massachusetts
Museum of Fine Arts, Boston, Massachusetts
Boston Public Library, Massachusetts
The Lord Brabourne
Joseph Brant Museum, Burlington, Ontario
Trustees of the British Library, London
Trustees of the British Museum, London
Trustees of the British Museum (Natural History), London
Anne S. K. Brown Military Collection, Providence, Rhode
Island
Bibliothèque Raoul et Jean Brunon, Salon-de-Provence,
Bouches du Rhône
Buckler's Hard Maritime Museum, Beaulieu, Hampshire
Camden Historical Commission, South Carolina
Cameronian Scottish Rifles, Hamilton, Lanarkshire
Public Archives of Canada, Ottawa
Musée de Carnavalet, Paris
Mr Edward Charol
Society of the Cincinnati, Washington, D.C.
Brigadier T. F. J. Collins
National Society of the Colonial Dames of America in Connecticut, Wethersfield
Library of Congress, Washington, D.C.
Connecticut Historical Society, Hartford
Courage Limited, London
Courtauld Institute Galleries, London
The Earl of Dartmouth
Davison, Newman and Company Limited, London

The Earl of Derby
Derby Museums and Art Gallery, Derbyshire
Dorset Natural History and Archaeological Society, Dorchester
Mr Robin Duff
East Yorkshire Regiment Museum, Beverley, Humberside
Edinburgh University Library
The Lord Egremont
Musée de l'Empéri, Collections du Musée de l'Armée (Anciens
Collections Raoul et Jean Brunon) Salon-de-Provence,
Bouches du Rhône
Essex Institute, Salem, Massachusetts
Fidelity Union Trust Company (as Executors of the Estate of
the late Mrs Geraldine R. Dodge), New York
Fogg Art Museum, Harvard University, Cambridge,
Massachusetts
Sir Andrew Forbes-Leith
The Viscount Gage
Georgia Historical Society, Savannah
Gibbes Art Gallery, Charleston, South Carolina
Glasgow Museums and Art Galleries
The Trustees of the Goodwood Collections, Chichester, Sussex
The Duke of Grafton
Greensboro Historical Museum, North Carolina
Guthman Collection, Westport, Connecticut
Mrs M. W. Guild
The Earl of Halifax
Major Basil Heaton
Mr Mervyn Herbert
Mrs A. J. G. Hope
The Earl Howe
Independence National Historical Park, Philadelphia,
Pennsylvania
Mr Peter Jackson
Mr J. A. Kevill (as Executor of the Estate of the late Auberon
Herbert)
King's Landing Historical Settlement, Fredericton, New
Brunswick
City of Kingston upon Hull Museums and Art Galleries
Regimental Headquarters (Increment), The Queen's
Lancashire Regiment, Warrington, Lancashire
The Trustees of the late Mrs Leavett-Shenley
The Leger Galleries Limited, London
Lloyds Bank Limited, London
Mr Francis A. Lord

227

Luffness Limited, St Peter Port, Guernsey
McCord Museum, Montreal, Quebec
Mr A. B. Macnab
The Earl of Malmesbury
Manchester Art Gallery
Maryland Historical Society, Baltimore
Massachusetts Historical Society, Boston
Merseyside County Museums, Liverpool
The Metropolitan Museum of Art, New York
The Honourable Society of the Middle Temple Library,
London
Mr Crosby Milliman
Montagu Ventures Limited, Beaulieu, Hampshire
Mount Vernon Ladies Association of the Union, Virginia
National Army Museum, Chelsea, London
National Gallery, London
National Gallery of Canada, Ottawa
National Gallery of Ireland, Dublin
National Gallery of Scotland, Edinburgh
National Maritime Museum, Greenwich, London
National Museum of Man, Ottawa
National Museum of Wales, Cardiff
National Portrait Gallery, London
The National Trust
New Brunswick Museum, St John
Provincial Archives of New Brunswick, Fredericton
New York Historical Society, New York
New York State Archives, Albany
New York State History Collections, Schenectady
North Carolina Division of Archives and History, Raleigh
The Duke of Northumberland
Nova Scotia Museum, Halifax
Public Archives of Nova Scotia, Halifax
Mr Andrew Oliver
Trustees of the Oxfordshire and Buckinghamshire Light
Infantry Museum, Winchester, Hampshire
Musée de la Marine, Paris
Miss Amelia Peabody
Pennsylvania Academy of Fine Arts, Philadelphia
Historical Society of Pennsylvania, Philadelphia
Mrs Rosamond Phillips
Public Record Office, London
Literary and Historical Society of Quebec
The Lady Reigate
Rhode Island Historical Society, Providence
The Earl of Rosebery
Royal Academy of Arts, London
Royal Artillery Institution, Woolwich, London
Royal Botanic Gardens, Kew, Surrey
Royal Ontario Museum, Toronto, Ontario
Royal Society of Arts, London
Royal Thames Yacht Club, London
Isaac Royall House Association, Medford, Massachusetts
The Lord Sackville
Scottish Infantry Depot Museum, Penicuik, Midlothian

Scottish National Portrait Gallery, Edinburgh
Scottish United Services Museum, Edinburgh
Smithsonian Institution, Washington, D.C.
Smithsonian Institution National Portrait Gallery,
Washington, D.C.
Mr Peter Sonerville-Large
The Speaker of the House of Commons, London
The Trustees of the Tate Gallery, London
Fort Ticonderoga, New York
Metropolitan Toronto Central Library, Ontario
The Armouries, H.M. Tower of London
The Marquess Townshend of Raynham
United States Naval Academy, Annapolis, Maryland
University of London Library
University College, London
University of South Carolina Institute of Archaeology and
Anthropology, Columbia
Brigadier H. R. W. Vernon
Victoria and Albert Museum, London
Virginia Historical Society, Richmond
Mr J. M. A. Wallace
Wallis and Wallis Military Heritage Museum, Lewes, Sussex
The Lewis Walpole Library, Farmington, Connecticut
Royal Warwickshire Regimental Museum, Warwick
Washington Navy Yard, Washington, D.C.
The Wellcome Institute for the History of Medicine, London
West Point Museum, United States Military Academy,
New York
Captain W. C. Wickham
The Colonial Williamsburg Foundation, Williamsburg,
Virginia
Mrs Margaret Wood
Woodland Indian Centre, Brantford, Ontario
Worcester Art Museum, Massachusetts
The Worshipful Company of Makers of Playing Cards, London
York County Historical Society, Pennsylvania
Fort York, Toronto, Ontario
The Marquess of Zetland

Grateful thanks are extended both to the lenders listed here and
to those who have chosen to remain anonymous.
Many generous lenders have contributed a variety of items in
order to furnish the London coffee house, the American tavern
and other set-pieces in the exhibition. We would like to thank
the American Museum in Britain, Claverton Manor, Bath,
Avon; Anne of Cleves Museum (Sussex Archaeological
Society), Lewes, Sussex; Blaise Castle House Museum of Social
History, Bristol; Bristol City Art Gallery; the Commanding
Officer, H.M.S. *Victory*, Portsmouth, Hampshire; the Geffrye
Museum, London; the Guildford Museum, Surrey; Harvey's
of Bristol Wine Museum; Hudson's Bay and Annings Limited;
Justerini and Brooks Limited; Mr Philip Poole; and the Victoria
and Albert Museum, London. Thanks are also due to many
institutions for research facilities, particularly the Army Mus-
eums Ogilby Trust.

Select Bibliography

General

Agniel, Lucien   *The Late Affair Has Almost Broke My Heart: The American Revolution in the South, 1780–81*, Chatham Press, Riverside, 1972

Ayling, Stanley   *George the Third*, Collins, London, 1972

Boatner, Mark Mayo   *Cassell's Biographical Dictionary of the American War of Independence*, Cassell, London, 1973 (published in America as *Encyclopaedia of the American Revolution* by McKay, New York, 1966)

Boatner, Mark Mayo   *Landmarks of the American Revolution*, Stackpole, Harrisburg, 1973

Boylan, Brian Richard   *Benedict Arnold: The Dark Eagle*, Norton, New York, 1973

Brooke, John   *King George III*, Constable, London, 1972; McGraw Hill, New York, 1972

Furneaux, Rupert   *The Seven Years War*, Hart-Davis, MacGibbon, St Albans, 1973

George, Dorothy   *London Life in the 18th Century*, Kegan Paul, London, 1925

Griswold, Wesley S.   *The Night the Revolution Began*, Stephen Greene Press, Brattleboro, 1972

Gruber, Ira D.   *The Howe Brothers and the American Revolution*, University of North Carolina Press, Chapel Hill, 1972

Hume, Ivor Noël   *1775: Another Part of the Field*, Eyre and Spottiswoode, London, 1966

Mackesy, Piers   *The War for America 1775–1783*, Longmans, London, 1964; Harvard University Press, Cambridge, 1964

Marshall, Dorothy   *Dr Johnson's London*, John Wiley, New York, 1968

Pearson, Michael   *Those Damned Rebels: Britain's American Empire in Revolt*, Heinemann, London, 1972

Plumb, J. H.   *England in the Eighteenth Century*, Penguin, Harmondsworth, 1950

Plumb, J. H.   *The First Four Georges*, Batsford, London, 1953; Fontana, London, 1966

Quarles, Benjamin   *The Negro in the American Revolution*, University of North Carolina Press, Chapel Hill, 1961

Rudé, George   *Hanoverian London*, Secker and Warburg, London, 1971

Summerson, John   *Georgian London*, Pleiades Books, London, 1945; Penguin, Harmondsworth, 1962

Van Doren, Carl   *Secret History of the American Revolution*, Viking Press, New York, 1941

Warner, Oliver   *With Wolfe to Quebec*, Collins, London, 1972

Wickwire, Franklin and Mary   *Cornwallis and the War of Independence*, Faber and Faber, London, 1971

Wright, Esmond   *Washington and the American Revolution*, English Universities Press, London, 1957; Penguin, Harmondsworth, 1973

Ideology and Politics

Bailyn, Bernard   *The Ideological Origins of the American Revolution*, Harvard University Press, Cambridge, 1967

Barnes, M. J. (Ed.)   *Politics and Personality*, Oliver and Boyd, Edinburgh, 1967

Beloff, Max (Ed.)   *The Debate on the American Revolution*, Black, London, 1949

Fortescue, Sir John W.   *The Correspondence of King George the Third, 1760–1783* (six volumes), Macmillan, London, 1927–28

Guttridge, George H.   *English Whiggism and the American Revolution*, Cambridge University Press, London, 1966; University of California Press, Berkeley, 1942

Malone, Dumas   *The Story of the Declaration of Independence*, Oxford University Press, New York, 1954

Miller, John C.   *The Origins of the American Revolution*, Stanford University Press, Stanford, 1943

Namier, Louis B.   *England in the Age of the American Revolution*, Macmillan, London, 1930; St Martin's Press, New York, 1961

Pares, Richard   *King George III and the Politicians*, Clarendon Press, Oxford, 1953

Ritcheson, Charles R.   *British Politics and the American Revolution*, University of Oklahoma Press, Norman, 1954

Rudé, George   *Wilkes and Liberty*, Clarendon Press, Oxford, 1962

Schlesinger, Arthur M.   *Prelude to Independence: The Newspaper War on Britain, 1764–1766*; Knopf, New York, 1958

Wright, Esmond (Ed.)   *Causes and Consequences of the American Revolution*, Quadrangle Books, Chicago, 1966

Army and navy

Billias, George Athan (Ed.)   *George Washington's Generals*, William Morrow, New York, 1974

Billias, George Athan (Ed.)   *George Washington's Opponents: British Generals and Admirals in the American Revolution*, William Morrow, New York, 1969

Darling, Anthony D.   *Red Coat and Brown Bess* (Historical Arms Series No. 12), Museum Restoration Service, Ottawa, 1970

Fortescue, Sir John W.   *A History of the British Army, Vol. III, 1763–93*, Macmillan, London, 1902

Guthorn, Peter J.   *American Maps and Map Makers of the Revolution*, Philip Freneau Press, New Jersey, 1966

Guthorn, Peter J.   *British Maps of the American Revolution*, Philip Freneau Press, New Jersey, 1972

Jackson, Melvin H., and de Beer, Charles   *Eighteenth Century Gunfounding*, David and Charles, Newton Abbot, 1973

James, Sir William M.   *The British Navy in Adversity; A Study of the War of American Independence*, Longmans, Green, London, 1926

Lloyd, Christopher   *The British Seaman*, Collins, London, 1968

Miller, Nathan   *Sea of Glory: The Continental Navy Fights for Independence*, McKay, New York, 1974

Mollo, John   *Uniforms of the American Revolution*, Blandford Press, London, 1975

Moore, Warren   *Weapons of the American Revolution*, Funk and Wagnalls, New York, 1967

Peterson, Harold L.   *The Book of the Continental Soldier*, Stackpole, Harrisburg, 1968

Preston, Antony, Lyon, David, and Batchelor, John H.   *Navies of the American Revolution*, Prentice-Hall, New York, 1975

Shy, John W.   *Toward Lexington: The Role of the British Army in the Coming of the American Revolution*, Princeton University Press, 1965

Loyalists

Brown, Wallace   *The Good Americans: The Loyalists in the American Revolution*, William Morrow, New York, 1969

Calhoon, Robert McCluer   *The Loyalists in Revolutionary America, 1760–1781*, Harcourt, Brace, Jovanovich, New York, 1965

Norton, Mary Beth   *The British-Americans: The Loyalist Exiles in England*, Little, Brown, Boston, 1972; Constable, London, 1974

Robinson, Helen Caister   *Joseph Brant: A Man for his People*, Longman, Toronto, 1971

Smith, Paul H.   *Loyalists and Redcoats: A Study in British Revolutionary Policy*, University of North Carolina Press, Chapel Hill, 1964

Original Sources

Brown, Marvin L., Jr. (Trans. and Ed.)   *Baroness von Riedesel and the American Revolution: Journal and Correspondence of a Tour of Duty*, University of North Carolina Press, Chapel Hill, 1965

Lydenberg, Harry Miller (Ed.)   *Archibald Robinson, His Diaries and Sketches in America, 1762–1780*, Arno Press, New York, 1971

Oliver, Andrew (Ed.)   *The Journal of Samuel Curwen, Loyalist. Vols. I & II*, Harvard University Press, Cambridge, 1972

Scheer, George F. and Rankin, Hugh F.   *Rebels and Redcoats*, World Publishing, New York, 1957

Catalogues

George III: Collector and Patron, The Queen's Gallery, London, 1974

The American War of Independence, The British Library, London, 1975

A Pageant of Canada, Roy Strong, National Gallery of Canada, Ottawa, 1967

Thomas Davies, R. H. Hubbard, National Gallery of Canada, Ottawa, 1972

In the Hearts and Minds of the People: Prologue to the American Revolution, 1760–1774, text by Lillian B. Miller, New York Graphic Society for the National Portrait Gallery, Washington, D.C., 1974

The Die is Now Cast: The Road to American Independence, 1774–1776, text by Lillian B. Miller, Smithsonian Institution Press for the National Portrait Gallery, Washington, D.C., 1975

Paul Revere's Boston, Museum of Fine Arts, Boston, 1975

To Set A Country Free, Library of Congress, Washington, D.C., 1975

American Print Making: The First 150 Years, Wendy J. Shadwell, Smithsonian Institution Press, Washington, D.C., 1969

Fiction

Roberts, Kenneth   *Arundel*, Doubleday, New York, 1930; Fawcett Premier, New York, 1973

Roberts, Kenneth   *Oliver Wiswell*, Doubleday, New York, 1940; Fawcett Premier, New York, 1973

Roberts, Kenneth   *Rabble in Arms*, Doubleday, New York, 1933; Fawcett Premier, New York, 1972